Pharmanomics

Pharmanomics

How Big Pharma Destroys Global Health

Nick Dearden

VERSO
London • New York

First published by Verso 2023

1 3 5 7 9 10 8 6 4 2

Verso
UK: 6 Meard Street, London W1F 0EG
US: 388 Atlantic Avenue, Brooklyn, NY 11217
versobooks.com

Verso is the imprint of New Left Books

ISBN-13: 978-1-80429-145-0
ISBN-13: 978-1-80429-146-7 (UK EBK)
ISBN-13: 978-1-80429-147-4 (US EBK)

British Library Cataloguing in Publication Data
A catalogue record for this book is available from the British Library

Library of Congress Cataloging-in-Publication Data

Names: Dearden, Nick, author.
Title: Pharmanomics : how big pharma threatens global health / Nick Dearden.
Description: London ; New York : Verso, 2023. | Includes bibliographical references and index.
Identifiers: LCCN 2023013755 (print) | LCCN 2023013756 (ebook) | ISBN 9781804291450 (hardback) | ISBN 9781804291474 (ebk)
Subjects: LCSH: Pharmaceutical industry – Moral and ethical aspects.
Classification: LCC HD9665.5 .D396 2023 (print) | LCC HD9665.5 (ebook) | DDC 338.4/76151 – dc23/eng/20230512
LC record available at https://lccn.loc.gov/2023013755
LC ebook record available at https://lccn.loc.gov/2023013756

Typeset in Fournier by Hewer Text UK Ltd, Edinburgh
Printed and bound by CPI Group (UK) Ltd, Croydon CR0 4YY

Contents

Introduction: Bad Apples

Nearly eighteen months into the Covid-19 pandemic, Albert Bourla, the chief of one of the world's biggest pharmaceutical corporations, Pfizer, sat down with a journalist in an upmarket Greek restaurant in New York.[1] Bourla had, by anyone's estimation, enjoyed a successful year. And in August 2020, over a $324 lunch for two, he talked to the *Financial Times* about the global health crisis that had made his company a household name.

Bourla now sat on the most lucrative medicine in the history of the pharmaceutical industry, expected to bring in $36 billion for its producers in a single year. Pfizer was also working on another blockbuster – an antiviral treatment for Covid-19 – which would, if it came off, net billions more dollars a year for the corporation. All in all, Bourla told the journalist, his company had become 'the most efficient machine' possible for converting raw materials into vaccine doses.

But sales were not the only important consideration during the pandemic. Just before Covid-19 struck in winter 2020, the sector, known as 'Big Pharma' by its critics, was regarded as the least trusted industry in the US, while Pfizer itself was seen as the least trustworthy of the well-known Big Pharma firms.[2] The pandemic was an opportunity not simply to profit, but to improve the industry's tarnished reputation.

What's more, it seemed to be working. In New York, as Bourla tucked into a $32 Greek salad, he was interrupted by the restaurant's head of marketing, who gushed: 'It is due to you that we can be open.' There were stories of revellers toasting Pfizer in Tel Aviv and cocktails named after his company's vaccine in London. The president of the United States referred to Bourla as a 'good friend', while prime ministers and presidents from across the world begged for a little time with the great man.[3]

The pandemic, Bourla said, had given pharmaceutical companies like the one he ran a 'stage' on which to prove their detractors wrong.[4] As Bourla had told the media a month earlier, 'I'm satisfied that the company is doing financially very well, but even more satisfied when I go into a restaurant and get a standing ovation because everybody feels that we saved the world.'[5] But he warned, as if to show his humility, 'We should never take it for granted. It can change very quickly.'[6]

And change it did. Within a few months of Bourla's *FT* interview, concern about the role of corporations like Pfizer in perpetuating the now deep levels of global vaccine inequality was becoming increasingly mainstream. While rich countries had vaccinated most of their populations, many countries in Africa, Asia and Latin America had barely been able to start their vaccine programmes. By November 2021, the number of booster shots being administered in rich nations outstripped the total number of vaccines administered in low-income countries by nearly two-to-one.[7]

All Western companies involved in vaccine production had failed to some extent. But particular anger was reserved for the producers of new generation mRNA vaccines. These vaccines were proving particularly effective at preventing the hospitalisation and death of Covid-19 patients. But mRNA vaccines were produced by just three companies – Pfizer and its German partner BioNTech, and another US-based corporation called Moderna.

Pfizer, in particular, stood accused of sending a measly 1 per cent of the vaccines it had delivered to COVAX, the international body set up to try to ensure all countries got a reasonable amount of the vaccines on offer.[8] What's more, these companies had sold their vaccines almost entirely to the richest countries in the world, and they were making eye-watering amounts of money on those sales – an estimated $1,000 per second from just two vaccines, with profit rates that would make the most cutthroat of financiers salivate.[9] So lucrative was Covid-19 that, within just over a year of the pandemic being declared, Big Pharma's vaccines had created nine new billionaires.[10]

It started to dawn on policymakers that a small handful of for-profit corporations with no public accountability could decide how many vaccines could be made in a given year, who got to buy them, and at what cost. They got to dictate, in other words, who lived and who died in the most serious public health emergency in living memory.

A barrage of allegations surfaced. Pfizer was accused of denigrating the vaccines of one of its competitors, with a potentially disastrous impact on vaccine hesitancy.[11] The company was accused of blatant profiteering, trying to charge the United States $200 for a vaccine course that cost, at the very most, $13 to produce.[12] It was accused of bullying governments, forcing them to change their national laws to protect Pfizer's profits, or even mortgaging national assets to cover any compensation claims against the firm.[13] Perhaps most serious of all, they were accused of stringing lower-income countries along, holding out the possibility of vaccine sales that they had no intention of delivering, simply to improve their bargaining position with richer countries.[14]

Suddenly a wide range of experts and insiders, not people used to badmouthing Big Pharma, started to speak out. One academic told the media that this represented 'really an extreme form of rapacious capitalism'.[15] A documentary maker trying his hardest to take a balanced approach on the positives and negatives of the company was forced to conclude that the most generous thing any of the people he'd talked to had found to say about Pfizer was 'they're a bunch of shitbags. They're not the only ones, but they're cleverer than the rest.'[16]

To add insult to injury, these vaccines had not, for the most part, been invented by the corporations now in charge of producing them. 'It's not even their vaccine', one former US government official complained, adding that the fact it had become the 'Pfizer' vaccine was 'the biggest marketing coup in the history of American pharmaceuticals'.[17]

In the pharmaceutical world, scandals – and there are plenty, as we will see in the coming pages – are often put down to a bad apple in a barrel of otherwise pretty good fruit. And for every negative story that emerges in the world of medicines, we, the public, are told: Sure, there are always a few who take advantage, but don't throw the baby out with the bath water – without Big Pharma, there would be no medicines.

But what the Covid-19 pandemic showed clearly is that, while the pharmaceutical world is certainly diverse, with a wide range of companies exhibiting more or less extreme behaviours, the problem is not individual greed. It goes much deeper than that, lying at the very heart of how these firms are structured. Once you start to pull at this thread, you discover that Pfizer, while certainly at the more unpleasant end of the Big Pharma spectrum, cannot simply be dismissed as a 'one-off'. Rather, the rules and incentives by which Big Pharma operates have created a deeply dysfunctional industry, which in turn prolonged the pandemic and ensured that the way the world has dealt with Covid-19 has entrenched global inequality, possibly for a generation.

Just look at Pfizer's rivals. There's Moderna, the new kid on the block, whose Covid-19 vaccine was developed entirely with public funds but whose CEO, Stéphane Bancel, became a billionaire after privatising that knowledge.[18] Not content with the billions of dollars Moderna made selling vaccines – almost entirely to rich nations – he refused to transfer the know-how behind the Spikevax vaccine to the World Health Organisation, preventing the production of many more doses, thereby prolonging the pandemic and costing countless lives.[19]

Then there's US corporate giant Johnson & Johnson, which produces a huge range of healthcare products, as well as a Covid vaccine. The corporation licensed doses of this vaccine to be made through a South African company, but then insisted that those doses were exported out of South Africa, just as that country was entering a major Covid-19 outbreak, and sent instead to the already highly vaccinated rich world.[20]

And it isn't only vaccines. US corporation Gilead discovered that one of its already existing antiviral drugs could be useful in the treatment of Covid-19. It then tried to obtain a special 'orphan status', which could bring the company additional monopoly privileges over the medicine, allowing the company to further boost the profits it could make.[21] 'Orphan status' is a category used for rare diseases, and was designed to help incentivise drug research into conditions that affect very few patients. The idea that a pandemic could constitute such a rare disease was so ludicrous that even Gilead ultimately rescinded its claim.

These are not simply examples of poor behaviour by individual chief executives. The problem, at its heart, is that Big Pharma companies behave more like hedge funds than medical research firms.

There has been a trend in recent books to look back to a golden age of the pharmaceutical industry, when chief executives were more likely to be scientists, and when researching medicines for the public good, even if it generated tiny profits, was seen as the right thing to do by these companies.[22] This case is somewhat overblown. Back in the early 1960s, Harold Wilson, who would go on to be British prime minister, spent years in parliament bemoaning the eye-watering profits of 'an industry which has grown fat at the expense of the public purse'.[23]

In the United States, anti-monopoly crusader Senator Estes Kefauver held a series of groundbreaking hearings, in which he hauled Big Pharma executives in front of his committee and berated them for profiteering by marking up drugs by thousands of per cent. Kefauver suggested the pharmaceutical industry was making twice the profit margin the average US manufacturer enjoyed at the time. He would go on to launch a full-scale assault on the patent system that underlay these profits, only to be halted by the power of the industry and its friends in Congress.

So, in reality, there was never a social contract between Big Pharma and the public it supposedly served. But it is true that the global economy that arose from the late 1970s onwards, and which incorporated a financial logic at its very heart, turbo-charged the worst elements of the pharmaceutical industry, transforming it almost beyond recognition.

Perhaps no one represents this new industry more honestly than the ultimate bad boy of the pharmaceutical sector, Martin Shkreli.

Shkreli is something of a pantomime character because, far from trying to avoid negative publicity, he seems to embrace it with glee. The rap-loving businessman was not born to wealth. When Donald Trump called him a 'spoiled brat', Shkreli countered, 'My parents were immigrants and janitors. [Trump] inherited wealth! Fuck him.'[24]

Shkreli was a hedge fund manager, but started up a pharmaceutical company when, by his own admission, he realised there was not enough money to be made in hedge funds. His strategy for making money from his pharmaceutical company was simple: buy up expired drug patents for important medicines, control the supply of those medicines, and hike the price.

In 2015, Shkreli became infamous when his company, Turing Pharmaceuticals, acquired a simple-to-make but lifesaving anti-parasitic medicine, used particularly by Aids patients and pregnant women. He then jacked the price up by 5,000 per cent. True to form, when Shkreli was asked at the end of 2015, and after being labelled 'the most hated man in America', about any regrets he might have, he replied that he should have raised the price higher. In the highly divisive world of US politics, Shkreli managed to unite Hillary Clinton, Bernie Sanders and Donald Trump in their opposition to him.[25]

Of course, Big Pharma moved to distance itself from Shkreli. He was just another bad apple, they said, but you cannot judge the whole industry by his standards. 'I think it's really important for our industry to make it clear that he is not us. We are a research-based pharmaceutical industry,' one Big Pharma CEO told the press.[26]

Yet, for all these denunciations, Shkreli's behaviour really was not so abnormal in the modern pharmaceutical industry, except in one respect: Shkreli did not hide what he was doing behind a wall of public relations. As he himself told a healthcare summit, 'My shareholders expect me to make the most profit. That's the ugly, dirty truth . . . no one wants to say it. No one's proud of it. But this is a capitalist society, capitalist system and capitalist rules. My investors expect me to maximize profits. Not to minimize them or go half or go 70 per cent but to go to 100 per cent of the profit curve.'[27] One of Shkreli's former employees added that, while pharmaceutical companies might like to pretend they are in a different category, 'they don't have any higher moral ground to comment on what we do!'[28]

As I will show, many of Shkreli's activities are indeed pretty mainstream in an industry renowned for price gouging, for buying up the intellectual property of other people, for acquiring or shutting down competitors, for playing the financial markets, for making insignificant changes to existing drugs and pretending they have made something new and important, and for lobbying for an even more favourable regulatory environment.

Far from being a necessary evil, which in spite of profit-hungry behaviour at least keeps us healthy, Big Pharma today is in fact one of the most financialised industries in our heavily financialised global economy. Big Pharma has little interest in keeping us healthy, and often an interest in the very opposite. It acts as a parasite on public research and public health systems; a super-efficient vehicle for channelling public resources into the pockets of the already superwealthy.

Indeed, Big Pharma has almost forgotten how to make useful medicines. What often surprises people most about the industry is that the big corporations we associate with production of medicines do so little research into the medicines we need. These are not, by and large, companies that develop vital drugs and then make obscene profits off the back of the drugs they create. Rather, the drug creation is done by others, often bankrolled by the public sector.

In this Big Pharma is not alone – though, perhaps because medicines are so important to all of us, they make the aversion we feel that much more acute. But the way in which medicines are made says something much more profound about our economy as a whole, giving us a glimpse of a deeply broken system. Wherever we look, our economy has been hollowed out, with corporations more interested in the diktats of the financial markets than in focusing on what they were set up to do. The results cannot be overstated. Under the rubric of 'letting the market decide' what gets made, we have built a system of monopoly capitalism, with inequality so extreme and the power of big business so great that it threatens to overwhelm what remains of our democratic rights.

Along the way, this model has fuelled extraordinary levels of inequality in medical access at a global level, as well as putting unbearable burdens on public health services in the Global North.

Meanwhile, for public health advocates across the Global South, the real scandal of the pandemic is that anyone might ever think putting Big Pharma in charge of a global vaccination effort could produce anything other than obscene inequality. For those who lived through the HIV/Aids epidemic in Southern Africa, the lesson should have been clear: do not trust Big Pharma when it comes to a major public health emergency.

In the early 1990s, while Big Pharma was in the middle of reinventing itself into the beast we know so well today, many at the top of the industry saw that their biggest asset was not their research expertise or their manufacturing know-how. It was, instead, their intellectual property – the patents and trade secrets that gave them monopolies, allowing them to control supply, production and prices over a wide range of medicines. Regardless of whether the underlying medicines were ultimately produced or not, the intellectual property was an incredibly profitable commodity in its own right, open to being moved around to hide profits or avoid regulation, or bought and sold on financial markets.

The key to cementing this power was making this intellectual property sacrosanct. Throughout the 1980s and '90s, Big Pharma worked to increase these monopoly powers. The industry lobbied and funded US politicians, supported new laws, integrated itself into European decision-making, and repeatedly fought court battles to set new legal precedents, all giving the industry ever more rights to extend their patents and keep their data secret. But perhaps their greatest achievement was a new trade deal, the Agreement on Trade-Related Aspects of Intellectual Property Rights – known as TRIPS. Described by journalist Alexander Zaitchik as 'a brute and profoundly undemocratic expression of concentrated corporate power', TRIPS extended US-style patent protection to the entire world.[29] Whereas before, countries across the Global South could produce medicines far more freely, TRIPS enforced monopoly protection everywhere. And while there were exemptions built into the agreement, as South Africa was soon to discover, those exemptions were particularly hard to apply in practice.

By the early 2000s, HIV/Aids was having a catastrophic effect across Southern Africa, with as many as 4.5 million – or one in nine people – living with HIV in South Africa, and 1,700 people being infected every day.[30] By this date, there were life-saving drugs on the market that could suppress the virus, halting the development of Aids and preventing the spread of HIV. The problem was that the patents on these drugs were held by pharmaceutical corporations that, as in the case of Covid, were able to set the price and decide who could produce the medicines.

In practice, that meant HIV medicines were priced at $10,000 per patient per year, rendering the drugs unaffordable both for South Africa's health service and for most individuals in the country.[31] But the situation was not insurmountable; fortunately, the medicines did not cost anything like that much to make. By producing the medicines in the Global South, it was estimated South Africa could cut the cost by 90 per cent. Fortunately, at the same time, the government had introduced legislation which would have given them the power to override patents and import generic versions of desperately needed medicines from elsewhere.

Big Pharma saw things differently. Accusing South Africa of 'piracy', thirty-nine firms, including some of the biggest corporations in the world, sued the South African government.[32] Together with senior figures from the United States and European governments, they pulled out all the stops to prevent South Africa introducing the legislation. The corporations were ultimately forced to back down. The case was also a disaster for the industry's image, sparking a movement that lives on to this day, and has been a critical part of the battle for equitable Covid-19 drugs.

But the battle was important precisely because it went to the heart of how the industry now made money – not from developing important new medicines, but from the monopoly power that patents, or intellectual property, conferred on them. We will see how this power laid the ground for the sort of pharmaceutical system that exists today: one where fortunes can be made without ever setting foot in a scientific laboratory, and where far more money can be made by playing the financial markets and exploiting access to desperately needed public knowledge than by inventing an important new medicine.

The consequences of such a system are bad for almost all of us. We have seen how they make a pandemic harder to end. And we will see how they are also making new health emergencies – like antibiotic resistance – unsolvable.

In fact, the problems of this intellectual property regime go well beyond medicines. This system of monopoly power has not only helped restructure our wider economy away from invention or production and towards financial markets. It has also fundamentally reshaped the relationship between richer and poorer countries, formerly the colonisers and the colonised. The latter have been rendered dependent on having to rent – or do without – the vital technologies that are necessary for building a modern society. Unless they can control and utilise these technologies, dispending with the rules of the financialised global economy, they will remain subservient to the power of the richest corporations in the richest countries on earth.

This book is not intended to push readers into despair – far from it. The chapters that follow will lay out the problem of the pharmaceutical system in detail; but they will also point the way to a very different sort of medical research and development. Such a model will be essential if we are to deal with the public health emergencies that lie ahead. But such a model is also closer now, precisely because of the failures of Big Pharma to deal with Covid-19, than it was ten years ago. That is because the movements that have arisen against the injustices of vaccine inequality, among ordinary people but also between governments around the world, are not only growing in power; they are starting to sow the seeds of that new system here and now.

This change is currently on a small scale. It will need to be nurtured and supported. But it is there, and it holds out the promise of more transformative change not only to the way medicines are produced and distributed, but to the economy as a whole. Such change will be vital, too, if we want to halt climate change, build a better food system, and create a more democratic society. Because the current way we are doing things is driving us towards the abyss at breakneck speed.

The purpose of this book is to open more minds to the possibility of that change. After all, all of the arguments made against reform are the same arguments that could have been made against the creation of the National Health Service in Britain after the end of the Second World War. But if, here in Britain at least, we take it for granted that our hospitals and clinics should be publicly controlled, why not the medicines that are administered by them? If our healthcare is too important to be left to the market, then that must include the research and development of medicines that keep us well.

It is true that, during a major pandemic, we developed – thanks to massive public investment in a short period of time – incredible medicines to deal with the emergency. Sadly, those medicines were ultimately doled out on the basis of power and wealth. Now imagine what might have been achieved if the drive of the pharmaceutical corporations for ever greater levels of profit was removed from the equation. Imagine if we could replace cut-throat competition and secrecy with collaboration and openness. Imagine if our research was driven solely by the desire to rid the world of disease and suffering, starting with the most serious and deadly conditions. When combined with our technological know-how, the dedication of our brilliant researchers, and the trust that such a model could inspire in the population at large, there is no telling how much more could be achieved.

Huge thanks are due to Kieran Burch, Emma Dowling, James O'Nions, Christa Hook, Max Lawson, Martin Drewry, David

Legge, and Mohga Kamal-Yanni, as well as all the campaigners who worked on People's Vaccine here and around the world, who have provided so much of the information, analysis and inspiration for this book.

1
A History of Scandal

Legendary American artist Nan Goldin made her name documenting the queer subculture of which she was a part in 1980s New York. Her photographs offer a shockingly honest portrayal of life outside the mainstream; she refused to gloss over the sex, violence and drug use that were a routine part of the life of her and her friends. But the real low of Goldin's life, the experience that prompted her to become a nearly full-time activist, came nearly thirty years later, in the form of a prescription painkiller called OxyContin.[1]

In a 2018 article in *ArtForum*, Goldin revealed how an OxyContin prescription she had be given for tendonitis in her left wrist sent her overnight into a dark spiral of addiction.[2] She described the black market in 'Oxy' when she returned to New York City, the gateway that Oxy provided into other drugs, the overdose and the pain of withdrawal: 'I survived the opioid crisis. I narrowly escaped. I went from the darkness and ran full speed into The World. I was isolated, but I realized I wasn't alone. When I got out of treatment I became absorbed in reports of addicts dropping dead from my drug, OxyContin.'[3] Goldin went on to describe finding out that she was not alone. In fact, OxyContin had become an epidemic in the United States by 2017, one which had already killed hundreds of thousands. By 2017, of the ninety-one people dying every day from drug overdoses in the United States, 60 per cent involved opioids like Oxy.[4]

But Goldin learned something else too. As an artist, she knew the name Sackler very well. The Sackler family were a major source of philanthropic funds for art galleries and museums across the world. But what she now realised was that their money came from the very drug that nearly killed her:

> I learned that the Sackler family, whose name I knew from museums and galleries, were responsible for the epidemic. This family formulated, marketed, and distributed OxyContin . . . The Sackler family and their private company, Purdue Pharma, built their empire with the lives of hundreds of thousands . . . They have washed their blood money through the halls of museums and universities around the world.

As part of a new activist group called Prescription Addiction Intervention Now, or PAIN, she set out to expose them.

The Sackler family has been in pharmaceuticals since the 1950s, when Arthur Sackler and his two brothers bought a small company called Purdue.[5] But Arthur Sackler's real talent was in selling drugs, and he is credited with inventing modern forms of pharmaceutical marketing in the United States. In particular, he was expert at marketing to doctors directly, understanding the role that doctors played not only in the prescription process, but as symbols of trust in society.

Sackler helped Pfizer – before then mostly a chemical company – to become a profitable drug company with a particularly successful marketing campaign on antibiotics.[6] But his real triumph came in marketing a new drug, Valium, in a way that turned it into a blockbuster for pharma giant Roche in the 1960s and '70s.

Reflections of Arthur Sackler's approach to marketing can be seen all over the modern pharmaceutical industry. First, and perhaps most far-reaching, was the suggestion that virtually everyone should be taking really strong medicines on a regular basis. People with perfectly standard levels of anxiety were encouraged to take Valium, even though no testing had been done into its addictiveness. One piece of marketing encouraged Valium for people with no psychiatric symptoms at all: 'For this kind of patient – with no demonstrable pathology – consider the usefulness of Valium.'[7]

As Patrick Radden Keefe, author of *Empire of Pain: The Secret History of the Sackler Dynasty*, puts it, Arthur Sackler has a 'Don Draper–style intuition for the alchemy of marketing'.[8] He recognised that doctors were perceived to be paragons of truth, whose words were rarely questioned by patients. If you could get to the doctor, the patient would surely follow. Keefe's work details the techniques used, from adverts masquerading as weighty scientific opinion in medical journals, through giving payments to regulators to support their products in, for instance, ghostwritten scientific studies, to blatant deception: pretending doctors endorsed products when they did not, for example.

The campaigns worked spectacularly well. Valium, popularly branded the 'mother's little helper', was prescribed to millions of people in Britain alone. It was the first real blockbuster prescription drug, and its producer, Roche, brought in sales of $750 million a year through the 1970s, making it one of the biggest pharmaceutical corporations in the world.[9] The drug was indeed a medical breakthrough compared to its predecessors. But there was a dark side: Valium was highly addictive. In the late 1970s, with nearly 45 million Valium prescriptions being written a year in the United States, the US Senate looked into the impact of the drug, Senator Edward Kennedy declaring it had created 'a nightmare of dependence' for some.[10]

Arthur Sackler died in 1987, before OxyContin was invented. But his marketing techniques were used to sell that drug when the Sackler-owned company, Purdue, started to produce it in the 1990s. Purdue was already making a strong painkiller called M. S. Contin in the 1980s; but as the patent on that drug was about to expire, it began to search for a new drug that could replace its income stream. Purdue came up with OxyContin, a very strong painkiller with a slow-release mechanism that meant, in theory, only two pills could give pain relief for serious conditions for an entire day. In 1996, Oxy went on sale, and America's biggest modern drug scandal began.

As with Valium, the problem was not that OxyContin was not a useful and important medicine. For cancer and end-of-life pain, such drugs can be an important weapon in a doctor's armoury. The problem was that OxyContin, like Valium, was aggressively marketed as a medicine that was not addictive, and that was appropriate for nearly anyone, even with moderate pain. Unfortunately, that was far from the case.

The company went out of its way to dispel the idea that OxyContin was addictive or open to abuse, recognising that this could be a central reason why doctors might be hesitant to prescribe the drug, inventing the term 'opiophobia' to describe an unwarranted fear of using opioids.[11] Sales reps from Purdue told doctors that fewer than 1 per cent of patients developed addiction. They played on the common misperception that OxyContin was less potent than morphine. They sent physicians on all-expenses-paid trips to learn about the benefits of the drug, creating merchandise like fishing hats and cuddly toys to promote the drug, and incentivised sales staff to help maximise prescriptions.

Within five years, OxyContin was generating over a billion dollars a year in sales. By now, real stories of addiction and deaths from overdoses were emerging. It was clear that some doctors were prescribing vast quantities of the drug. At this point, Purdue switched tactics, insisting, in an echo of the gun lobby, that the problem was not with the medicine but with the people taking it. For anyone who died or developed an addiction, well, the problem was that they were an addict, and were therefore taking the medicine inappropriately. Keefe quotes from Purdue's senior medical adviser, J. David Haddox, comparing the drug to a vegetable: 'If I gave you a stalk of celery and you ate that, it would be healthy. But if you put it in a blender and tried to shoot it into your veins, it would not be good.'

Of course, the reality was different. OxyContin is very addictive. A drug like this should be prescribed very sparingly. The problem is that profit-seeking businesses like Purdue don't behave like this. Their imperative is to maximise sales, and shift any resulting costs onto wider society.

The impact of OxyContin on many communities in the United States is hard to overestimate, and the story has even been turned into miniseries – Netflix's *Painkiller* and Disney's *Dopesick*. Exact figures are difficult to come by, because addiction and overdoses are rarely attributable to a single drug. OxyContin is not the only synthetic opioid on the market; other drugs like fentanyl – believed to have killed the pop star Prince, among others – are also major contributors to the opioid epidemic.

But the trends are clear. The rise in prescription opioids like OxyContin, aggressively promoted with unprecedented amounts of money by Purdue, fuelled a major drug epidemic estimated to have cost 300,000 lives since 2000.[12] In 2019, an average of thirty-eight people died each day from overdoses involving prescription opioids.[13] Research suggests that three-quarters of America's heroin addicts started out using prescription opioids. Some areas of the country were decimated by the epidemic.[14] In south-west Virginia, the number of deaths related to opioid prescriptions increased 830 per cent, from 23 in 1997 to 215 in 2003.[15] In one story that captured the media's imagination in neighbouring West Virginia in 2006, 28 people overdosed in just one town over a period of four hours.[16]

As the scale of the crisis became clear, Purdue doubled down on its attempts to blame 'bad patients', hiring former New York Mayor – and future Donald Trump lawyer and cartoon villain – Rudolph Giuliani, to limit the damage to the company's fortune.[17] And that fortune was huge. OxyContin generated $35 billion for Purdue since its release in 1995.[18] In 2015, the Sackler family entered the top twenty of *Forbes Magazine's* 'America's Richest Families' list, with $14 billion of wealth built on the success of OxyContin.[19]

What's more, despite the bad press, Purdue did everything possible to keep sales going. As OxyContin's patents were due to expire, they made small tweaks to the drug so they could file new patents and retain their monopoly on the drug – a very common tactic in the industry's playbook, as we shall see. Although OxyContin's patents were due to expire in 2013, this so-called 'ever-greening' saw Purdue file new patents thirteen times in the United States alone, extending its exclusive rights to 2030.[20]

As the opioid epidemic became mainstream news in the United States, OxyContin's producers looked overseas to maintain sales. British-based Mundipharma is a Sackler-owned company that deals with sales outside the United States and Europe. Through the business, China has become the second-largest market for OxyContin. In 2019, the company's CEO Raman Singh, a former vice president at GlaxoSmithKline, told the *Nikkei Asian Review*, 'This is where the growth is coming from. By 2025, I'm hoping [China] will become the largest market, overtaking the US.' Singh continued, 'We have been very, very successful in commercializing for pain.'[21]

Leaked internal documents suggest the company is using the same discredited tactics to market opioids in China, including telling doctors that OxyContin is less addictive, pushing ever larger doses of the drug, disguising sales staff as medical professionals, using outdated figures that have subsequently been debunked, and giving doctors gifts.[22] This turn to foreign markets has been described by a former US regulator, David A. Kessler, as 'right out of the playbook of Big Tobacco. As the United States takes steps to limit sales here, the company goes abroad.'[23]

Nor is this problem confined to China. A study in the esteemed medical journal the *Lancet* warned that the opioid crisis had 'got a good chance of spreading globally' in the Global North and South, with 'pharmaceutical companies based in the USA actively expanding opioid prescribing worldwide, and . . . using fraudulent and corrupting tactics that have now been banned domestically'.[24] Australia recorded a fifteenfold increase in opioid prescriptions, while a 'criminal investigation [was] ongoing in Italy, where two Mundipharma executives [had] been sentenced for involvement with a leading physician, who promoted opioids and allegedly laundered large cash payments from Mundipharma'.[25]

In countries like Brazil, which has seen a 465 per cent increase in prescriptions in the six years between 2009 and 2016, the company is accused of using 'pain ambassadors' to run training seminars with doctors to overcome 'opiophobia', encouraging people to seek medical treatment for chronic pain, and offering patient discounts to make prescriptions affordable.[26] It also used 'first prescription free' coupons, just as Purdue had in the United States – an almost direct emulation of the tactics of illicit drug pushers. Direct marketing to patients included a celebrity-led campaign in Spain urging viewers not to be afraid of painkillers.[27] And in South Korea, a company executive said Korean doctors 'worry too much' about addiction.

Pharmaceutical scandals are often brought to light by the victims themselves, as well as by relatives of patients who have died as a result of inappropriately sold medicines. Often, ordinary people are transformed into incredibly brave and effective campaigners by their ordeals and their loss. The opioid crisis has thrown up a generation of such campaigners, and Nan Goldin is only one of the more famous. But she has used her platform to build pressure on the art galleries and museums that have sometimes hosted her work to remove the Sackler name from their buildings.

In 2018–19 Goldin's group undertook actions at the most prominent of these galleries. At the Guggenheim in New York, activists took as their starting point a remark by Richard Sackler that 'the launch of OxyContin tablets will be followed by a blizzard of prescriptions that will bury the competition. The prescription blizzard will be so deep, dense, and white.'[28] The activists filed into the gallery and took up positions along the space's concentric walkway, dropping hundreds of fake white prescriptions for OxyContin into the central hall. Each one contained a controversial claim Sackler had made about the drug, including one in which he called addicts 'criminals': 'We have to hammer on the abusers in every way possible. They are the culprits of the problem. They are reckless criminals.'

At the V&A in London, campaigners placed bottles of pills and 'Oxy dollar' bills stained red on the floor and lay down for a 'die-in'. At the Louvre in Paris, they unfurled a banner standing in one of the museum's water features, exposing the words 'Take down the Sackler Name'. And at New York's Metropolitan Museum of Art, they floated pill bottles labelled 'OxyContin, 200,000 dead' in a pool in front of the ancient Egyptian Temple of Dendur.

It worked. The Sackler name started to disappear from galleries, including the Met in New York, which also pledged to take no more Sackler money. Tufts University in Massachusetts also removed the name, explaining, 'Our students, faculty, staff, alumni, and others have shared with us the negative impact the Sackler name has on them each day, noting the human toll of the opioid epidemic in which members of the Sackler family and their company, Purdue Pharma, are associated.'[29]

After a number of lawsuits and settlements, Purdue filed for bankruptcy in 2019, and a settlement was devised whereby the company was to be sold off, with some funds being channelled to help deal with the opioid crisis. Mundipharma will also be sold, and the proceeds used to pay for the settlement. However, the legal protection that the settlement extends to the family and much of their fortune caused anger among campaigners, and in late 2021 a federal judge rejected the settlement. The Sackler family had withdrawn over $10 billion from Purdue in the decade leading up to the firm's bankruptcy.[30] And so, as the Purdue scandal continues, it remains to be seen whether the victims of the opioid epidemic will receive the justice they deserve.

A Lancet–Stanford University commission into the opioid crisis concluded, 'To manage pain, greed must be managed as well.'[31] That's true. But greed is often taken as an individual moral failure.

The problem that the opioid epidemic exposes goes beyond individual bad behaviour. Rather, we have a system that incentivises, or even requires, this sort of behaviour. Changing this does not simply require bringing Purdue down, but transforming the architecture of which Purdue is a part. To achieve this, it must be understood what it is about the pharmaceutical model that is pushing its protagonists towards such antisocial behaviours.

In 2020, investigative *Times* journalist Billy Kenber wrote an exposé of the pharmaceutical industry, *Sick Money: The Truth about the Global Pharmaceutical Industry*.[32] Kenber's book is an examination of the development of this dysfunctional and unsustainable industry. Kenber explains, through a series of scandals and case studies, how Big Pharma has become increasingly obsessed with maximising profits and channelling wealth to shareholders. He lays much of the blame for this firmly at the door of an economic process known as 'financialisation' – a phenomenon that has affected not only the pharmaceutical industry but the whole global economy, with profound social implications globally. Kenber explores the way these processes have transformed the pharmaceutical industry into something more akin to a set of enormous hedge funds than a group of companies researching and developing important medicines.[33] It is tempting to see all of the problems of the industry through the lens of financialisation. Indeed, it is easy to fall into a trap of thinking that there was a golden age of the pharmaceutical sector, when scientists headed up the Big Pharma companies and the chief motivation of the industry was a deep sense of social responsibility. In fact, this is very wide of the mark. In many ways, the opioid scandal is an old-fashioned scandal, as well established as the industry itself.

It is certainly true that there was a time, in the middle of the twentieth century, when major medical science breakthroughs were bigger and more transformative, and when research funding was therefore more productive. At that time, the figures tell us, it took less money to create a more transformative medicine – famous examples including antibiotics, steroids, chemotherapy drugs and the polio vaccine.

There was also a time when the regulatory framework – hard-won laws secured by the public and governments to control the industry – meant that some of the excesses of a previous period were curtailed, including tougher safety standards and better price controls. In fact, the battle to improve standards in the industry was ongoing throughout the course of the twentieth century.

But none of this ensured a socially responsible industry whose interests were at one with those of the wider public, as the story of the Sacklers vividly demonstrates. Valium and OxyContin represent genuinely important and useful breakthroughs in medical knowledge. One was developed a long time before the phenomenon of financialisation took hold, the other at the beginning of that trend. But both show an industry determined to use any mechanism available to it – whatever the risk to the end user, whatever the cost to society – to maximise its profits. They point to the much deeper problem of delegating decisions about how lifesaving medicines are developed and used to the market.

Purdue was not alone: other companies were also making opiates. While Arthur Sackler was a pioneer, his marketing techniques became commonplace across the industry. In fact, the history of the pharmaceutical industry is a history of scandal – of misinformation and deception, of kickbacks to doctors and dodgy marketing techniques, of selling products regardless of cost; and of the medicalisation of the human condition. The few exceptions to this pattern are precisely the result of this ongoing battle between the public, defending its right to decent healthcare, and an industry pushing the boundaries of what it can get away with.

Diarmaid McDonald of campaign group Just Treatment believes you can apply the same argument to Martin Shkreli, the 'pharma bro' who, as I explained in the Introduction, became a public hate figure for his eye-watering price hikes to vital Aids-related drugs he had acquired. 'Nothing Shkreli did was that unusual', McDonald told me when I spoke to him:

> He did it in a more extreme manner and he wasn't pious about his behaviour. But really he just got too greedy and he did it with a grin on his face. The methods and techniques he used to maximise profits are mainstream. Everyone else does the same but when they get caught out they go on about how much they care. Look at GlaxoSmithKlein – giving kickbacks in China, poor safety standards, getting fined all over the place – the scandal is there in plain view and we accept it. We're so used to this industry behaving like this. We don't even notice.[34]

So the question for us is how the pharmaceutical industry is able to behave in this way, with what often seems like impunity. How did they become such powerful players in society? This question is important if we are to understand how the sector was able to reinvent itself as the dysfunctional industry we see today.

Part of Big Pharma's power lies in its major lobbying efforts. The *Lancet*'s opioid crisis report concludes, 'The power that lobbying and unconstrained political donations give the pharmaceutical industry is hard to overstate.'[35] It found that, over a decade, groups attempting to place limits on opioid prescribing spent only $4 million on lobbying and campaign contributions in US state legislatures, while the pharmaceutical industry spent $880 million 'to serve their business interests'.

In the United States this lobbying firepower is particularly pronounced. The pharmaceutical and health industries together spent $352 million lobbying the US Congress in 2021, the pharmaceutical industry donating to two-thirds of congressional representatives in 2020.[36] A *Stat News* report found that Pfizer alone donated to 228 American lawmakers ahead of the 2020 election, noting, 'Even after years of criticism from Congress and the White House over high prices, it remains routine for the elected officials who regulate the health care industry to accept six-figure sums.'[37]

Lobbying is intense in Europe too – another massive market for the industry, where separate safety standards apply and drug firms must also work to secure approval of their drugs and associated patents. Based on publicly available information, Corporate Europe Observatory – an independent research group monitoring corporate lobbying power – found in 2021 that at least $36 million was spent on lobbying by Big Pharma, while pharma companies and lobby groups reported employing 290 lobbyists directly.[38] The true figures are probably much higher.

Then there is the 'revolving door' between industry and government, through which Big Pharma attracts experienced officials to work for it by offering lucrative salaries. The *Lancet* gives a particularly extreme example of how this results in regulatory capture: 'Former US Congressman Billy Tauzin, for example, led the crafting of Medicare legislation that substantially expanded the US Government's purchasing of pharmaceutical products while simultaneously forbidding the Government from bargaining for lower drug prices. The day after his term ended, Tauzin became a leading pharmaceutical industry lobbyist, earning more than ten times his congressional salary.'[39]

There is a myriad of other ways in which Big Pharma builds its power, too, including direct marketing both to the health profession and to us as current or potential patients. Again, the lax US regulatory regime means this activity is particularly extreme there: doctors are routinely provided with free samples and gifts, paid for giving speeches or professional opinions on a drug, and treated to special 'educational' conferences at high-profile destinations and top restaurants. In 2012, the industry spent $24 billion marketing to American doctors.[40] This problem pertains even in more tightly regulated markets: companies spend around £40 million a year on British doctors in service fees, flights, and hotel and other travel expenses.[41] There has also been a whopping increase in direct marketing to patients, often through TV advertising, which tries to convince patients that they need help for conditions they were unaware they had, in a practice that has been termed 'disease mongering'.[42]

But this too is insufficient to explain the sheer scale of the industry's power. We need to look deeper still, into how a recognisable pharmaceutical sector developed after the Second World War, and how it developed roots across all relevant sections of society, until it was able to frame its own interests as being at one with those of the political establishment, academia and the health profession, as well as citizens and patients.

After the Second World War, a recognisably modern pharmaceutical industry emerged, comprising many of the same names familiar today. This was driven partly by the optimistic post-war belief that science and technology could solve any problem that humanity faced – that the future would inevitably be better for everyone. Few areas of life justified this optimism more strongly than the advancement of medical knowledge. The development of a new wave of breakthrough drugs, not least antibiotics, transformed our medical institutions. And the development of a range of other drugs – from antidepressants and tranquilizers through to vitamin supplements – changed the way we thought about our health, while also increasing the number of pills we took as a matter of routine.

By becoming more important in our lives, the pharmaceutical industry became more profitable; and as it grew, it consolidated. A traditional division between research and manufacturing started to disappear, and through a series of mergers the industry became more concentrated among a handful of major, vertically integrated players. In addition, the industry built a formidable sales and marketing arm, which developed increasingly sophisticated methods of selling not just products, but illnesses. A handful of massive pharmaceutical corporations came to oversee all aspects of producing medicines, working hand in hand with universities and regulatory authorities. This integration was certainly useful for planning, but the private nature of these corporations meant that public interest took a back seat to private returns. These companies did spend a great deal on research, but they also made huge profits.

Like all corporate sectors that become this powerful, the industry began to attract criticism. Rather like the big automotive industry that exercised such a powerful pull on the politics of countries like Germany, Italy and the UK, or indeed the Big Tech corporations like Amazon and Google today, the sheer power of these companies was beginning to have a major impact on the economy and society in general. In particular, with more people taking ever more costly pills, the prices of their products came under the spotlight. So began a series of battles between the pharmaceutical sector and the public. One of the most dramatic took place in the late 1950s, when a then well-known US politician called Estes Kefauver publicly took on the industry and demanded change.

Kefauver was a Democratic senator from Tennessee. Unlike many of his fellow Southern politicians at the time, who tended to be conservative, Kefauver was a 'new deal' Democrat, aligned with President Roosevelt in his concern at the concentration of economic power within private monopolies, and with the corruption of politics that this power fostered. As he remarked, 'I have long believed that it is only a step from the loss of economic freedom to the loss of political freedom.'

Keafauver's lifelong crusade against big business made him a thorn in the side of both the industry and the political elite in his party. In fact, he had to take on his own party bosses to become a senator. When a Democratic political boss accused him of pursuing communist political sympathies with the 'stealth of a raccoon', Kefauver donned a raccoon-fur hat to show his fearless independence from the party machine. It became a prop that he used in all subsequent elections.

In the early 1950s – when many Americans were first acquiring televisions – Kefauver ran a series of televised hearings into organised crime. A range of mafia bosses appeared before him, most famously the mobster Frank Costello. Parts of the hearings were even screened in cinemas, watched by an estimated 20 million people. Kefauver used the publicity generated to make a run for the presidency. He lost, though he ran for vice president on the failed 1956 ticket, beating the young John F. Kennedy as the party's candidate.

In 1959, with his hopes of winning the presidency dashed, Kefauver turned his guns on the pharmaceutical industry. He used his Senate antitrust and monopoly subcommittee, through which he had already taken on other big business sectors, to launch a series of hearings into the prices of medicines. One industry insider called it 'the pharmaceutical industry's own

"Pearl Harbor Day"'.[43] As the hearings unfolded, they uncovered a wide range of problems in the industry that are familiar to us today, from unaffordable and unjustified medicine prices to aggressive and unethical marketing, patent abuse, and the focus on so-called 'me-too' drugs, which were barely any different to medicines already on the market.[44]

Through 1959 and 1960, the chief executives of the pharma giants of the day – Merck, Pfizer, Bristol-Myers and Smith Kline – were publicly berated for the prices of their blockbuster drugs, including antibiotics, steroids, antipsychotics and tranquilisers. Pointing out that the pharmaceutical sector then earned twice the profits of the average manufacturing corporation at the time, with mark-ups of up to 7,000 per cent on some drugs, Kefauver told Merck's president, 'If you lower your profits and forget about some of these expensive methods of selling and expensive stock options, you could lower the price of drugs, too.'[45]

Arthur Sackler also appeared before the committee, though he managed to evade all blows aimed at him. But Patrick Radden Keefe reports that Kefauver was especially intrigued by Sackler, quoting from a staff memo that reads:

> The Sackler empire is a completely integrated operation in that it can devise a new drug in its drug development enterprise, have the drug clinically tested and secure favorable reports on the drug from the various hospitals with which they have connections, conceive the advertising approach and prepare the actual advertising copy with which to promote the drug, have the clinical articles as well as advertising copy published in their own medical journals, [and] prepare and plant articles in newspapers and magazines.[46]

For Kefauver, this was surely a perfect example of the unrivalled power of this industry.

The hearings were the most detailed public investigation into the pharmaceutical industry to date, and provided a sensational exposé of the way the drug corporations worked. They also showed those corporations that they could not take public support for granted – that they needed to advance better arguments and develop a better public-relations infrastructure if they were to hold onto their wealth.

Kefauver brought forward proposals to make radical changes to the way medicines were produced and sold. As well as improving safety regulation, he wanted the state to impose restrictions on important new drugs, and to strip the corporations of their monopoly privileges, making them face generic competition after three years. Kefauver also proposed a provision that went to the heart of Big Pharma's profiteering, trying to prevent the proliferation of 'me-too' drugs by only granting patents for medicines that represented a significant improvement over medicines already on the market. And he wanted to stamp out collusion between pharma companies to stitch up the market. In other words, Kefauver's bill could have transformed the drug industry. Presenting it in 1961, Kefauver declared, 'The time has arrived for action by the Congress to reduce the excessive and unwarranted charges upon those who are least able to afford them – the Nation's sick and afflicted.'[47]

Unsurprisingly, Kefauver faced immense pushback. First, pharmaceutical bosses and their friends in Congress hinted that Kefauver was actually pushing an anti-American line. In the febrile atmosphere of the Cold War, just a few years after Senator McCarthy's anti-communist hearings, this was a potent suggestion. But underlying the Cold War rhetoric was a very real concern: that Kefauver was actually pushing the United States towards some sort of national health service, the socialisation of medicine, which would kill all that was successful in the American dream. The socialisation of medicine was painted as a dangerous step towards communism that, in the public imagination, conjured up visions of doctors being told what to do by big government, of endless queues to get an operation, and of the impossibility of getting access to new medicines.

Of course, none of this reflected Kefauver's opinions. The senator's philosophy was as much about empowering small business and making competition work for the consumer as it was about big government. But the fear that the PR offensive engendered worked, and Big Pharma learned to use its most effective argument with the general public: that higher prices were necessitated by the high costs of medical research. As a health policy academic put it, 'They were advised that whenever the senators mentioned high prices, just mention research and how difficult it is, how expensive it is.'[48] Without the price tag, you risked having no effective new medicines at all.

For politicians and policy thinkers, the argument was further developed. Without new medicines, the United States risked being outcompeted by other economies. America was only as strong as its national champions, and it needed to back these champions, whatever the cost.

Former intellectual property lawyer Tahir Amin believes this link was vitally important in explaining the capture of policymaking by the pharmaceutical industry. 'Really in the US the industry seized on this idea that they were the drivers of innovation', he told me:

> And this all became part of the battle to defeat socialised healthcare in the US, actually. So you've really got to go back almost to the Second World War if you want to find the moment when we could

have gone a different way. At that point, science was at its crossroads, and the state still had the power to do things differently. Some did. India had the highest drug prices in the world in the 1950s – that's what gave India the impetus to develop its own pharmaceutical industry, including not granting patents on pharmaceutical products in the 1970s.

But in the US it was different. Innovation is seen almost as part of the American dream. And so any industry at the forefront of that is also going to be driving forward technology, growing the American economy – it's good for all of us. But we need to know that by innovation they meant something very specific. It was basically about making things slightly different – maybe marginally better, maybe not – but the important thing was getting people to *buy* more and more. Innovation equals more consumption, more growth. That's not the same as progress. But it's how Big Pharma justifies its power.[49]

The facts seem to bear Amin out. One 2020 study found that, over roughly forty years and across American industry, the pace of 'innovation', measured by patented products, had grown enormously. But during this period the gains of that innovation had been distributed far more unequally, with over 50 per cent of new US patents awarded to the top 1 per cent of patentees. Moreover, most patents were generated in just five US states: California, Texas, New York, Washington and Massachusetts[50]

Back in the 1950s, however, the success of the pharmaceutical industry at positioning itself at the heart of American innovation meant that Kefauver's proposals seemed doomed. But then something happened that underlined the importance of change.

In the late 1950s thalidomide was invented, and began to be marketed as a sort of super-drug. It was said to be a sedative that supposedly cured insomnia, coughs and headaches. Most importantly, it was also found to relieve morning sickness in pregnant women, and began to be heavily promoted for that purpose. But the drug had not been properly tested on pregnant women. Within a few years there was an epidemic of children born with deformities of their arms and legs, many of whom died. Before long these birth deformities were linked to the use of thalidomide in pregnancy. Ironically, thalidomide had never been formally approved in the United States, though many women had been given the drug as part of a clinical testing programme. Elsewhere, particularly in West Germany and Britain, there were a huge number of cases. High costs were one thing, but it now became clear that the pharmaceutical industry was not properly regulated to ensure the safety of patients.

In the wake of the scandal, there was a push for new regulations, and new life was breathed into Kefauver's proposals. However, the Kennedy administration, in no mood to go to war with the pharmaceutical industry, was determined to strip Kefauver's bill of its most far-reaching measures. Instead, it chose to focus on safety and effectiveness regulations. Kefauver himself was bypassed for the most part, even though the final piece of legislation bore his name. The new law did change the way drugs were approved, and created a more robust system to prove the effectiveness of new medicines, as well as introducing better inspections and certification.

But despite Senator Kefauver's best efforts, he did not manage to go make any further progress in pushing back the power of the industry. In fact, the bill actually had a negative impact on pricing, as drug companies could now argue that their medicines were even costlier to make, laying the basis for an even longer patent pathway to be introduced in the 1980s.

Kefauver would die after suffering a heart attack on the floor of the Senate while engaging in another fight to challenge monopolies. However, he left a huge legacy. His attempts to reform the pharmaceutical industry were repeated by progressive lawmakers on a regular basis up to the present. Mostly they have failed, but the torch has today been picked up by politicians like Katie Porter, Elizabeth Warren and Bernie Sanders, who are now closer to achieving meaningful change than at any point since Kefauver's time.

On the other side, Big Pharma learned a great deal from the hearings. It recognised that it needed to spread its influence deep into society if its power was to be preserved. This certainly meant cementing its arguments that high prices were justified by the costs of research. And the corollary of this argument was the claim – pressed by the industry upon policy-makers – that the interests of Big Pharma were at one with the interests of the US economy as a whole. But it also meant convincing doctors, medical students and patients that the pharma industry was 'on their side'. This required the industry to become a ubiquitous presence both within the state and in wider society.

Across the Atlantic a similar battle was brewing. In Britain, too, the spiralling costs of medicines was causing concern, particularly because so many of the medicines the NHS was purchasing were produced by foreign-owned companies. British governments were especially irked by the price of the new wonder-drug 'antibiotics', which they believed had essentially been a British invention but had been patented by American firms that were now overcharging Britain for the drugs. Britain therefore issued 'compulsory licenses', authorising the overriding of patents so they could purchase cheaper versions of the same antibiotics from Italy, which enjoyed a lax patent regime on medical products. In doing so they made use of a provision that still exists in British law, known as 'crown use'. In fact, the United States had done the same thing when it regarded an antibiotic, and many other drugs, as over-priced, saving the taxpayer a substantial amount of money.

Then, in 1965, Pfizer sued the British government for overriding its patents, arguing that use of drugs by the NHS was not 'for' the Crown as such.[51] The British courts disagreed, though they stipulated a 5 per cent royalty for Pfizer and left doubt as to whether the nominally more independent GP surgeries should be treated in the same way as NHS hospitals.[52]

Nonetheless, concern was such that a commission was established under Lord Sainsbury to look into the relationship between the pharmaceutical industry and the National Health Service, including the price of medicines. Sainsbury conducted a thorough and lengthy investigation, which even included visiting pharmaceutical factories. His commission found ample evidence of inflated costs draining NHS funds, and made a set of proposals not hugely different from those of his American counterpart. They would have forced the industry to be fully transparent about its costs, ended the selling of medicines by their brand names, and set up a powerful committee to oversee the sector.

As in the United States, Britain's Labour government balked at the proposals. Legislation followed, and the government did extract some promises of price constraints and more transparency on pricing, though this was achieved by tightening up an already-existing voluntary scheme. But the industry convinced the government that abolishing brand names would place British industry at a competitive disadvantage globally. The government duly accepted that pharmaceutical corporations should remain free in the way they promoted their products to doctors, albeit making clear they expected a 'very substantial reduction in the amount of promotional expenditure'. After all, they pointed out in 1965, the industry's 'cost of promotional representatives amounted to an average of £250 per doctor in the country per year'.

Overall, though, even the opposition Conservative Party welcomed the 'extreme caution' of the government's position.[53] As in the United States, the industry had convinced the government that further regulation would destroy the industry. In fact, the promotion of 'a strong and profitable pharmaceutical industry' became an explicit objective.

Again echoing the US pattern, the issue did not go away. But nor did the government's caution about taking measures which could have transformed the situation. It is instructive to look back at some of the British debates about Valium in the early 1970s. In 1973, the British parliament's Monopolies Commission examined the cost of Valium to the taxpayer, and 'reached the clear conclusion that United Kingdom prices for some years have been manifestly too high and that the Roche group has accordingly obtained from the sale of the drugs in this country profits far in excess of what is justifiable'.[54] Finding that Roche had made up to a 60 per cent profit on sales, with a 70 per cent return on capital, the commission ordered a reduction in the price of Valium and its sister drug Librium. So, while British governments, like their American counterparts, proved too timid to restructure the pharmaceutical industry in a fundamental way, there were limits to the toleration of its blatant profiteering.

As a result, the industry's approach to socialised healthcare was somewhat contradictory. On the one hand, a publicly funded National Health Service provided it with a massive market for its products, paid for by the state. In effect – even throughout Thatcher's premiership when government intervention and subsidy were dirty words – the British state continued to support the pharmaceutical industry through the NHS. What's more, this protected Big Pharma from undue public scrutiny of prices, because ordinary citizens generally had no idea how expensive the drugs they used were.

But there was a problem with this: being the biggest purchaser of new pharmaceutical products gives governments power, and a keen interest in controlling prices. The British government's interest in overriding patents and purchasing generics where possible, and its ability to negotiate directly with the industry, were important tools wielded by the British government. This gave the pharmaceutical industry a reason to be very wary of socialised healthcare.

In the United States, Big Pharma tended as a result to push back hard against socialised medicine. To this day, the federal government has a very limited ability to control prices – and hence the United States is the most lucrative market in the world for the industry, with prices many times higher than those found in other advanced markets. In fact, the key concessions that the industry won in the debates on Obamacare embedded this principle that the federal government must not interfere with the market price of medicines.

In *Pills, Power, and Policy*, Dominique Tobbell documents this post-war history of Big Pharma and the attempts to regulate it. Tobbell details the industry's growing power as it built a network of influence that encompassed medical students, universities, doctors, health workers and patients themselves, politicians, and regulatory bodies. In some ways, her argument runs, they went beyond being just an external actor exerting a powerful pull on Western governments, becoming deeply intertwined within the state itself. Even when regulation was improved, its effectiveness was compromised by the reach of the industry into the regulatory process.

The industry started using researchers to discredit scientific evidence that did not suit its interests – a tactic that Tobbell believes later inspired the tobacco industry.[55] Doctors became concerned at the sheer quantity and quality of advertising they received, which was indeed enormous. While Kefauver's committee found an average spend of just over 6 per cent of sales income on research and development in the United States, the largest pharmaceutical corporations spent between five and eleven times that much on advertising and sales costs. As the corporations came under ever greater scrutiny, so political donations ramped up, and the industry became increasingly involved in securing the election of pro–free market representatives to Congress. But an even more pernicious form of leverage was that exercised over academics, scientists and universities.

Dr Nancy Olivieri is one of world's leading experts of thalassemia, a blood disorder that causes your body to produce too little haemoglobin, resulting in anaemia. In severe cases, patients need regular blood transfusions.[56] There are medicines that can help, but they can be difficult to take, requiring lengthy, sometimes nightly, infusions.

Back in the 1990s, Olivieri was desperate to find a different type of medicine that could be taken in pill form, which might make living with thalassemia much easier. And she thought she had found one: a medicine now known as deferiprone. Working at the Hospital for Sick Children, a research-intensive hospital affiliated with the University of Toronto, she began testing the drug, working with a Canadian pharmaceutical company called Apotex, which agreed to trial it.

Everything started well enough, but after many months Olivieri began to notice some worrying longer-term side-effects of the drug. Recognising the huge step forward the pills represented for her patients, Olivieri was very reluctant to end the trials, but thought she had a duty at least to warn patients about the dangers and amend the consent form they were given. She told Apotex of her intention to inform those on the trial of the dangers. Later, Olivieri became even more concerned after some patients seemed to be suffering an alarming deterioration in their liver function, forcing her to conclude that taking the drug was unsafe. Again, Olivieri saw it as her primary duty to inform her patients.

But Apotex disagreed with Olivieri and told her to keep quiet, and then announced it would terminate the trials. Olivieri returned home one Friday night to discover a message on her answerphone. It was the vice-president of Apotex informing Olivieri that it would be ending her tests and bringing the drug to market as soon as possible. What's more, they warned Olivieri of the confidentiality agreement she had signed: she could not divulge her concerns about the drugs even to her own patients – indeed, the company threatened legal action should she do so. Olivieri's career was on the line.

This was the beginning of a long campaign of disinformation, threats, harassment, humiliation and legal action that could easily have driven Olivieri over the edge. She risked losing everything. Far from receiving the support she was due from her employer, Olivieri was cast out, and lost her position and reputation, before being reinstated after a difficult campaign for justice in which she was supported by experts from around the world. Although it has never been proved that this was the reason for her treatment by her employer, many have pointed out that Apotex had promised Olivieri's university a multimillion-dollar investment for a new building, the biggest donation it had ever received at that time.

Olivieri endured lengthy legal battles with Apotex, which took over a decade to resolve. Both she and those supporting her started receiving anonymous threatening letters, making them concerned for their safety. It was later discovered, after taking DNA evidence from the envelopes of the hate mail, that they had been sent by a senior colleague whose own work was being funded by the company. He kept his job throughout.[57]

Olivieri was later reinstated and cleared of all charges against her. Meanwhile, an independent investigation found that

> Apotex acted against the public interest in issuing legal warnings to Dr Olivieri to deter her from communicating about risks . . . Apotex's legal warnings violated Dr Olivieri's academic freedom. The Hospital for Sick Children and the University of Toronto did not provide effective support either for Dr Olivieri and her rights, or for the principles of research and clinical ethics, and of academic freedom, during the first two and a half years of this controversy.[58]

In 2009 Olivieri was again dismissed from her position at the university, with no reason given. Further investigative work suggested that, almost immediately after her dismissal, the university had begun to switch thalassemia patients to the controversial drug deferiprone, that Apotex was supplying unrestricted educational grants to the thalassaemia programme, and that the company had strategised with her replacement about how to license the drug.[59]

Since then, Olivieri has dedicated her life to trying to uncover the insidious power of the pharmaceutical industry over researchers and medical practitioners. Her determination meant that many people came to know of her case. Olivieri was an inspiration for John le Carré's famous novel about the pharmaceutical industry,

The Constant Gardener, later made into an acclaimed film starring Ralph Fiennes. Le Carré wrote in the book's foreword, 'I came to realize that, compared to reality, my story is as tame as a holiday postcard.'

These events forced people in the field to begin questioning the power of the pharmaceutical industry. Although Olivieri's case took place in Canada, and involved a relatively unknown pharmaceutical company, it is far from isolated. Olivieri herself says that she used to believe she had been unlucky, but after receiving hundreds of letters she knows there are many people in similar situations who have simply received less publicity – people who have faced threats, dismissals and harassment simply for doing their job.

One expert who has documented the case draws a parallel with US President Eisenhower's warnings about a military-industrial complex, in which the

> ties between the American military and the arms industry had become so intimate and extensive that Eisenhower – by no means a Marxist revolutionary – felt compelled to speak publicly of his fears for the future of American democracy. It is not implausible to speculate that were Eisenhower alive today, he might be tempted to issue a comparable warning against 'the scientific/industrial complex' . . . The dramatically increased role of for-profit corporations in the funding of medical and life sciences research is, arguably, a trend that threatens to undermine both the traditional values of science and the public's trust in our research universities and teaching hospitals.[60]

Apotex is not as big as Pfizer, and indeed makes more generic drugs than anything else. In other ways, its behaviour was similar to that of the bigger players with a global footprint, a history of takeovers of other firms, and a huge budget for fighting legal battles over patents. Until 2017, Apotex was run by Barry Sherman, a billionaire who also had major investments in a casino, a gold mine, commercial real estate, a jewellery company and a range of B-movies. In that year, Sherman and his wife were brutally murdered in their home.[61] No one has ever been convicted for the murder, but speculation is rife. Sherman upset a lot of people.

But the factors behind the Olivieri case go beyond the people involved. They are systemic, stemming from the fact that research has become increasingly dependent on a highly self-interested group of corporations. Today, universities are encouraged to enter deep 'partnerships' with corporations, which allow these businesses, directly or indirectly, to set priorities, oversee the design of research projects, terminate projects they dislike, ghost-write academic pieces for reputable scientists and exert influence on appointments. As one academic puts it, 'In the long run and overall it cannot serve the public interest to have the research agenda dictated by the corporate imperative of short run profitability.'[62]

The problems with the industry's stranglehold on research extend also to the regulatory approval process. Olivieri is critical of the speedy approval of deferiprone by the US regulator, the FDA, albeit as a last-resort drug. She says it went against the FDA's own acknowledgement that her evidence was valid, and was approved on very insubstantial proof of effectiveness: 'Asked whether the FDA had ever issued approval based on data of such poor quality, an FDA official responded as follows: "Not that I am aware of. I want to make sure this doesn't establish a precedent." '[63] More recently, an Alzheimer's drug was approved in a controversial move that saw the FDA overrule the near-unanimous view of its own advisory committee, causing the resignation of three of its members. The drug is priced in the United States at $56,000 per person per year, and although the producer of the medicine has to show evidence of effectiveness over the next decade, that is plenty of time to make huge profits.[64]

Of course, this is not an argument for foot-dragging in the approval of medicines. Some diseases are indeed very rare, with very severe symptoms. If there is reasonable evidence new drugs might make a difference, it seems perverse to wait for certainty before dispensing the drugs to those most in need. The salient question, as with so much in the production of medicines, is who is pulling the strings.

A substantial portion of the FDA's own funding comes from user fees charged to the very corporations seeking approval for their drugs – the companies the FDA should be holding to account.[65] And a majority of the drug-review funds come from the industry itself. The whole purpose of the FDA moving to this model was to ensure the approval of drugs more quickly. But it has raised serious concerns that the FDA is increasingly willing to approve drugs on the basis of insufficient evidence of benefit. Journalist Caroline Chen claims the FDA 'is increasingly green-lighting expensive drugs despite dangerous or little-known side effects and inconclusive evidence that they curb or cure disease'. She makes a powerful case that the regulatory body itself has become a public–private partnership.[66]

'Very few of the poor benefit from the potential of modern medicines.' So proclaimed an influential book, published by Dianna Melrose with the backing of Oxfam, back in 1982.[67] *Bitter Pills* raises a litany of charges against the post-war pharmaceutical industry's impact on the Global South – or Third World, as it was known at the time. For most of the world, at least, the notion that the golden age of pharmaceutical research was guided by enlightened and socially responsible corporations is very wide of the mark. For the post-war pharmaceutical industry, the developing world was pretty much irrelevant. Markets were too limited, the potential profits that could be earned there too small, to justify devoting research capacity to the diseases that mainly affected those countries.

But this didn't mean these countries – the majority of the world, of course – were somehow less harmed by that industry. Most obviously, it meant that diseases that should have been perfectly treatable with modern medical knowledge were simply ignored. As Big Pharma chased more lucrative markets, so-called 'diseases of poverty' were much less important objects of research than relatively minor inconveniences suffered by those with money in advanced consumer markets – hair loss, for instance.

But, of course, some Western medicines were in fact extremely useful to people in these countries. Yet such medicines were hard to come by, and very expensive. At the time, three-quarters of the world's population in the Global South only had access to around 20 per cent of the world's drugs – 15 per cent if you took China out of the equation. Melrose quotes an Indian doctor who sums the situation up well:

> The drug industry, like any other industry, produces only to the extent that drugs can be sold at a reasonable profit in the market, irrespective of the needs of the people. The majority of our population is very poor. It is precisely this poor section that requires more medical attention and hence larger quantities of drugs. But since these people do not have money to buy the drugs, the industry neglects this section of the populace.[68]

Where medicines were available, they were often priced well out of reach of the majority of the population, particularly because so many drugs were imported from the rich world. Although the pharmaceutical industry as a whole was big and fairly diverse, 90 per cent of the trade in medicines was done by around 100 manufacturers, dominated by huge Western multinationals. The cost of these drugs was rising rapidly, just as in the West, but buying in foreign currency was a special problem when countries were hit with high inflation or currency devaluation.

We have already seen that the drug industry developed a clear rationale justifying high prices in terms of the need for innovation, which in turn incentivised the production of many more drugs with very little difference between them. When you build into this equation that most countries of the Global South had nothing to gain from these drugs, it seems particularly unjust that they were paying for such 'innovation'. Out of total research and development expenditure of around $5 billion in 1980, an industry analyst reckoned the international pharmaceutical industry spent just 1 per cent of that on diseases that specifically afflicted the poorer world.

Moreover, medicines were sometimes sold in a way that ignored basic safety standards. This last point was of major concern for agencies like Oxfam at the time. 'On open market stalls in Upper Volta [Burkina Faso] red and yellow capsules of antibiotics are displayed for sale alongside equally colourful sweets. Poor people buy just one or two capsules at a time to treat themselves', writes Melrose. To take a different example,

> In 1980 governments and aid agencies all over the world responded to the plight of the Kampuchean people by rushing in a mass of drugs they had well-meaningly scrambled together. But this jumble of medicines, labelled in dozens of different languages,

> created chaos. In the absence of a team of multilingual pharmacists to sift through them, many potentially useful and useless drugs alike had to be discarded.[69]

When illness struck, those in poverty often tried anything to get their hands on Western medicines, spending everything they had on them – money that would go much further spent on food, water and sanitation than on overpriced medicines. Given that these drugs were sometimes completely uncontrolled, people often struggled to take them properly.

This included taking medicines that had been deemed too ineffective or dangerous to be on market in the West, since 'When a decision is made to withdraw a drug in Europe or the US, the evidence suggests that it by no means follows that manufacturers will always voluntarily remove their product from the Third World market.' As Melrose posits, 'Some rich world manufacturers appear to have actively encouraged the misuse of powerful and potentially dangerous antibiotics for mild infections.' She uses the example of selling diarrhoea medication to mothers of dehydrated babies. As Melrose notes, these babies needed water more than anything, and in fact the drugs concerned might actually have masked signs of dehydration, for which reason they were not prescribed for babies in Britain. But, of course, pharmaceutical corporations are not going to recommend water when they can sell a pill.

Marketing spend was often relatively large. Just to take one example, in Tanzania Melrose found that the amount pharmaceutical companies 'spend each year on "educating" doctors about which drugs to use is more than the annual budget of the Faculty of Medicine, which is used to educate doctors in every other sphere including how to use drugs properly'.[70] More insidious were adverts from India designed to discredit the cheaper generic medicines that the Indian government was desperately trying to promote.

We might like to think such behaviour is the product of a less enlightened time. But the abuse continues today. In 2002 I worked with comedian and campaigner Mark Thomas and Médecins Sans Frontières on a television programme about 'drug dumping' – the phenomenon of pharmaceutical corporations taking advantage of tax loopholes to offload useless or expired medicines on less wealthy counties, often in the middle of humanitarian disasters.[71] This was usually cheaper than paying to dispose of the medicines properly – particularly as the companies involved could earn tax relief, as well as adulation for their altruism, by claiming they were donations.

Drugs that had expired – some were several years out of date – or which contained instructions in a language not spoken in the country were common. In some cases the results could be serious, as people were prescribed the wrong medicine. The report contained details of tons of useless drugs, including appetite stimulants dumped in the middle of a famine in Sudan and silicone breast implants donated to Malawi's health service.

There is another way in which developing countries were found to be useful to pharmaceutical companies: as test sites. Perhaps the most famous example comes from Kano, Nigeria, during a terrible meningitis outbreak. Anxious to test a new drug that had never been trialled on children before, Pfizer had leapt on the serious outbreak and sent scientists to the region. The *Washington Post* described a medical camp in Kano at the height of the epidemic as follows:

> Behind a gate besieged by suffering crowds stood two very different clinics. A humanitarian charity, Doctors Without Borders, had erected a treatment center solely in an effort to save lives.

> Researchers for Pfizer Inc., a huge American drug company, had set up a second center. They were using Nigeria's meningitis epidemic to conduct experiments on children with what Pfizer believed was a promising new antibiotic – a drug not yet approved in the United States.[72]

Some people on the trial died – including both those given Pfizer's new drug and those given the standard drug. Other children were left with permanent damage to their limbs. Pfizer claims it was not the drug that killed the children, but the meningitis. After all, it is a horrible disease, and it was an epidemic. But as more and more parents came forward, as journalists and investigators came to look at the case, there was growing disquiet, because Pfizer appeared to have behaved very differently from how it would have been obliged to behave in the West. At the centre of the concern was the different standards of consent and care that Pfizer appeared to have used in Kano. No consent forms were obtained from patients.[73] Pfizer says it was simply not possible, as parents did not write or speak English. But some of the parents involved deny this.

There was also criticism of the doses given, and of Pfizer's failure to switch drugs when the new medicine failed to work, as well as holes in the data and the decision to launch an experiment very quickly in very difficult conditions. As one nurse working for Médecins Sans Frontières in the Kano emergency said, 'In an epidemic, where you have a very high number of cases who will die, you don't go and experiment. You are talking about human beings, after all.'[74]

Perhaps the most damning piece of evidence was that one of Pfizer's childhood disease specialists wrote to the director of the programme protesting in the strongest term about the trial.[75] He claims he was sacked as a result.

There seems no way of proving whether the deaths and injuries were a result of the trials or of the underlying disease that it was intended to fight. But Pfizer was sued by families who believed the corporation had behaved unethically.[76] Furthermore, the drug was never authorised for use in children in the United States. A secret Nigerian government report concluded that Pfizer had undertaken an 'illegal trial of an unregistered drug'.[77] To this day, the people of Kano remain understandably sceptical of Western medicines – something that has further hampered the Covid-19 vaccine rollout. One college student from the area told the *Washington Post*, 'I don't trust anything from the West, because of what happened here.'[78]

Perhaps most frightening of all is the realisation that Kano was not unique. A *Washington Post* investigation at the time into corporate drug experiments in Africa, Asia, Eastern Europe and Latin America revealed 'a booming, poorly regulated testing system that is dominated by private interests and that far too often betrays its promises to patients and consumers. Experiments involving risky drugs proceed with little independent oversight. Impoverished, poorly educated patients are sometimes tested without understanding that they are guinea pigs. And pledges of quality medical care sometimes prove fatally hollow.'[79]

The post-war period can hardly be held up as a golden age of social responsibility and ethical behaviour by the pharmaceutical industry. It was a period of empire building, when the industry sunk its roots into every aspect of society to cement its power. The key argument deployed again and again was the claim that their cutting-edge research meant they were a national asset, conferring international competitiveness on the country where their headquarters were located. There was no difference, the argument ran, between the interests of the pharmaceutical sector and the national economic interest of the state.

What started out as a Cold War argument about the necessity of developing the technology necessary to outcompete the eastern bloc played just as well during the economic crisis of the mid 1970s. As countries faced economic downturn, it made no sense, so the story went, to kill off the goose that laid so many golden eggs. Far from decrying the excessive profitability of the industry, governments should be celebrating it – and any regulation would stifle the innovation necessary to grow.[80]

These arguments laid the ground for the two most important pieces of US regulation to affect the industry since the 1960s. First, the Bayh–Dole Act, passed in 1980, gave private bodies the right to patent their work when those discoveries had been contracted and funded by the government. Before then, such breakthroughs were either owned by the state or placed in the public domain. This led to an enormous increase in the number of patents issued across the board. According to a report by think tank Common Wealth, 'in the United States, the Patent and Trademark Office took 155 years to issue its first 5 million patents, and just 27 years for it to issue the next 5 million, but there's little evidence of a great explosion of exponential innovation in that 27 year period'.[81]

Then, in 1984, the Hatch–Waxman Act was passed. Although supposedly concerned with making it easier to register generic medicines, the act gave patent holders a tighter form of market exclusivity and longer patent terms, implicitly conceding the argument that previous regulation had hampered Big Pharma's ability to profit.

But these acts did not simply hand more power to big pharmaceutical corporations – they also helped change the nature of the industry. We have already seen that, from the 1950s, marketing, advertising and PR often accounted for a far bigger share of the pharmaceutical industry's budget than research and development. Still, that research, along with the industry's manufacturing base, was at the heart of the industry's power. Together, these were the main assets of the industry. What happened next would change all that.

From the 1980s, as I will show in the next chapter, an economic transformation took place that went far beyond the pharmaceutical industry. New economic thinking took hold, embraced most enthusiastically by Ronald Reagan in the United States and Margaret Thatcher in Britain. The idea of government intervention, even as a last resort, was regarded as folly. In future, faith was to be placed in corporations to regulate themselves. Markets were seen as the best mechanism for making economic and social decisions. Financial markets were seen as the purest form of market, and their influence was to be expanded across the economy, giving a much-needed jolt to what was perceived as a wasteful and inefficient public sector.

What was important to those financial markets was less research and manufacturing than the intellectual property that corporations held. Research and manufacturing were therefore scaled back. Research scientists were replaced by lawyers and financiers. For society at large, this left a huge gap in research funding that – at least to some extent – had to be filled by public funds. On the manufacturing side, the gap was to an extent filled by countries like India. But such developments were patchy, and Big Pharma ultimately used its political power to ensure that it retained full control.

As a consequence, the corporations now had us in a headlock. Increasingly they did less of what made them socially useful in the first place; but still they remained in control of the production of medicines. As we will see, the dysfunctional nature of this relationship became obvious when governments needed to scale up research and manufacturing of Covid-19 medicines in 2020.

Today, for the first time since the 1970s, we may be at a turning point where we can again reimagine the system of making medicines, and tear down the power of these drug giants. That is because, ultimately, despite all its loci of power, the pharmaceutical sector depends on political good will. And that good will is in short supply. The *Lancet* echoed the editorials in many newspapers across the world over the last couple of years when, taking aim at the core of the pharmaceutical sector's operating model, it said, 'The profit motives of actors inside and outside the health-care system will continue to generate harmful over-provision of addictive pharmaceuticals unless regulatory systems are fundamentally reformed.'[82]

The journal looked at how the pharmaceutical sector's power in the United States – at both federal and state levels; in regulatory bodies, in universities, the health sector, patient advocacy groups and professional bodies – has played an active role in worsening the opioid crisis. One example is particularly chilling:

> when the US Drug Enforcement Administration caught opioid distribution companies breaking the law by not reporting massive, suspicious shipments of opioids to particular communities, the companies asked Congress to pass a law curtailing the organisation's power to conduct such investigations. The pharmaceutical industry contributed US$1·5 million to the campaigns of 23 lawmakers who sponsored the new law, including US$100 000 to Representative Tom Marino, who led the law's passage in the House of Representatives.[83]

The report made detailed recommendations about how to fix the problem, including curtailing promotional activity, removing industry influence over medical education, closing the revolving door between regulators and industry, and making drug monitoring and risk-mitigation functions of government. In addition, it made broader points about the need to 'restore caps on political donations [and] prevent the pharmaceutical industry from covertly funding advocacy organisations'. These proposals, like those of Senator Kefauver sixty years ago, struck at the heart of the state–industry complex protecting Big Pharma. While many of the recommendations were aimed at the US government, the report had relevance for all countries that played host to major pharmaceutical players.

I will leave the last word in this chapter to Diarmaid McDonald of the patient advocacy group Just Treatment, because it gives me hope, showing, as it does, that ultimately, the industry's power is limited, and that it can be challenged. He told me:

> You can take away the tax breaks, the supportive regulations, the public financing and so on, and most industries can still function. But if you strip away the regulatory space which gives Big Pharma its power, [its] business model crumbles as its profits and sky-high prices rely on the artificial scarcity created by government-granted monopolies. There's nothing else. That's why they spend so much money trying to influence the political process.[84]

2

A Hedge Fund with a Pharmaceutical Firm Attached

In 2007 luxury car manufacturer Porsche was celebrating success. Its leader, Wendelin Wiedeking, had taken the company from the doldrums – a loss-making manufacturer on its last legs – to being one of the most profitable car companies in the world. By late 2007, Porsche announced whopping half-year profits of over €5 billion.[1]

But, as successful as Porsche had undoubtedly become, a closer inspection of the corporation's accounts showed that all was not as it first appeared. Financial journalists revealed that the firm had earned three times as much trading derivatives as it had selling cars. A year later, that ratio had become even more extreme.[2] The BBC reported that the car maker had made six times as much on the stock market as it had making cars. Indeed, the article quoted insiders as only half-joking when they claimed that Porsche was now 'a hedge fund with a carmaker attached'.[3]

Under the radar, Porsche had been buying up Volkswagen stock in an attempt to take over the much larger car company, massively driving up the price of that stock in the process.[4] But in order to finance this buy-up, the company had gone deep into debt. In fact, the size of this debt at just the time the economy crashed in 2008 finally led to the collapse of the whole takeover. But along the way

Porsche had been sitting on a mountain of over-inflated stock that was, on paper, making the firm a fortune – though of course the value of this stock would collapse if Porsche ever tried to cash it in.

In early 2008, at the height of financial exuberance in the global economy, luxury car-making was a lucrative activity. But, as one analyst put it, 'the car business was good, but the financial engineering business was even better'.[5] And this was great news for Porsche CEO Wiedeking, who had negotiated a contract that tied his salary to corporate profits, which meant the financial trading led to his becoming the highest-paid corporate executive in Germany. Even when Wiedeking's gamble failed and the deal collapsed, leaving Porsche with €10 billion of debt, he received a cool €50 million severance package. Still, one business paper wrote, 'He was worth the money.'[6]

The Porsche case became something of a cause célèbre among those concerned about a trend in the global economy known as financialisation. While many of us might not care much about how a luxury car-maker runs its operations, the example of Porsche was by no means a one-off. In fact, a similar trend was taking place right across the economy. And that mattered not simply at the level of individual companies – it was also having a profound impact on the economy and society as a whole.

Financialisation is a hotly contested term, and many thousands of pages of academic research have been produced trying to define it. Those debates will not be rehashed here, but I will explain some of the core elements of this phenomenon, in order to explain more fully the changes taking place in the pharmaceutical sector.

While it is difficult to imagine financialisation without large and powerful banks, the process is by no means confined to them. Britain has had an overly powerful financial sector for many decades, but that did not amount to the financialisation of its economy until the 1980s. Financialisation refers to the extension of the logic of financial markets *beyond banks*, to the economy as a whole. This means subjecting ever more parts of our economy and wider society to financial motivations, and treating everything we value as if it were a gigantic financial market.

As the logic of finance comes to dominate non-financial industries, companies are increasingly forced by their investors, most importantly holders of their corporate stock, or their creditors to prioritise profit-maximisation over all other considerations. In turn, shareholders have become less interested in investment in a specific industry or sector, and more driven to invest in whatever makes the highest return. This is closer to short-term speculation – betting on the rise and fall of prices – than genuine long-term investment, and forces companies to compete against each other for ever higher returns.

Of course, profits have always been important to companies in the capitalist economy, but financialisation is something different. Whereas in the past a drug company was primarily competing against other drug companies to make more profitable medicines, in the modern economy drug companies are competing against all profit-making enterprises – whether they make cars, biscuits or financial services – for investors and creditors. They are not judged by the standard of the products they make, but by the short-term returns their operations can generate for their investors. If higher profits come from trading derivatives, or buying up and asset-stripping other companies, or trading your own shares to keep your stock price high, so be it: the financialised economy will instruct firms to do so, rather than produce anything tangible.[7]

That means not only that car companies might make more money buying shares than making cars, but that supermarkets might make higher profits through buying and selling land, or mobile phone companies might make more from selling insurance than selling phones. Wherever you look, speculation and rent becomes a better investment bet than productive activity.

Does this matter? Yes, because it distorts what a company chooses to invest in – rather than creating a more sophisticated workforce or a more productive plant, it will plough money into supremely unproductive parts of the economy, in turn driving their value up even further. This will also, for example, change what ambitious young graduates choose to study and apply their talents to. In other words, it alters how our society chooses to use its resources.

Financialisation does not just change the way companies think and behave – it changes the way governments behave too. Under financialisation, financial markets have become the answer to everything, from funding healthcare to stopping climate change – even if, in reality, social problems might be better served by greater *regulation* of finance, not its further liberalisation.

Financialisation also means more money flowing around the world – much, much more money. We are used to thinking of the globalisation of the 1980s and '90s in terms of a huge increase in trade, but it was in fact far more about an increase in financial power. Between 1980 and 2007, international capital flows expanded from $500 billion to $12 trillion.[8] In 1973, the ratio of the value of foreign exchange transactions to global trade was two-to-one; by 2004 it had reached ninety-to-one. And by 2017, while the total value of global trade was $18 trillion *a year*, the foreign exchange transactions that were making this trade possible accounted for $5.1 trillion *a day*. In other words, this money is not flowing for the purpose of making the production and distribution of goods possible, but represents money becoming an end in itself, in turn undermining the value of production. This increase in the mobility and scale of money flowing around the world has created enormous volatility in the global economy, with more frequent crises, whose cost is paid disproportionately by the poorest.

Finally, financialisation creates much more debt. Debt has ballooned since the 1970s, not just at a government level, but also at the level of individual households – everything from credit cards to payday loans, mortgages and university debt – and the corporate sector, where companies increasingly use debt to finance their operations and enrich their shareholders. In 2021, global debt stood at $226 trillion, more than twice the value of the world economy.[9]

This has serious consequences for economic stability. But at a political level, debt is also important because it provides a disciplining mechanism in the economy.[10] To pay your debt, you need to do what your creditors demand: make as much money as possible, regardless of the consequences. Furthermore, the logic of finance is forced upon governments, companies and households through debt. The power of debt has played an important role, as we will see, in laying the basis for the neoliberal economy from the 1990s through to the present.

Perhaps unsurprisingly, this has exacerbated inequality hugely, both within and between countries, because those who hold capital are able to lend it, while those who do not must borrow it. So, the 'haves' get richer – and while debt allows the 'have-nots' to go on spending, keeping the consumer economy afloat, the underlying inequality gets worse and worse. In effect, it both defers a reckoning with inequality while also intensifying it.

I will return to the bigger social implications of financialisation again, but it is worth noting here that this process has had very profound consequences for society. It has shifted economic activity from production and invention, which rely on a talented and educated labour force, towards 'making money from money', and what is known as the rentier economy: producing wealth from money rather than from making real things. In turn, this has shifted power from labour towards capital, from ordinary people towards the superrich, with profound implications for economic stability, for our democratic rights, and even for how individuals think about their role in society.

A team of University of Sheffield researchers, including radical accountant and tax-justice campaigner Richard Murphy, has looked in detail at how this process of financialisation has affected individual non-financial companies.[11] Their work is important for understanding what this all means for the pharmaceutical sector. They note three major changes in the way companies work.

First, companies have put far more emphasis on paying shareholders. In the last twenty years or so, we have seen historically high returns to shareholders and investors. The team found that an average big business in the United States has handed 87 per cent of its income to shareholders in the ten years leading up to 2019. That is a huge amount – and it is all money that cannot be reinvested and spent on improving the business. At the extreme end, things are even worse. In a sizeable minority of cases, returns to shareholders *exceeded* the profits that the company in question had made.

Pharmaceutical corporations are particularly extreme in this regard. In a separate study that looked only at companies listed on the British stock market, both UK-based Big Pharma giants GlaxoSmithKline and AstraZeneca fell into this category, returning over 100 per cent of their net income to shareholders.[12] I repeated the exercise for the five companies examined in this chapter – Abbvie, Gilead, Pfizer, GSK and AstraZeneca – for the years 2016–20. All of them returned more to shareholders in that period than their net income, AbbVie returning a huge 165 per cent.[13]

This seems counterintuitive. How on earth can a corporation possibly return more to its shareholders than it made during the year? There might be several answers to this question, but it likely involves the second and third traits of financialisation that the Sheffield researchers identify – the growth of cash and debt, and the growth of something called 'intangible assets'.

I have mentioned debt already. Financialisation has seen the ballooning of cheap and often very risky debt. Usually, the bigger you are, the more you can borrow, and within our economic model there are huge incentives to borrow. In theory, firms use their debt to invest and generate a good return, allowing them to repay their debt and make a reasonable profit. In practice, they can use debt to bankroll their shareholder bonanza – and effectively make up the difference between what the company is making in a given year and what they are handing over to shareholders. They can also use debt to gain leverage, buying out their competitors, and thereby becoming even bigger and more powerful. As likely as not, this will attract even more investors. Using debt to pay shareholders rather than investing in improving the business is not a great long-term strategy if what is needed is a more productive company. But this is what happens practically in the financialised economy.

To understand the scale of this problem, it is worth quoting from the findings of a study by Rodrigo Fernandez and Tobias J. Klinge.[14] Examining the accounts of twenty-seven of the world's largest pharmaceutical corporations between 2000 and 2018, including most of the corporations mentioned in this chapter, they found that debt had ballooned from $60 billion to $520 billion. This trend was particularly pronounced in the top ten companies, where debt had increased from $50 billion to $310 billion, well in excess of the growth of those same companies during this period. The financial reserves of these companies had also increased massively, from $83 billion to $219 billion, with most of the increase again accounted for by the top ten largest corporations.

The researchers suggest this shows that, by holding more debt and cash, these corporations are not reinvesting profits in better medicines, equipment or staff, but hanging on to cash so they can buy up other companies, stash money in tax havens, or use it to enrich wealthy shareholders. When they compare this pile of cash to the amount of 'real' assets owned by the companies, like factories or labs, they find that 'the largest pharmaceutical companies increasingly hold more financial reserves than physical means of production for drug manufacturing'.

The fact that so much money is chasing proportionally less research and fewer drugs explains why the price of medicine has increased so much. It is not to do with the cost of making the drugs – in fact, medicine prices are entirely unrelated to research costs; rather, it is hard-wired into the financialisation of the industry.

But there is a third aspect of financialisation: the growth of intangible assets. I am going to explore this in much more detail in Chapter 5, but for now, I will simply note it refers to a whole host of assets businesses own that you cannot quite put your finger on, but which have become increasingly important to their profits. It includes things like a company's brand, its reputation, or the know-how embedded in whatever it produces and that its competitors cannot use. It is not as simple as, say, owning a factory, or even having workers on your payroll; you can assess the value of those things relatively easily. But how do you assess the value of owning, say, the Levi's brand? How can you put a figure on what McDonalds's name-recognition might mean for your profits over the next ten years?

Frankly, it is almost impossible to do so. But that doesn't mean there are not accounting techniques dreamed up to put very precise figures on this sort of thing. For some companies, including Big Pharma, this stuff has become really important – in particular, when it comes to the so-called intellectual property that protects recipes and know-how and technologies over which their owners enjoy a monopoly. In fact, this stuff is considered more important than their scientists or laboratories – and so they assign a value to it. And because it is quite difficult, many of these assets end up overvalued – which is great news for investors in the short term, because it means the company looks better off than it actually is.

That might all be acceptable if you are about to invest in some amazing new technology or in improving your productivity. But if you are simply using it to make your wealthy shareholders even richer, then, just as with debt, what you are really doing is hollowing out your own firm, leaving little real value in the underlying company.

In fact, this massive concentration of the pharmaceutical industry – with ever fewer and bigger corporations – has been shown to be bad for drug development. A piece in *Science* magazine tells the story of a very important cancer drug that languished in the fridge for years because it went unnoticed.[15] The reason was that, through buying out a potential competitor in 2003, Pfizer found itself in possession of an enormous amount of research, which it did not adequately assess for medical potential. Several years later, some scientists outside the company were doing cutting-edge research that forced Pfizer to sit up and take notice. They looked through the research sitting on their shelves and turned it into an important medicine. It ended well, thanks to independent research, but years had been lost in which many patients could have been helped if everyone at Pfizer had not 'been so preoccupied with merging, buying, moving, rearranging, and figuring out if they were getting laid off or not'.[16]

Intangible assets, particularly intellectual property, are at the heart of the pharma model.[17] For the twenty-seven biggest pharma companies, intangible assets increased from $48 billion in 2000 to a staggering $857 billion in 2018. The latter figure is not far off the GDP of a very rich country like the Netherlands. The concentration of such assets in the ten largest firms was particularly pronounced, increasing from $38 billion to $522 billion. As a proportion of a company's total assets, intangible assets had ballooned from 13 per cent to 51 per cent. Meanwhile, the growth of physical productive capacity (such as factories and labs) has sharply declined as a share of total assets.

This means, in turn, that Big Pharma spends more and more of its resources trying to bolster the value of its intangible assets, rather than engaging in productive activity. One report looks at the twelve best-selling drugs in the United States, and finds that drug makers filed nearly 1,500 attempted patent claims on them – the vast majority successful – simply to extend their monopolies far beyond the twenty years of protection they enjoy by right.[18]

One example of this trend is the patenting of the currently illegal drug psilocybin, the psychoactive component in magic mushrooms, which is increasingly seen as a groundbreaking medicine for treating depression. One group, Compass Pathways, funded by major investors including Peter Thiel, the PayPal co-founder and right-wing political financier, has issued a huge number of controversial patents to try to corner the market.

There is enormous controversy around these patents, because magic mushrooms are a naturally occurring organism that theoretically should not be patentable. But Compass is trying to patent the *processes* around extracting the drug, and even some of its therapeutic applications. Some of these are so general as to be absurd, such as a blanket patent covering the therapy setting specifying that 'the room comprises soft furniture', 'the room is decorated using muted colors', 'the room comprises a high-resolution sound system' and 'the room comprises a bed or a couch'.[19] One leading shareholder noted, 'Many psychedelic companies out there will never be able to bring a product to market as they will hit the patents,' while a journalist remarked that the psilocybin patent race 'demonstrates the breakdowns in the patent system, and how it can be twisted to the benefit of monopolists'.[20]

The Sheffield researchers argue that this process is not making our economy as a whole any more efficient, effective or productive – quite the reverse. In essence, it 'presents a picture of corporate America effectively eating itself'.[21] The same also applies to corporate Britain and – to only a slightly lesser degree – corporate Europe. Far from building a sustainable enterprise, this trend represents something more like a scorched-earth strategy, which leaves corporations unable to serve the function we assume they are fulfilling, instead becoming gigantic cash machines for their investors.

Financialisation carries huge risks, too. As Murphy and his colleagues write, the crisis-prone economic model will make 'recessions deeper, the costs to governments larger'.[22] An economy that makes less useful products and employs less skilled people will find itself ever more fundamentally weakened, less resilient and nearer to total collapse. In turn, this will 'accelerate the uneven societal distribution of income and risk', because the pain will be felt by ordinary people, not by those who have gained from this crazy casino model. In this society, it is workers who bear the risk.

Far from being the 'national champions – R&D powerhouses and drivers of UK productivity', pharma companies have instead become 'increasingly flimsy', 'increasingly intangible, and don't appear to be improving the underlying productivity of each firm'.[23] Nevertheless, because of the way our economy now works, they remain extremely powerful actors, 'and maintain an effective gatekeeper position in final markets due to their extensive marketing operations' that actively prevents smaller competitors from challenging their dominance. We will see below just how damaging this model was throughout the pandemic, but it should not have surprised anyone. Big Pharma was an industry already steeped in scandal and addicted to profiteering long before the era of financialisation. Its business model made it a natural candidate to adopt a turbo-charged version of this process, turning its players into hedge funds with pharmaceutical companies attached.

It is May 2021. Richard A. Gonzalez, chairman and CEO of pharmaceutical giant AbbVie, looks bemused as he sits before a US Congressional committee taking questions on drug pricing. Covid-19 restrictions mean that Gonzalez is speaking via video link, but this seems to do little to mitigate his discomfort when Representative Katie Porter of Orange County reaches for her whiteboard and sticky notes.

Porter has become an online sensation for the way she lectures CEOs about their pay and corporate activity, placing sticky notes on a board to drum home messages of corporate profiteering, like a primary school teacher telling off an errant school pupil. As Rolling Stone magazine puts it, 'There are few things in Washington more dangerous than Katie Porter with a white board.'[24]

Today, Porter is on particularly fruitful ground, as she quizzes Gonzalez about the price hikes his company made on a cancer drug called Imbruvica. She starts out by asking about the price of Imbruvica. A standard three-pill-a-day course would have cost a cool $98,000 a year in 2013 – high enough, you might think. But what Porter really wants to know is how, in only eight years, the price has jumped to an eye-watering $181,000.

The answer, as usual, appears to be the research and development costs that AbbVie has incurred. But Porter has heard this one before and is having none of it. After all, she asks, what has the effect of this R&D spending been? Are there now fewer side-effects, perhaps? No, answers Gonzalez. Do patients require fewer pills now? No, not that either.

In fact, it transpires that AbbVie has not improved Imbruvica at all. What's more, it did not in fact even invent the medicine, but rather bought up the much smaller company that created the drug. As Porter puts it, 'AbbVie took zero risk to develop this drug, you bought it approved for the market knowing it would be profitable, you hiked the price to pay for R&D but you haven't made the drug any better even as you doubled the cost.'

Then come the sticky notes. Porter sticks a little pink circle onto the white board representing the $2.5 billion AbbVie has put into research and development on Imbruvica between 2013 and 2018. She suggests, given that Imbruvica does not seem to have improved in that time, that much of this 'research' is really 'innovations and indications which are designed to keep competitors off the market and develop new sales opportunities', rather than anything that the average person might regard as genuine 'research and development'.

Porter is right. AbbVie filed 165 patents for Imbruvica to keep competitors outside the market, giving the firm an additional nine years on what is considered the normal exclusivity period.[25] Experts predict that, during those nine years alone, American patients will spend $41 billion on the branded drug.[26] Big Pharma likes to pretend that sky-high research costs justify the cost of medicines. In the case of Imbruvica, sales of the drug in a single year dwarf anything the company has put into research and development.

Porter now reels off a number of other figures that the company has spent in the period 2013–18. They include a budget of $1.6 billion for litigation and settlements – partly in enforcing and defending the company's monopolies. They include a marketing and advertising budget of $4.7 billion, plus $334 million for executive compensation – the pay and other benefits of senior leadership.

Especially staggering is a massive blue sticky note representing $50 billion, which includes money directly returned to shareholders (dividends) and money spent buying by the company in buying its own stock, which drives up share prices and thus returns even more money to shareholders. It is this huge pot of money more than any other that tells us that the pharmaceutical industry is not struggling to recoup its sky-high research costs. In fact, as Porter concludes, 'The big pharma fairy tale is one of groundbreaking R&D that justifies astronomical prices, but the pharma reality is that you spent most of your company's money making money for yourself and your shareholders.

Katie Porter is far from the only US politician concerned with the pharmaceutical model. In fact it has become a major issue in US politics, and with good reason. Britain, like many Western countries, has some ability to negotiate down the price of new medicines, most importantly by refusing to list them as available through the NHS if they are not considered good value for money.

What's more, the British public is shielded from the behaviour of the pharmaceutical industry by the NHS, which buys the drugs on behalf of patients. One reason the British love the NHS is precisely that it removes the market from healthcare decisions. When it was formed, in the wake of the Second World War, Britain adopted a fully socialised system in which the money you earn has no bearing on the standard of care you receive. In the words of a friend of mine, 'I've had to use the NHS many times, including for serious surgery, and money has never even been mentioned. All that matters is the care you need.' No wonder that many British people seem to feel it is the greatest achievement of any government, and that, in spite of many attempts at partial marketisation that have certainly damaged the service, full privatisation has been resisted.

This does not mean there are no problems. Unavailability of new and important medicines is clearly a major issue for patients who need access to them. The cost of medicines to the NHS is rising much faster than the NHS budget, putting severe strain on an already overstretched public service.[27] Between 2011 and 2016, the amount that NHS England gave to private drug companies rose by £3.8 billion, which was more than twice the NHS's total deficit (£1.85 billion).[28] In 2020, the price of medicines on the NHS increased to £20.9 billion, a year-on-year increase of nearly 10 per cent – while the cost of medicines used in hospitals rose by a whopping 14 per cent.[29] In short, the pharmaceutical model is creating a major problem for the British health system, in turn threatening to intensify the push to privatise parts of the service.

The US healthcare system, by contrast, is built on the notion that the market, left to its own devices, will provide. In practice, this means patients are preyed upon by gigantic corporations that charge whatever the market will tolerate. The result is catastrophic for almost everyone: this is the most expensive health system in the world, and delivers the worst health outcomes of any industrialised country.[30]

In line with this overall healthcare system, pharmaceutical corporations charge the US market the highest prices in the world.[31] Neither the government nor individual hospitals have much if any ability to negotiate these prices down, and the lack of regulation more generally gives enormous power to corporate giants. As a result, financialisation of the industry is more extreme in the

United States than anywhere else in the world, and patients are directly exposed to the resulting costs in multiple ways – from the pressure of advertising, to the corruption of healthcare professionals, to the unaffordable out-of-pocket expenses of treating life-changing illnesses. This helps explain why medicine prices have become a doorstep election issue in the United States, and why politicians like Katie Porter, Bernie Saunders and Nancy Pelosi have taken such a keen interest in precisely how the industry makes its money.

In a congressional report published in July 2021, representatives discovered that Porter's accusations against AbbVie were applicable across the sector.[32] Between 2016 and 2020, the top fourteen drug companies spent $577 billion on stock buybacks and dividends – $56 billion more than they spent on research and development.[33] One company, Amgen, spent nearly six times as much on buybacks, dividends and executive compensation as it did on R&D in 2018. Assuming the same rate of spending continued, the report projected that these fourteen companies would spend $1.15 trillion on buybacks and dividends between 2020 and 2029.

A separate report confirms this trend across Big Pharma, showing that payouts to shareholders in the twenty-seven biggest corporations increased by almost 400 per cent, from $30 billion to $146 billion a year, between 2000 and 2018.[34] These twenty-seven firms transferred a mind-blowing $1.5 trillion to shareholders over that period. In other words, as in the wider economy, the unleashing of debt has not made society more productive or more equal. As House Speaker Nancy Pelosi pointedly asked during a press call to launch the report, 'How can pharma say with a straight face after spending $577 billion on buybacks and dividends in the last five years that lowering drug prices for Americans will have to come at the expense of research and development?'[35]

The congressional report noted some other related trends. First, although research costs were still not negligible for many of these companies, the definition of R&D covered a multitude of sins, and often simply referred to 'finding ways to suppress generic and biosimilar competition while continuing to raise prices, rather than . . . innovative research.'[36] We will see more examples of this later in the chapter.

Second, the authors of the report noticed a sharp upward trend in the pay of the leaders of these corporations. From 2016 to 2020, executive compensation totalled $3.2 billion, annual compensation growing by 14 per cent over those five years. AbbVie paid its CEO Richard Gonzalez over $66 million from 2018 to 2020, while at the same time hiking the price of cancer drug Imbruvica by 14 per cent. This is important not simply because it is obscene, but because there is a causal link that goes to the heart of how financialisation works in practice. As the authors of the congressional report make clear,

> drug company executives are incentivized to raise drug prices in the United States through bonus structures that increase revenue targets year after year. These executives publicly justify price increases as being necessary to fund R&D, but the Committee's investigation shows that a significant portion of drug company revenues are being funneled to shareholders and executives in the form of buybacks, dividends, and executive compensation.[37]

It is not just that pay is benchmarked to financial performance, but that a large amount of CEO compensation comes directly in the form of shares. Moreover, when CEOs have been in place for several years, previous shares awarded will also benefit from dividends and stock buybacks. In some cases, this will add tens of millions of dollars to a CEO's multi-million-dollar salary.[38] It is no wonder that, while executive pay has ballooned across the corporate world over the last four decades, pharmaceutical CEO pay has accelerated well beyond the average.[39]

So far we have assumed that research and development are the 'good' part of what pharmaceutical corporations do. But, as Katie Porter noted when she questioned the head of AbbVie, a large proportion of Big Pharma research budgets in fact represent 'innovations and indications which are designed to keep competitors off the market and develop new sales opportunities'.

In other words, when the industry speaks of the research it does, it is often not what we assume it to be: scientists working to develop new chemical combinations that can treat or cure disease. Much research is actually geared towards increasing the value of the company's intangible assets by making negligible changes to drugs so that patents can be renewed and lengthened, thus suppressing competition. These are the 'me-too' drugs mentioned above, which tweak existing knowledge but offer little or no new benefit over what is currently on the market. One example is Asacol, used to treat Crohn's disease and other illnesses that involve inflammation of the intestines. When the medicine was reaching the end of its patent life, the producers created a new drug called Delzicol – an Asacol tablet inside a capsule. As one expert in innovation remarked, 'If the capsule was cut open, the original Asacol tablet fell out.'[40]

These drugs bring substantial profits owing to the much lower financial risk involved. Research suggests that only around 2–3 per cent of new drugs represent genuine breakthroughs, while around 10 per cent offer a modest advantage over existing treatments.[41] According to one German study in 2017, the majority of new medicines – 57 per cent – offered no added therapeutic value at all.

A further 16 per cent had only minor benefit, a non-quantifiable amount of benefit, or were in fact less effective.[42] Another study shows that only one out of four new drugs launched in the UK between 2001 and 2011 were 'highly innovative'.

What useful research there is tends to be heavily skewed towards chronic diseases suffered by rich people, or people in rich countries. One area where there is a large amount of research is cancer – a field seen as a lucrative source of blockbuster drugs. Billy Kenber documents just how much of this research is based on tiny incremental changes. Given the emotions invested in a very modest extension of a cancer patient's life, pharma companies can charge sky-high prices, face lower regulatory burdens, and can bully health services into adopting medicines that represent very poor value for money. As Kenber notes, 'More than half of 68 approved by the European Medicines Agency between 2009 and 2013 had not established that they could prolong survival or improve quality of life. Among those which improved survival rates, half had gains that were so small – sometimes just a few weeks – that they were not held to be clinically meaningful.'[43]

Meanwhile, diseases not seen as being able to generate blockbuster medicines are ignored – including, as we shall see, many diseases likely to cause a pandemic. Between 2000 and 2011, only 4 per cent of newly approved products – 37 of 850 – were for neglected diseases that affect middle- and low-income countries.[44] While tuberculosis and malaria kill millions, their victims are mostly poor, and there is thus little profit to be made from anything produced to treat them. In the last fifty years, only two new treatments for tuberculosis have been developed, while fourteen new treatments have been developed for a condition that kills no one: hay fever.[45]

One expert, William Lazonick, told the *New York Times* that the problem is not that there is little important research taking place, but that it is not taking place inside Big Pharma companies: 'there really is very little drug development going on in companies showing the highest profits and capturing much of the gains'.[46] Research often takes place in small companies and university departments, backed by massive state funding: 'The US government has put in place the most formidable national system of innovation in history.'[47] This has not encouraged Big Pharma to invest, but rather the opposite: in-house R&D has declined within Big Pharma. One study found that just ten of Pfizer's forty-four leading products and two of Johnson & Johnson's eighteen leading products were discovered in-house.[48] Large drug companies in the United States have only initiated research on 20 per cent of drugs approved in the ten years since 2009.[49]

Big Pharma's research budgets are notoriously opaque, but when we try to dig into them, we find R&D budgets stretch the definition of 'research' to breaking point. Consider this obtuse passage in AbbVie's 2018 annual report as an example of how far the pharmaceutical industry's conception of 'R&D' extends:

> Research and Development expenses in 2018 increased principally due to a $5.1 billion intangible asset impairment charge related to IPR&D acquired as part of the 2016 Stemcentrx acquisition following the decision to stop enrollment in the TAHOE trial. The impairment was primarily due to lower probabilities of success of achieving regulatory approval across Rova-T and other early-stage assets obtained in the acquisition.[50]

The sum of $5.1 billion represents *half* of the corporation's R&D budget for 2018 – a massive amount of money – so it is worth disentangling the language here. What AbbVie appears to have done is acquire a company, paying well over the odds on the basis that said company owned some research that was assumed to be highly profitable. In reality, the acquisition proved much less lucrative than supposed, and so they wrote down the value of their acquisition. This bears no relationship to most people's definition of research and development; in fact, it is completely divorced from productive activity. Including the costs of taking over other businesses as 'R&D' has become commonplace, while around a fifth of R&D costs are 'uncategorised', making any attempt at examining their validity impossible.[51]

We are told again and again that companies need high prices to produce profits that can be reinvested in innovation, to improve their equipment, and to invest in staff. But in the age of financialisation, exactly the opposite is true: alongside sky-high shareholder returns and executive pay, we also have a crisis in drug discovery, with big companies living off patented medicines, and doing little to replace them when those patents run out.

As US president, Donald Trump passed a massive tax giveaway in 2017, slashing the tax rates on corporate America. The cuts were supposed to encourage on-shoring, generating both research and jobs with the resulting new wealth. Oxfam analysed what four of the biggest drug companies did with the cash they saved. They discovered that Johnson & Johnson, Merck, Pfizer and Abbott Laboratories received a combined sum of around $7 billion as a result of the tax cuts.[52] They found little early evidence that the corporations had ended their use of offshore tax havens, or meaningfully invested in the United States; rather the companies prioritised investor returns, handing $52 billion out in stock buybacks and dividends, while their R&D spend flat-lined. In other words, they treated the newly released funds as a cash machine for investors.

As 2022 dawned, there was every sign that Big Pharma was about to go on another spending spree with the piles of cash these firms were sitting on.[53] Swiss giant Novartis announced plans to buy back up to $15 billion worth of its shares over two years, while US-based Bristol-Myers Squibb also authorised a $15 billion buyback.[54]

In a previous age, for all that Big Pharma companies may have profiteered, unethically pushed drugs, corrupted medical professionals and over-medicalised normal human emotions, they did at the same time actually invent and manufacture new medicines. All that has changed. These companies buy the rights to produce medicines that other companies have invented. They take over these smaller companies, using a vast stash of cash and debt to do so, and in the process push up the price of any medicines whose intellectual property they own. They then channel huge sums of money to their shareholders, disproportionately benefiting the superrich. As a direct result, medicine prices are pushed to unaffordable levels, and scientific innovation and collaboration are stifled. Given the deep integration of these corporations with the financial markets, they represent increasingly volatile entities in an ever more crisis-prone global economy.

In the short term, the financial results have been spectacular for shareholders. Big Pharma was already a highly profitable industry. Between 1954 and 1999, its average profit margin was more than double the average for big business at the time – good enough, you might think.[55] But since 1999, as the industry has become increasingly financialised, this has rocketed, and drug companies now enjoy more than three times the average profit margin. The authors of this finding make clear that 'even if drug companies lost a fifth of their profits they would still outperform 75% of other sectors, and losing nearly a third of their profits would leave them earning no less than the average industry. Remember: these profits are, by definition, left over after paying for research and development.'[56]

Another study concurred, finding that, between 2000 and 2018, thirty-five large pharmaceutical companies had brought in $11.5 trillion, $8.6 trillion of which – 77 per cent – was profit. This represented a massively greater level of profitability than the US-based big business sector in general, with its average profit margin over this period of 37 per cent.[57] This was hardly a sign of an industry scraping around for R&D funds.

The effects of this business model ripple out well beyond the production of medicines. Although leaders like Margaret Thatcher promised to create a 'shareholder democracy' in which small investments by many ordinary individuals would give everyone a stake in the fortunes of the stock market, this does not describe the society we live in, and never has. In fact, the concentration of wealth is getting worse, with the primacy of shareholder interests intensifying wealth disparity.

In the United States, the richest 10 per cent of Americans now own 89 per cent of all stocks, with the top 1 per cent accounting for over half.[58] Perhaps unsurprisingly, this reinforces other forms of inequality in society – men own much more stock than women, white people more than black and ethnic-minority people. The massive increase in stock market wealth during the pandemic has further fuelled the astonishing levels of wealth inequality across society, and the behaviour of the pharmaceutical industry is playing a role in driving this inequality.[59] Far from trickling down to the bottom, in the age of financialisation wealth has gushed to the top.

The Companies

So far, I have taken a bird's-eye view of the problems and economic changes affecting the industry. But what does all of this look like at the level of individual companies and individual drugs? The following discussions of three US corporations – Pfizer, Gilead and AbbVie – offer an insight into the impacts of financialisation within companies, but more importantly its consequences for the patients they are supposed to serve.

Pfizer

Thanks to Covid-19, Pfizer is now a household name, but it is also one of the oldest pharmaceutical corporations in the world, having started out in mid-nineteenth-century New York. The company boomed during the US Civil War, thanks to the high resulting demand for chloroform and painkillers, as well as disinfectants such as iodine. Pfizer's mass-produced citric acid became popular in soft drinks – its manufacturing process for this later helped it to become a major player in vitamin C and penicillin production.

We have already glimpsed Pfizer's role as perhaps the most aggressive of the Covid vaccine makers, but the company is no stranger to scandal. In 2009 the company was embroiled in a case in which it stood accused of ripping off the NHS and threatening access to epilepsy drugs. Pfizer made a drug called Epanutin – a brand-name for phenytoin, a drug first produced in 1908, which was found to be useful in controlling seizures as long ago as 1936. Nowadays it is usually not the drug of choice for doctors, but for many patients it offers a lifeline in preventing seizures, and it is still used as an emergency treatment for epilepsy. Despite its being overtaken by more modern medicines, around 10 per cent of epilepsy patients in the UK – tens of thousands of people – still depended on the medicine.[60] Fortunately, the drug cost the NHS very little: about 3p per capsule. But what was good for the NHS was bad for Pfizer – the drug simply was not making the company enough money. But, under a voluntary agreement with the NHS designed to help the NHS rein in spiralling drug prices, Pfizer had undertaken not to hike the price of branded drugs like Epanutin.

So Pfizer opened talks with a smaller company and hatched a plan. To get around the NHS agreement, they would 'debrand' the medicine, license its sale to a smaller company, and use the fact that the drug could then still enjoy a de facto monopoly for a few years to hike the price.

Billy Kenber documents how this trick of debranding drugs in order to hike prices was being widely deployed by highly financialised companies in the sector at the time.[61] What made phenytoin a particularly promising candidate for this trick was that controlling epilepsy often relies on precision, and changing medicines is therefore not advisable once you have found one that works for you. In other words, health professionals would be prepared to pay a premium in order to keep their patients on a drug they trusted and knew was effective. But this required some fancy footwork on Pfizer's part. On the one hand, it had to convince the NHS that this was a *different* drug, and so a price rise was acceptable, while on the other hand asserting that it was also the *same* drug, to maximise the natural monopoly it enjoyed among the patients who relied on it.

Pfizer ultimately did a deal with a pharmaceutical company called Flynn. Under the deal Pfizer would still make the medicine, but Flynn would buy it, 'debrand' it and market it on to the NHS. Unsurprisingly, British regulators were far from happy with this scheme. Kenber documents negotiations with Flynn in which British health regulators warned that debranding the drug could cause patients alarm and confusion. But Flynn played hardball.

They threatened, in effect, to discontinue supplying the product. Kenber quotes a regulatory official writing to the Department for Health: 'Whilst this is completely irresponsible of Flynn, we do not see an easy way out of this.'[62] The plan was approved.

The price hike that Flynn applied was astonishing. NHS expenditure on phenytoin capsules rose from about £2 million a year in 2012 to about £50 million in 2013, the price of 100mg packs of the drug rising from £2.83 to £67.50, before falling again to £54 by May 2014.[63] UK wholesalers and pharmacies faced price hikes of between 2,300 and 2,600 per cent.

The Competition and Markets Authority investigated the case, initially concluding that prices in the UK were far higher than in any other European country. In December 2016, Pfizer was handed the highest fine ever levied by the CMA – £84.2 million. Meanwhile, Flynn was fined £5.2 million.[64] Pfizer and Flynn appealed, and in June 2018 the Competition Appeal Tribunal upheld the decision that the firms held dominant market positions, but concluded these positions were not abused, therefore quashing the fines. In March 2020, the Court of Appeal upheld the decision to quash the fines, but reopened the question over whether the CMA's ruling as to the firms' pricing was excessive. The judge in the case stated, 'It was quite easy to lose sight of a stark reality, which was that, literally overnight, Pfizer and Flynn increased their prices for phenytoin sodium capsules by factors of between approximately seven and twenty-seven, when they were in a dominant position in each of their markets.'[65] In August 2021 the CMA provisionally ruled once again that Pfizer and Flynn had broken competition law, exploiting a loophole to overcharge the NHS illegally.[66] What's more, the case prompted a rethink in government, which closed the loophole Pfizer had used, passing legislation that allowed ministers to impose lower prices on unbranded generics.[67]

Pfizer was one of the companies that embraced financialisation early on, putting the desire for short-term profit ahead of long-term drug research. At the time of the epilepsy drug price gouge, Pfizer was making over one-third of its revenue growth from increasing prices on existing drugs, and had little by way of new research in its own pipeline.[68] The CEO at the time, Ian Read, slashed research by one-third and massively reduced staff in order to bolster returns to shareholders.[69] Wall Street loved it.[70] As the world's largest pharmaceutical corporation devoted ever less of its resources to medical research, its profits only grew.

With blockbuster drugs of its own in short supply, Pfizer tried to buy innovation elsewhere. In 2014 the corporation attempted a hostile takeover of AstraZeneca, citing its desire to avoid US taxes as a core reason for the move, which would have allowed Pfizer to keep vast amounts of its cash outside the United States in 'a competitive tax environment'.[71] When the bid for AstraZeneca failed, Pfizer tried to use another takeover – this time of Allergan – to make Ireland its home for tax purposes. Pfizer's CEO remarked that the company was at a 'tremendous disadvantage' because of its US tax bill.[72] In fact, Pfizer's plan was for Allergan to 'take over' Pfizer – and then change its name to Pfizer.[73] The plan was scrapped after a rule change in the United States that prevented the tax dodge.[74]

Pfizer's tax 'disadvantage' didn't stop the corporation distributing nearly five times as much to shareholders as it paid in US tax. In fact, Pfizer distributed well over 100 per cent of its profits to shareholders during that decade.[75] This was perhaps no wonder, when Pfizer's then CEO's own fortune was so closely tied to the fortunes of the corporation's investors. In 2014 Ian Read enjoyed a payout of $22.6 million, 77 per cent of which came from stock awards and options.[76]

As financialisation experts William Lazonick and Öner Tulum said at the time, 'If Pfizer is cash-constrained, it is far more likely that it is the golden handcuffs of stock-based executive pay that are the source of the problem.' The model continues to this day. Pfizer's share buybacks and dividend payments totalled a mind-blowing $70 billion in the five years up to 2020, dwarfing the $41 billion spent on R&D.[77]

Gilead

In March 2015, world-renowned professor of economics Jeffrey Sachs wrote in the *Huffington Post*, 'Gilead has the cure for Hepatitis C . . . Now we need a cure for Gilead.'[78] Labelling the corporation 'a ruthlessly crude monopolist', Sachs laid out how Gilead was 'leaving millions to die both in the US and abroad' while the company made a killing on a vastly overpriced hepatitis C drug on which it was not even paying its proper share of tax.

Gilead Sciences was founded in 1987, specialising in selling antiretrovirals to treat HIV. For a few years the company was chaired by Donald Rumsfeld, who would go on to be George W. Bush's infamous defence secretary during the 'War on Terror'. The company's strategy, in keeping with the financialisation model, was always based on acquiring other companies and the intellectual property they held, and then producing drugs based on that knowledge at enormously inflated costs. In 2017, the Institute for New Economic Thinking wrote, 'Gilead has built its business by acquiring companies.'[79] Five companies in particular had 'discovered and largely developed the drugs that have generated virtually all of Gilead's revenues over its 30-year history'.

One of the most important drugs Gilead now owns is Hepatitis C cure sofosbuvir, sold under the brand names Sovaldi and Harvoni. Hepatitis C is caused by a blood-borne virus that damages the liver. Some patients can get rid of the virus without treatment, but 70 per cent develop a lifelong infection, and some of these will cause severe, life-threatening liver disease. It is estimated that 58 million people around the world have chronic hepatitis C. About 1.5 million new infections occur every year; nearly 300,000 died from the disease in 2019. Drugs like sofosbuvir have profoundly changed the outlook for patients, curing the majority of patients of the virus. The problem is that very few people can afford it.

Even in a wealthy country like Britain, the NHS balked at the huge price of the drug, which was expected to cost £1 billion for every 20,000 people treated.[80] That meant only the very sickest people were able to access the drug. Claire Groves, who became an activist with patient advocate group Just Treatment, endured an agonizing three-year wait for the medicine: 'I was repeatedly told by my doctor that I am sick, but not sick enough to qualify for the treatment under the public health program'.[81] Fifty-two-year-old mother of three Michelle Tolley was in an even worse state when she found out she had Hep C.[82] The disease had already led to cirrhosis of the liver and she was very unwell, but the price of the drug had led to such rationing that Michelle was still told she could not be treated immediately.

Sofosbuvir was developed by university scientists who received public funding in the United States, but spun out to a small biotech company called Pharmasset.[83] Pharmasset spent $62 million on the medicine, and projected that completing the development would cost an additional $216 million. Gilead bought Pharmasset for just over $11 billion in 2011. It turned out to be a lucrative purchase, because after only around nineteen months on the market Sovaldi and Harvoni had brought in double the purchase price – a massive $22 billion. Public Citizen predicted, 'Gilead's executives will continue to make out like bandits.'[84]

Gilead introduced Solvadi to the US market at $84,000 for a twelve-week course of the treatment – which works out at $1,000 per pill. According to Sachs, the cost of making the medicine was more like $1 per pill – something borne out once generic competition was introduced in some countries producing the drug.[85] The public backlash against this exorbitant price was so great that it resulted in an eighteen-month US Senate committee investigation, which involved scrutiny of 20,000 pages of company documents. The Senate Finance Committee's ranking member, Ron Wyden, concluded:

> The evidence shows the company pursued a calculated scheme for pricing and marketing its Hepatitis C drug based on one primary goal – maximizing revenue – regardless of the human consequences. There was no concrete evidence in any document – in emails, meeting minutes, or presentations – that basic financial matters such as R&D costs or the multi-billion dollar acquisition of Pharmasset, the drug's first developer, factored into how Gilead set the price . . . Gilead knew these prices would put treatment out of the reach of millions and cause extraordinary problems for Medicare and Medicaid.[86]

The committee noted in particular that Gilead's price was set so high partly as a device to raise anticipated prices for its next Hepatitis C formulation, Harvoni, which was priced at an even more staggering $94,500 per course. The result, of course, was a severe limit on who could access the breakthrough drug in the United States.

The Hep C drugs were transformative for Gilead.[87] Between 2013 and 2015, global revenues for the company trebled, rising to $32.6 billion, while total corporate profits increased fivefold to

$21.7 billion. Combined sales for Solvadi and Harvoni represented 56 per cent of the company's total revenue in 2014 and 2015, and the Hep C drugs generated nearly $62 billion in sales between 2013 and 2020. No wonder, as the Senate committee discovered, that Gilead was determined to face down any public pressure. In an e-mail seen by the committee from days before the launch of Sovaldi, a senior Gilead official wrote, 'Let's not fold to advocacy pressure in 2014. Let's hold our position whatever competitors do or whatever the headlines.'[88]

To add insult to injury, Gilead moved some of its intellectual property to Ireland to reduce its tax bill. According to the advocacy group Americans for Tax Fairness, this saved the company $10 billion between 2013 and 2015 – exactly when its profits were booming from the Hep C drugs, thanks particularly to public spending via the US healthcare system.[89]

Jeffrey Sachs was particularly concerned by the human cost of Hep C, which affects 5 million Americans and 160 million people around the world, telling readers that an epidemic was 'raging out of control in some communities'. The price meant denying medicines 'even to patients with advanced liver disease, delivering not a sentence of unnecessary prolonged illness, but of death'.[90] While Gilead did sign voluntary licenses with lower-income countries allowing the medicines to be produced more cheaply, the system remained under the corporation's control, with strict restrictions on access for the 49 million people living with Hep C in fifty middle-income countries.[91] In effect, said Sachs, Gilead and the US political system 'have turned the proper use of patents . . . into a veritable license to kill, which must never become acceptable in a sane society'.

In Britain, Michelle Tolley got the life-saving drug after taking to her local radio station to campaign for her right to be treated. Sadly, many around the world were not so fortunate. As Michelle remarked, 'I think it is disgraceful that pharmaceutical companies are allowed to monopolise the price of drugs. It is also very wrong that where you live can determine if you are eligible to be treated.'[92]

Gilead likes to boost its research and development budgets by including the R&D of corporations it has bought. But if you strip these figures out, Gilead's share buybacks and dividend payments exceeded its R&D budget over the five years from 2016 to 2020 – $33 billion compared to $22 billion – though in the years 2017 and 2020 the budgets were fairly close.[93] It paid its shareholders 114 per cent of its net income during this same period.

AbbVie

We have already seen Katie Porter take AbbVie's CEO to task for the price of cancer drug Imbruvica. AbbVie itself is a fairly new company, which in 2013 was spun out of a much older corporation – Abbot Laboratories, a corporation with its origins in nineteenth-century Chicago, where it specialised in medicines made from the active ingredients of plants, most prominently opiates. It continues to make medical devices and health-related products today.

AbbVie is a repeat offender when it comes to buying up other people's medicines and then using them to price-gouge. The company is perhaps best known for its drug Humira, which is used to treat autoimmune diseases like Crohn's and rheumatoid arthritis. A drug like Humira is a goldmine for a drug company: it treats a chronic, lifelong condition, and patients can be on the drug for years.

It is perhaps no wonder that, before Covid, Humira was the most lucrative single drug in the world, bringing in nearly $20 billion in 2017.[94] Humira was based on a revolutionary new technology known as monoclonal antibodies (or MABs), which are artificially created antibodies that can bind to a specific target. But that technology – like most such breakthroughs – had nothing to do with the corporation now making so much money from Humira. In fact, the technology was pioneered in Cambridge by Greg Winter, in the 1980s and 1990s.[95] The work was predominantly done at the UK's Medical Research Council Laboratory there, and funded with large amounts of public money. While the Medical Research Council does, as a result, receive royalties on the many MAB-based medicines, these are peanuts compared to the revenues AbbVie is raking in.

Humira itself was in fact devised by a spin-off company formed by researchers called Cambridge Antibody Technology, who worked with a German company called BASF Pharma. At the end of 2000, Abbott Laboratories, AbbVie's parent, bought the division of BASF that held the patents for the sum of $6.9 billion.

In its 2021 report, the US Congressional committee on oversight and reform took a look at what happened next.[96] They discovered that, as with the cancer drug Imbruvica, AbbVie's total R&D spending on Humira was 'only a small fraction of its net revenue from this drug'. AbbVie claimed it had spent just over $5 billion on R&D for Humira between 2009 and 2018, but the committee disagreed:

> internal documents show that a large portion of AbbVie's research expenditures on Humira were dedicated to extending the company's market monopoly by limiting biosimilar competition through 'enhancements' to Humira. An internal presentation emphasized that one objective of the 'enhancement' strategy was to 'raise barriers to competitor ability to replicate.' AbbVie's enhancement's strategy was successful, helping the company obtain or file for hundreds of patents on Humira that will delay competition from any lower-priced biosimilars in the US until at least 2023 . . . cost[ing] the US health care system at least $19 billion.[97]

Thus, although Humira's US patent expired in 2016, this 'research' helped to create new versions of the same medicine that could enjoy new protection and a huge number of patents related to different uses of the drug, manufacturing processes, ingredients and alternative formulations. The company was also accused of using 'pay for delay' tactics – effectively paying competitors to hold off selling their product until a later date, though an antitrust case found that AbbVie had not acted illegally.[98]

Secure in their control of Humira, AbbVie then jacked up the price year-on-year. In the United States, Humira costs around $77,000 for a year's supply – 470 per cent more than when the drug was launched in 2003.[99] In Britain it is cheaper, but still close to £11,000 per year, making it the highest expenditure for a single medicine on the NHS during 2014–16, with a total spend of nearly £800 million in just two years. Worldwide, the drug brought in $96 billion (£72 billion) up to 2016.[100]

The congressional report further accused AbbVie of tying executive compensation to drug price increases. Since 2013, it claimed, AbbVie had paid its highest executives over $480 million in compensation, with bonuses tied directly to Humira's net revenue targets.[101]

AbbVie has completed a huge number of mergers and acquisitions, and its combined dividends and share buyback packages were greater than their R&D budget for all of the five years from 2016 to 2020.[102] In those same years, it paid out to shareholders 165 per cent more than it made in net income. An unusual jump in the budget in 2018 can be explained by the footnote already referred to in the company's accounts – over $5 billion for an 'intangible asset impairment charge' related to R&D that was taking place when it purchased a company, which turned out to be less significant than hoped. Quite how this represents 'R&D' is anyone's guess.

~

In recent years it has become increasingly accepted by historians that the early development of modern medicine was not unrelated to the ancient practice of alchemy. Alchemy is a difficult subject to understand today, but one branch of this mystical art was interested in the development of a panacea, which could treat any disease and prolong life forever. Perhaps it is unsurprising that this practice played some role in the invention of chemistry and modern medicine.

Another belief of many alchemists, and one more commonly recalled today, was the idea of turning base metal into gold. This side of alchemy provides a fitting metaphor for the modern pharmaceutical industry – an industry that takes public resources and, through a secretive, almost mystical practice of which they would like us to believe only they are capable, creates huge quantities of money for its executives, investors and financiers.

A number of recent court cases have been cited as evidence of a turn in society's relationship with the pharmaceutical industry. Martin Shkreli was barred for life from the pharmaceutical industry – a ban later extended to all public companies – and ordered to pay $64.6 million of the money he had made from hiking the price of the lifesaving drug Daraprim.[103]

The Sackler family look set to pay $6 billion to address the damage caused by the opioid crisis, as part of a deal which would settle all outstanding claims against them, while families of the victims of the epidemic were given the right to formally confront the Sacklers and explain their story.[104] Other companies tied up in the opioid crisis, including Johnson & Johnson, are also in the process of making massive settlements. Meanwhile, as we have seen, the Flynn case even prompted a change to British law, allowing the government to lower the price of unbranded generics for which the NHS is being overcharged.

Do these cases represent a sea change, or just more of the same – fining bad apples and tinkering around the edges to close down one model of profiteering, only for another avenue to open up? Court battles and legislative tweaks have been a regular feature of the state's response to the industry's behaviour – yet that behaviour has only continued to get worse.

Perhaps, underneath the surface, something deeper is indeed beginning to stir: a recognition that the pharmaceutical model is simply no longer able to respond to the medical emergencies that pose a threat to us all. It has been hollowed out, eaten away by the disease of financialisation. The pharmaceutical sector is far from alone in embracing this model, but the nature of its activity and its particular dependence on intangible assets like intellectual property have made it an ideal vehicle for channelling wealth from society at large into the pockets of the superrich. Just like pharma companies, however, many other parts of the economy have also been hollowed out, unable to provide the resilience and security so many are crying out for. Delegating major decisions to the whims of the financial markets has brought us close to catastrophe. At some point, change becomes inevitable – the only question is what form it will take.

Nothing has demonstrated this more vividly than what happened during the Covid-19 crisis. In trying to tackle this pandemic, the worst the world has faced in 100 years, Big Pharma not only exposed its true nature to most countries – desperate for vaccines to deal with a virus that was causing death and illness on a scale rarely seen in modern history – it even lost them the trust of their once greatest ally, the president of the United States.

3
It Was Greed, My Friends

It was March 2021. British prime minister Boris Johnson had finished one of his regular Covid-19 press conferences, flanked by his scientific advisors, and headed to a Zoom call with his back-bench MPs. Britain was still under heavy restrictions, and the winter had been a hard and lonely one for many people. But there seemed to be light at the end of the tunnel. Effective vaccines had been created in record time, and Britain, the first country in the world to vaccinate a citizen, was now inoculating tens – soon to be hundreds – of thousands of people a day.

The popularity of Johnson's government had gone from boom to bust and back again, pushed along by the peculiar brand of shambolic showmanship that has characterised his career, with a famously disarming Teflon personality. But, over time, Covid-19 had worn down the patience of wider society. Johnson presided over one of the highest rates of coronavirus-related death in the world. First, the prime minister embraced a laissez-faire 'herd immunity' approach to the virus, seeming to believe that if every-one just caught it as quickly as possible, we might muddle through. When it became clear that such a strategy was on the verge of bringing the health system to its knees, he abruptly about-turned, implementing a long, strict lockdown. Johnson regained support when he came close to dying of Covid-19 himself, but that support again ebbed away when it became clear his senior advisor Dominic Cummings had broken lockdown rules when he himself had had coronavirus, and yet Johnson refused to censure him.

Towards the end of 2020, Johnson again threw caution to the wind, removing many protective measures, only to be forced once again into a dramatic about-turn and a long, dark, cold lockdown over the winter. But by late March the vaccine rollout was well underway, and it appeared Johnson had turned another corner.

Johnson was therefore in a bullish mood when he addressed his MPs, including his libertarian right wing who had chafed against the restrictions. Conducting the address via Zoom, he threw them some red meat, reportedly telling them, 'The reason we have the vaccine success is because of capitalism, because of greed, my friends.'[1] 'It was driven by big pharma – and I don't just mean the Chief Whip', he added, pointing to his colleague, a former farmer who was eating a cheese-and-pickle sandwich next to him.[2]

Johnson quickly thought better of it – 'Actually I regret saying it' he backtracked, 'forget I said that.' Britain and its now well-known pharmaceutical company AstraZeneca was, after all, at the time in the middle of an acrimonious dispute with the European Union precisely over the fact that EU leaders felt Britain had been given preferential treatment in early vaccine sales. Britain's rapid vaccine rollout success was coming, the EU felt, at the expense of the rollout in their own countries. It was an unedifying fight all round, especially given that most countries in the world were a million miles away from securing adequate vaccine doses.

Whether Johnson really regretted making the greed comment at that exact moment is impossible to know, but we do know that he did not regret the idea it reflected. Because it became a central plank in his speech to the Conservative Party conference later in the year, where he said:

> It was the private sector that made it possible. Behind those vaccines are companies and shareholders and, yes, bankers. You need deep pools of liquidity that are to be found in the City of London. It was capitalism that ensured that we had a vaccine in less than a year and the answer therefore is not to attack the wealth creators, it is to encourage them – because they are responsible for the aggregate increase in the country's wealth that enables us to make those Pareto improvements.[3]

Johnson was wrong, however. It was not capitalism or greed that delivered the vaccines which gave people such hope in March 2021. In fact, the highly financialised pharmaceutical corporations and their City of London investors did not create the British vaccine, or for that matter any other leading vaccines. But, as we shall see, greed and capitalism did indeed play an important part in the vaccine rollout, ensuring that access to the vaccines would be so deeply unequal that many activists started to refer to it as a 'vaccine apartheid'.

For many people, with enough to worry about in their daily lives, Covid-19 seemed to come out of nowhere. We had heard about epidemics in other parts of the world – bird flu, swine flu, Ebola, SARS, MERS, Zika virus – but they never touched the lives of most of us. We had had a few scares, some worrying outbreaks, a few apocalyptic articles heralding a new plague. But it never quite came to pass, and so we went about our lives as usual.

Or at least most of us did. But among the medical community, in the writings of academic experts, even among some of my activist friends, there was a belief that a world-changing pandemic was inevitable at some point, and that, far from mitigating this possibility, the structure of the global economy was driving us ever faster towards it.[4] There was also, for those who looked, plenty of warning that the impact of such a pandemic would be felt in a deeply unequal way across societies, and that the way the pharmaceutical industry worked might present a major obstacle to dealing with the pandemic in a speedy, never mind equitable, manner.

When you take a step back, you realise that it is not only the pharmaceutical industry, but the whole of our economy that seems geared towards making a pandemic likely. In fact, the era of financialisation has brought us perilously close to collapse on a number of fronts – most notably, of course, climate change. When short-term profit-maximisation is placed at the centre of an economic model, there are huge incentives to dump the costs of economic activity onto the rest of the world, the public sector, the environment or future generations. The financial markets are interested in what can be extracted today. The costs will be borne by other people, at another place or time.

It is not the first time our civilisation has confronted this problem. Back in the 1940s, one of the greatest writers on political economy in the twentieth century, Karl Polanyi, tried to articulate the lessons of the social upheavals of the previous decades in 'The Great Transformation'. For Polanyi, the problem centred on what happens when politicians 'allow the market mechanism to be sole director of the fate of human beings and their natural environment'. His conclusion was that this would result in 'the demolition of society'.[5]

For Polanyi, the catastrophic wars of the twentieth century, and in particular the horror of fascism, could not be explained without looking at the period of rapid globalisation, corporate monopolies and financial power that the First World War had brought to an end. The ideology of the market was entirely utopian, and for Polyani a market-controlled society represented the death of the human being, necessarily removed from the cultural and political contexts that make us human. It would also lead to the total commodification and destruction of our environment. No wonder Polanyi believed that, long before such a pure market society could be realised, people would reach for whatever force seemed able to protect them from these market forces. And this is precisely what gave rise to fascism.

For this reason, Polanyi has so much to teach us about the social, political and economic crises we are currently living through. The control of our economy and society by financial markets – the purest form of market – has indeed created massive social dislocation and unprecedented environmental destruction. And it is precisely these dynamics, rather than the old-fashioned assumption that there are 'too many people on the planet', that have laid the ground for pandemics. The highly financialised form of capitalism we have become accustomed to is making our societies, and our individual lives, far more precarious, fuelling the risk of pandemics by encroaching further on our environment, incentivising ever more unsustainable methods of farming, promoting the privatisation of healthcare while restricting provision, and forcing more people into cities with inadequate infrastructure. It is true, we still do not know exactly how Covid-19 developed; many still believe that the virus escaped from a lab in Wuhan. What is clear is that the spread of the virus and our inability to contain it owe much to our profit-driven economy, while the continued trashing of the planet means that new pandemics will remain a risk as long as we continue to live like this.

If we assume that Covid was, at least partly, a direct result of the dynamics of the global economy and the push towards profit-maximisation, then the way the pandemic played out also gives us deep insights into how that economy works. Even though the financial costs of the pandemic to the state have been astronomical, to say nothing of the non-financial costs of illness and death, the financial markets have made healthy profits that have further exacerbated inequality. In early 2022, Oxfam found that the world's ten richest men more than doubled their wealth, from $700 billion to $1.5 trillion, during the first two years of a pandemic – even as 99 per cent of humanity saw its income fall, and over 160 million more people were forced into poverty.[6] Greed and capitalism created the pandemic. And they were about to hinder efforts to deal with its effects.

American historian and activist Mike Davis made a career of exposing how leaving major social decisions to the market has had the most shocking consequences. In *Late Victorian Holocausts*, he explored how the introduction of new capitalist relations decimated support systems at a local level in the Indian subcontinent, while the extreme free-market ideology of Britain's imperial governments left it to the market to decide who would eat and who would starve.[7] The result was the loss of millions of lives to famine – not the result of 'backwardness' and ignorance, but of 'modernity', capitalism and the market.

In *The Monster at Our Door: The Global Threat of Avian Flu*, published in 2005, Davis argued that it was similar destructive tendencies within the modern global economy that made a pandemic inevitable.[8] A group of activists was so shaken by Davis's work that they set up a campaign group called Pandemic Action. Davis convinced them not only that the overdue pandemic had arrived in the form of avian flu, but that the nature of the global economy would ensure that it would be confronted in a radically different way depending on where you lived in the world. Among other demands, they called for 'an end to corporate patents that restrict access to critical medicines' and 'urgent funding by the rich world to boost health and surveillance systems in countries most at risk in Asia and Africa'. Their call was signed by leading activists, including Noam Chomsky, Naomi Klein, Walden Bello and Mike Davis himself.

Pandemic Action was ahead of its time. Avian flu turned out not to be 'the big one'. But the points they made about the actions needed to make a pandemic less likely, and to ensure that the highest costs of such a pandemic were not borne by the world's poorest, were prescient.

The problem Davis had identified was not only that we weren't taking radical action to restructure our societies in order to forestall the coming pandemic. It was worse and even more short-sighted than that. We weren't even researching the medicines that could rapidly deal with such a pandemic. And the reason? There was simply no money to be made. In an interview in April 2020, before any effective medicines to deal with Covid-19 had been invented, Davis explained, 'a drug company has no incentive to manufacture something that will only be used once, when it could invest in other areas that offer constant profits over many years, such as medication for heart disease or sexual dysfunction in elderly males like myself'.[9]

He was right. In crisis situations, the market has failed entirely, either seizing up, as in the financial crisis of 2008, or provoking the most horrific responses, such as shipping food *away from* where it was most needed in the late Victorian famines of the British Empire. During the Covid-19 pandemic, only massive state intervention in the economy prevented economic collapse. Just as in

2008, unprecedented public money was spent bailing out the banks that had created that crash in the first place. This suggests that all but the most fanatical free-market ideologues really do understand that the market is at best an extremely limited mechanism for making important social decisions.

When it matters, the state steps in. But in the financialised era there is a huge problem with how this takes place. First, the state only ever steps in to 'correct the market's failures'. Rather than using public resources to reinvent the system in a way that works effectively, state intervention saves the market from the consequences of its own disastrous behaviour, and then leaves financiers to get on with running society. Look at the way the British government routinely bails out the inevitable failures of rail privatisation, taking parts of the railway into public ownership, only to turn around and sell it off again when the system is stabilised. While the rich walk away, the poorest end up paying the price for these interventions through austerity and the decimation of public services.

The second problem is that not all states can intervene in this way. Over the last forty years, many countries have been instructed to undermine their own capacity to intervene or plan. They have been told – often forced – to leave everything to the market, giving up the state resources and state powers that allow them to intervene successfully. And so, in a situation like Covid-19, they literally were no longer capable of taking the actions necessary to protect their citizens. The end-result, in Chomsky's words, is a system of 'socialism for the rich, free markets for the poor'.

This logic applies not only to the general response of governments to Covid-19, but specifically to the vaccines that became so important if the pandemic was to be brought rapidly to an end. At every stage the market, in the form of the pharmaceutical industry, failed. It failed to create vaccines, it failed to produce vaccines in the quantities required, and it failed to distribute vaccines in anything approaching a fair and equitable manner. This latter failure meant we were not able to halt the spread of Covid-19 or prevent the rise of new and dangerous variants of the virus.

These failures were widely recognised by politicians. That is why governments and international bodies poured unprecedented public resources into vaccine development and production to correct 'market failures'. Certainly, without this intervention, things would have been much worse. But rather than using these resources to transform the system, the obsession with making the market work meant that governments ultimately used them to make a few very rich without producing a system that could have served the public better, and left us in a stronger position to deal with medical emergencies in the future.

Creating the Vaccine

The market failed us long before Covid-19 broke out. In January 2020, we could have been in a far better position to deal with a coronavirus outbreak – but the structure of the pharmaceutical industry prevented it.

It was not only radical academics and activists who knew a pandemic was coming. It was something that was causing increasing alarm among policy experts who advised governments. Several figures within the business world had voiced concern. Even within the US government, plans were laid out to deal with such a scenario, even though preparations were seriously disrupted by cuts made by Donald Trump's administration.[10]

But when it came to medicines, the pharmaceutical sector

had shown a near-complete indifference to coronaviruses, or indeed any likely candidate for a global pandemic, because they were considered too unlikely to be profitable. In fact, vaccines themselves had become a research backwater for the industry because they were not seen as sufficiently profitable. One reason these two key areas were not seen as profitable was that they were unlikely to create big enough markets among richer populations. As author Robin Henig wrote, 'Ask a field virologist what constitutes an epidemic worth looking into, and he'll answer with characteristic cynicism, "The death of one white person." '[11]

Throughout the early 2000s, the Global South was hit with several epidemics. Coronaviruses had caused two of these epidemics, making the leap from animals to humans in the form of SARS in China in 2002 and MERS in the Middle East in 2012. Both were contained before becoming pandemic. But they did sound the alarm in university departments and international institutions like the World Health Organization (WHO). In 2016, as healthcare journalist Charlotte Kilpatrick wrote, the WHO issued a warning 'intended to be a call to arms for the world's largest pharmaceutical companies'.[12] The body identified sixteen pathogens, including coronaviruses, that posed a serious threat to global health, all of which were seriously under-researched.

This moment exposed a deep-seated concern in the scientific community that the industry that was supposed to be creating the new medicines that might protect us from disease was not doing its job. Nonetheless, true to form, 'Two years later, in 2018, the pharmaceutical giants had zero research projects in development to fight coronaviruses.'[13]

As Covid-19 started to spread beyond China, a researcher at US campaign group Public Citizen, Zain Rizvi, was worried. He took another look into what research was being done into coronaviruses. He found that in the previous year, 2019, there had been only six active clinical coronavirus medicine trials involving pharmaceutical companies, all of them heavily dependent on public funding. He told me, 'I know it sounds strange, but we actually got really lucky with Covid-19. Given where we were there was no guarantee we would have come up with vaccines that fast.' Of course, he said, no one is arguing that we could have developed a Covid-19 medicine before the disease had even been identified. 'But with proper investment, with proper concern about the inevitability of some sort of epidemic, we could have been well ahead of where we were, we could have been in a much better place. The fact we weren't goes to the heart of the problems in the industry.'[14]

Even today, when coronavirus has obviously become a major concern for the industry, Big Pharma is doing almost nothing about other worrying emerging infectious diseases. Outside coronavirus, there are still only fifteen projects targeting the other diseases on the WHO's priority list – and ten diseases with no R&D in the pipeline at all.[15]

The industry's failures do not end there. By 2020, vaccines of any sort had become deeply uninteresting to Big Pharma. Once they had been a mainstay of the pharmaceutical industry, but the high costs of trialling drugs, combined with the low profit potential, meant the industry had prioritised more lucrative areas. To be clear, vaccines do not make no money at all – they just don't make enough for the profit-maximising pharmaceutical industry. In 2019, global vaccine sales brought in $54 billion.[16] Just compare that to the $92 billion total that the top-ten blockbuster drugs generated in 2019.[17] Vaccines are more risky, historically more difficult to make, and potentially less profitable – which is why the number of companies producing vaccines fell from twenty-six in 1955, to eighteen in 1980, and then to four in 2020. These four controlled some 80 per cent of the vaccine market.[18] One of those, British-based GlaxoSmithKline, had curtailed its epidemic response. GSK's head of vaccine research told the media: 'Our learnings from Ebola, from pandemic flu, from SARS previously, is that it's very disruptive and that's not the way that we want to do business going forward.'[19]

Part of the reason for this is that vaccines, at their best, immunise people for life. Even with fast-mutating viruses, most people do not require more than one injection a year. It is almost the opposite of the ultimate industry medicine, which will alleviate a chronic condition and be needed, ideally, for the rest of a patient's life. In 2018, only 1 per cent of the global pharmaceutical industry's R&D spending focused on emerging infectious diseases.[20]

In the spring of 2020, Tahir Amin and Rohit Malpani made clear that the pharmaceutical system was simply not able to deal with a world of pandemics: 'despite clear warnings that another viral pandemic could emerge, the pharmaceutical industry failed to sustain investment into new treatments and vaccines', because:

> In today's capital-driven market, investments in pandemic preparedness and in neglected diseases like tuberculosis and malaria are not, and never have been, a priority for pharmaceutical company drug development even though neglected diseases cause more than 2 million deaths per year, almost seven times the number of deaths caused so far by Covid-19 . . . A company executive deciding between investing in a novel treatment to address a potential pandemic threat or buying back company shares to boost a company's stock price will probably choose the latter.[21]

Had we had an industry that focused on developing our know-how around diseases like SARS, we might well have got ahead of the game on Covid-19.

To deal with these routine market failures, governments pour eye-watering amounts of money into pharmaceutical research, even in the absence of a pandemic. These resources are the reason we have useful drugs. As Rizvi puts it, 'Without this, we'd be in real trouble.'

In 2017, major charitable foundations like Gates and Wellcome, along with a host of governments, set up the Coalition for Epidemic Preparedness Innovations (CEPI) to finance research into vaccines against emerging infectious diseases. There would have been no reason to do this if the industry was believed to be doing its job. Even Bill Gates, a fierce proponent of the private sector and the pharmaceutical industry, admitted at CEPI's launch, 'The market is not going to solve this problem because epidemics do not come along very often – and when they do you are not allowed to charge some huge premium price for the tools involved.'[22]

The biggest spender on pharmaceutical research by a long way is the US government. Most of this spending goes through a body called the National Institutes of Health (NIH), a massive state-driven healthcare research agency. The NIH has its roots in the late nineteenth century. But it became particularly important in the period of President Roosevelt's New Deal. In 1940, FDR praised the NIH with characteristically stirring rhetoric as a symbol of peace:

> It has been devoted throughout its long and distinguished history to furthering the health of all mankind, in which service it has recognized no limitations imposed by international boundaries; and has recognized no distinctions of race, creed or color . . . Now

> that we are less than a day by plane from the jungle type yellow fever of South America, less than two days from the sleeping sickness of equatorial Africa, less than three days from cholera and bubonic plague, the ramparts we watch must be civilian in addition to military.[23]

Without the NIH, we would have very few medicines. It pushes tens of billions of dollars a year into medical research. One piece of research that looked at over 200 medicines approved in the United States between 2010 and 2016 found that NIH research had played some role in the development of every one of them.[24] Another study showed that more than 90 per cent of new or commonly prescribed drugs had received funding the from the NIH in their early, most risky stages of development.[25] Whatever decision-makers might claim for the pharmaceutical industry, they know that the market will not generate the research we need to keep us healthy.

One commentator in the business press sums up the situation as follows: 'While people are often sceptical of government, this is one instance where its involvement has changed the course of history for the better.'[26] There was alarm, when President Trump threatened to take an axe to NIH funding in 2017, that this could 'severely impair the development of new, life-saving drugs'.[27] Experts such as Michael S. Kinch at the Washington University School of Medicine in St. Louis warned that 'for decades, pharmaceutical companies [had] been moving further away from the earliest stages of research', and that even smaller biotech research companies were disappearing (many, of course, gobbled up and incorporated into the old Big Pharma companies), which leaves the NIH as the primary funder of early-stage research.[28]

Until 2020 the bulk of the work done on coronaviruses was that of the NIH. Since the SARS outbreak, the NIH had spent an estimated $700 million on research and development. While pharma companies had sometimes participated, that involvement was lukewarm at best, and as likely as not to be shelved. In 2017, drug giant Sanofi pulled out of a partnership with the US army to develop a vaccine for the Zika virus, despite having won $43 million in government funding and having developed a promising drug.[29]

European governments do not match the funding levels of the NIH, but they do still put substantial investment into research, even though Big Pharma has gained enormous influence over how these public funds are spent. In 2018, big business even pushed back against investing *public money* into the fast-tracking of vaccines for pathogens like coronaviruses, according to Corporate Europe Observatory, which wrote that Big Pharma's influence over public investment meant that public money was being spent on 'a vast array of projects to develop products, technologies, and processes primarily for the benefit of the companies involved, while the consequences for public health, people, and the environment are hardly taken into account'.[30]

As Rizvi remarked, 'no one knew coronavirus was going to be "the one". No one is saying we could have been ready to go on day one. But we could have been in a much better place'.[31]

And so it was that, in spring 2020, a dysfunctional industry was confronted with a global pandemic. What was required was a whole new level of public mobilisation. Despite its dysfunctional president, the US government again led the way. Operation Warp Speed was an $18 billion initiative to 'incentivise' Big Pharma to start researching, trialling and producing vaccines and treatments fast, as well as a commitment to purchase large quantities of doses produced.

Warp Speed was not an institution, but simply a mechanism for getting huge sums of money out of the door with the minimum bureaucracy. It was also a question of political expedience: despite often seeming to believe Covid was a conspiracy against him, Trump was desperate to get vaccines into citizens' arms before he faced re-election in November. In that, he failed – but Warp Speed did prove what can be achieved when virtually unlimited amounts of money are ploughed into medical research, development and production. Though well over a billion dollars was given out to smaller companies for non-vaccine work, the largest sums went to the Big Pharma players. Moderna was granted $2.5 billion, Sanofi and GSK $2 billion for their vaccine, which never materialised, Pfizer and BioNTech nearly $2 billion, Novavax $1.6 billion, Johnson & Johnson nearly $2 billion, and AstraZeneca $1.6 billion.[32]

If Boris Johnson's handling of Covid-19 left a lot to be desired, Trump's was a catastrophe of epic proportions – with one exception: Warp Speed. As Peter Hotez of the National School of Tropical Medicine at the Baylor College of Medicine in Houston told Bloomberg, 'The only part of the pandemic Trump responded to was things he could get companies to manufacture.'[33] Warp Speed didn't only give money for vaccines and treatments, but ensured there would be enough vials and syringes and inputs to make the vaccination programme work.

But while Warp Speed was necessary, it was nowhere near sufficient. At its heart, it was still about trying to correct, rather than replace, the market: throwing money at Big Pharma with little transparency, and seemingly few conditions around prices and access. Public Citizen even took legal action to try to improve the use of money. Eli Zupnick, a spokesman for Accountable Pharma, noted that Warp Speed 'led to a huge payday for many pharma executives. It's a perfect business. Their downside is covered by taxpayers, and their upside is already in their pockets.'[34]

This also demonstrated a key problem with the government's relationship to the industry. As we discovered in the previous chapter, Big Pharma is not only dysfunctional; it has also retained its role as a gatekeeper for our medicines. Even though the industry has failed to do its job, governments have failed to create the infrastructure required to do things better.[35] So we remain dependent on something that clearly does not work.

Warp Speed was just one component of the public spending that represented mobilisation beyond the norm. Overall, governments are estimated to have spent at least €93 billion on vaccines and treatments in just under a year.[36] Not all of that money went to the big players. But there was no attempt to use it to begin to transform an industry that, far from being our saviour, completely lacked the necessary incentives to respond to a pandemic.

As should be obvious by now, the companies that gave their name to the vaccines were not responsible for creating them. But since we have so often been told the opposite, I should make it very clear: these were all, to some degree, publicly funded vaccines.

It is understandable that the development of the vaccines during a global pandemic has made many people reluctant to criticise the industry that produced them. For some, perhaps, it did not seem to matter much who got the credit, or even who made the money: we needed vaccines, and everything else paled into insignificance. But as the pandemic wore on, it became clear that it really did matter. Because it was not simply a matter of who had invented what, or who was making money. By handing the vaccines to a select number of profit-making companies, we were also handing fundamental decisions to them – such as who got to make the vaccines, at what price, and in what order they would be sold. These questions were about to constitute one of the most important political issues we faced.

Moderna

Moderna is different from most of the Big Pharma companies that became major players in the pandemic in that it is a relatively new outfit. Before the advent of Covid, it had no products on the market. In fact, if not for the pandemic, it might have become just another biotech company that sold its work to a bigger player. But Covid changed all that, turning the company's ambitious CEO into a multibillionaire.

Moderna specialises in the mRNA technology that has become so important in the pandemic; the company's name is even based on the acronym mRNA. The technology has revolutionised vaccine development, and holds out the possibility of cutting-edge inoculations or treatments for a wide range of diseases, including HIV, cystic fibrosis, certain types of cancer and malaria.

Traditional vaccines use weak or inactive germs that need to be grown in animal cells on an industrial scale, often taking many months or even years. The technology behind mRNA vaccines is very different. It is based on a molecule that uses genetic code to teach our cells to make proteins that will trigger an immune response. In a sense, it allows you to give an instruction to your body to fight disease. That means there is no need for large factories or the time it takes to grow cultures: mRNA vaccines can be made much more rapidly and cheaply than traditional vaccines, and can be adapted very quickly, allowing vaccines to be promptly updated as viruses mutate.

Moderna's vaccine reportedly took a weekend to design, and

was completed before China had even acknowledged the disease was contagious in humans.[37] Of course, testing took much longer, but the fact that Moderna started producing vaccines rapidly in a facility that had never produced them before demonstrated the technology's potential. This led to other exciting possibilities. The adaptability of mRNA technology potentially means it can be used to deal with all manner of diseases, including rare conditions that affect only a small number of patients. Small batches of vaccines can be developed and produced in a highly decentralised way.

None of this is to say that figuring out mRNA technology was easy. Working out how to get mRNA vaccines into a the human body and ensuring they provided adequate protection without poisoning the patient has taken decades of research. At the beginning of the pandemic, many still believed it might not be possible. Now we know that it is, mRNA vaccines open up a world of possibilities, potentially transforming medicine as we know it. This means that ownership of the technology has become an important political question. Health campaigner Achal Prabhala calls mRNA a potentially very democratic technology. He uses an analogy to describe the difference between mRNA and traditional vaccines, explaining that if pre-pandemic vaccines were analogue, then mRNA vaccines are digital. 'Of course, vaccines are complex and hard to make', Prabhala says, 'But of all the vaccine technologies that are in use today, the oldest are in fact the hardest to make, and the newest – mRNA vaccines – the easiest.'[38]

We are told by free-market ideologues that risks are taken by entrepreneurs in order to drive innovation, while the public sector, rife with bureaucracy, is little more than a dead weight on the economy. This is perhaps one of the most widely believed myths of capitalism: the pharmaceutical industry shows it to be completely false. The story of mRNA goes back decades, long before Moderna was established. As so often, the earliest and riskiest research was carried out in universities using public funds. In all such breakthroughs, scientists stand on the shoulders of their predecessors, and the development of a vaccine is never a self-contained project.

In the 1990s, mRNA was regarded as such a scientific backwater that early scientists involved in it, like Katalin Karikó, struggled to obtain funding, ultimately even earning herself a demotion from the University of Pennsylvania.[39] Karikó is one of a handful of scientists who deserves the credit, if not a Nobel Prize, for her commitment to making mRNA work.

Moderna was formed in 2010 by scientist Derrick Rossi and his colleagues, who managed to raise sufficient funds to pursue some of this research. A year later, the company's investors hired Stéphane Bancel as CEO. Bancel was a very different beast from the scientists who had been working on mRNA up to this point. Driven by his ambition to run an important company, Bancel was a hard-nosed businessman whose early days at Moderna were characterised by secrecy, a high turnover of staff, and a determination to attract venture capital.[40] Moderna's engagement with the outside world seemed more attuned to generating investment than to open scientific enquiry. As one former employee put it, 'They're running an investment firm, and then hopefully it also develops a drug that's successful.'[41]

In a sector that richly rewards such behaviour – providing you have made the right bet – Moderna thrived. When the company went public in 2018, the sizeable shareholdings of Bancel and other senior executives meant they too were doing very well. When the vaccine itself proved effective, the rewards were piled high. At one point during the pandemic, Bancel was worth over $12 billion, and, while Moderna's stock has been volatile, he was still worth $5 billion at the start of 2022.[42] In Spring 2021, the People's Vaccine Alliance calculated that the Covid-19 vaccines had created nine new billionaires. Bancel topped the list, and two of Moderna's founders and its chair also appeared on the list.[43]

These fortunes were built on astonishing levels of profit. In early 2022, Moderna announced sales of its Covid vaccine the previous year had brought in $17.7 billion.[44] Of this, Moderna's $13 billion pre-tax profit – around $36 million a day in 2021 – gave it a profit margin of around 70 per cent. This was the kind of margin you should expect to see on luxury goods, not essential medicines. To put it in perspective, the average pre-tax profit margin of the 500 largest US companies in 2021 was around 15 per cent.[45]

But this was no surprise. Experts have calculated that Moderna's vaccines could be produced for as little as $2.85 a dose, yet they are in fact the most expensive vaccines on the market, averaging between $19 and $24 a dose – and up to $37 a dose to some customers.[46] In other words, the company was charging between four and thirteen times the estimated cost price of its vaccine.

Some might still say that none of this really matters. Bancel and friends might have made a killing, but ultimately we have a vaccine that has saved many lives – and a great deal of money. But in fact Moderna's profiteering is a problem for all of us, because it created an obstacle to ending the pandemic. As we shall see in Chapter 4, Moderna's business model is built on a set of perverse incentives that have encouraged secrecy and competition in place of collaboration; its vaccine represents poor value for money; and, worst of all, it has created disastrous inequality in access to vaccines, damaging our ability to overcome the pandemic.

Perhaps the thing that most clearly illustrates the waste and folly of Moderna's pharmaceutical model is the string of lawsuits the company is now involved in. Litigation is a major item in the budget of most Big Pharma companies, because maintaining full control of intellectual property is essential for maximising profits. Moderna seems at pains to conceal the basic truth about the public funds it has relied on, even to the point of legal action. It has been accused of breach of contract for not transparently stating the proportion of public funding for its vaccine.[47] And it refused even to recognise three federal scientists as co-inventors on some of its patent applications, prompting a legal challenge on the part of the American government.[48] Scientists have said they feel Moderna's attempts to sideline their work is a 'betrayal' by the corporation.[49]

This is about more than recognition. Excluding the three scientists who the public body says were critical to the drug's development from the principal patent application helped Moderna block the US government from having authority over who could produce the vaccine. As Zain Rizvi of Public Citizen noted, 'It's not just about bragging rights. It's also about supply. Patents are development monopolies, and in a pandemic it is a terrible idea to have a private corporation have a monopoly on part of a lifesaving technology.'[50]

While legal wrangling was underway with the US government, a company called Arbutus also lodged a legal case against Moderna, claiming the company infringed its patents in the use of its vaccine.[51] More recently, Moderna itself took legal action against Pfizer and BioNTech, arguing that their vaccine infringed Moderna's patents.[52]

The fact that these companies have spent huge sums on litigation to maintain the sanctity of their intellectual property, rather than collaborating in the improvement of their medicines, shows just how perverse the incentives in this system really are. No one company can possibly claim to have created such broad technological developments. So much public funding has gone into developing the vaccine Moderna produces that it was labelled 'the NIH vaccine' by Public Citizen. According to experts, 'the vaccine was jointly developed with the NIH, and . . . US taxpayers are financing 100 percent of the vaccine's development'.[53] Peter Maybarduk of Public Citizen said of Moderna's vaccine, 'This is the people's vaccine. The NIH's vaccine. It is not merely Moderna's vaccine. Federal scientists helped invent it and taxpayers are funding its development. We all have played a role. It should belong to humanity.'[54] Or as economist Adam Tooze noted, 'Given Moderna's heavy dependence on public funding, it is astonishing that the company should have any bargaining power whatsoever. It would not exist as a serious vaccine producer without public support of every kind.'[55]

One of the scientists who played a role in the mRNA revolution put it succinctly when talking about his own contribution to the mRNA delivery system: 'You really can't claim credit, we're talking hundreds, probably thousands of people who have been working together.'[56] Or as Katalin Karikó put it, 'Everyone just incrementally added something – including me.'

Moderna was far from alone in having taken public money. Pfizer claimed not to have taken public funding – a claim it used to justify the profits it made on the vaccine. But Pfizer's vaccine was partly developed by partner company BioNTech, with which Pfizer has shared its profits. BioNTech received $445 million from the German government for its research. But public support did not stop there.[57] As we have seen, Warp Speed's $2 billion was theoretically paid for 'advanced orders', radically reducing the financial risk to the producer.

One exasperated former US government official told the *Financial Times*, 'It's not even their vaccine', adding that the fact it was now known as the 'Pfizer vaccine' was 'the biggest marketing coup in the history of American pharmaceuticals'.[58]

In Britain, it was well known that the home-grown vaccine was invented by the University of Oxford. Its scientists included, most prominently, Sarah Gilbert, who had worked on Ebola and then MERS, and was able to apply the approaches she had learned to Covid-19.[59] AstraZeneca was a latecomer to the party, yet the vaccine it was involved in producing still came to bear its name in the public mind.

A groundbreaking piece of work by medical students at the Universities Allied for Essential Medicines looked into the funding of the Oxford vaccine in detail. While hampered by a lack of transparency that is routine in the area of medical funding, they drew the conclusion that public or charitable funding contributed between 97 and 99 per cent of the funding for the Oxford–AstraZeneca vaccine – around 37 per cent of R&D funding coming from the UK government and 25 per cent from foreign governments.[60]

The final 'Big Pharma' vaccine, produced by Johnson & Johnson, had likewise been given substantial public funding, including the enormous sum of close to $2 billion from Warp Speed, which included funds for both R&D and manufacturing.[61] The NIH also helped with clinical trials, developed the technology on which the vaccine was based, and had bankrolled the Ebola vaccine candidate that had first used this platform.

Between a Rock and a Hard Place: The Story of Covax

Thanks to the massive injection of public funding and a healthy dose of luck, effective vaccines and other treatments were produced fairly rapidly. The power of the state had to some degree corrected the failures of the market.

But then another problem arose: how to produce the *quantity* of vaccines the world needed. This was not helped by the fact that the three biggest vaccine producers – Merck, Sanofi and GlaxoSmithKline – all failed to produce an effective Covid-19 vaccine. It has been argued that this was because intellectual property law incentivises corporations to focus on developing technologies they already control, rather than branching out into new areas. But, whatever the truth of the matter, intellectual property exacerbated the situation: most of the world's biggest vaccine-makers were not using their capacity to produce Covid-19 vaccines because their own candidate vaccines had failed to make the cut.

As Oxfam's Anna Marriot noted in February 2021, 'The three biggest global vaccine-producing pharmaceutical corporations by market value are GlaxoSmithKline (GSK), Merck and Sanofi and between them they have only pledged to produce 225 million vaccines this year.' UN Aids chief Winnie Byanyima added, 'Every company with capacity to manufacture vaccines must be drafted in to support the herculean effort that is required.'[62] But that is not how the world of Big Pharma works. The same intellectual property model that meant vaccines could only be developed with massive quantities of public cash also hindered the production of vaccines in the quantities required. Yet again, the nature of Big Pharma was hindering rather than helping, just when its production capacity was needed most.

This problem was never resolved. While some deals were signed to increase production of vaccines, the world simply had to deal with the fact that far fewer were being produced than were needed. But this led to a third market problem: With massive demand and limited supply, how could it be ensured that the rich countries would not simply buy up all the vaccines on the market?

Just as intervention had been required to correct market failures in research and development, so it was believed, it would also be needed to correct the market failures that might be the inevitable consequence of allowing the market to decide who could buy the vaccines and who could not. This is where Covax came in.

Covax was the brainchild of two men, Seth Berkley and Richard Hatchett. They came up with the idea chatting at the Hard Rock hotel bar in the elite Swiss ski resort of Davos in January 2020.[63] Davos has become famous for hosting the annual World Economic Forum, an annual gathering of the great and the good, where business leaders and politicians take a step back from their immediate duties and discuss the trends, opportunities and the challenges in the system. It is a sort of awayday for capitalism that became particularly prominent in the 1990s, when the institutions of the global economy were being created.

In hindsight it seems incredible that Covid-19 did not dominate proceedings, but in January 2020 it was still unclear how serious it would be for the world as a whole, and thus the global economy. Instead, delegates were treated to a speech by Donald Trump telling them to ignore the prophets of doom, and that climate change was a conspiracy intended to destroy the US economy.

But Berkley and Hatchett were concerned. Each of the two ran a powerful international institution devoted to creating more and better medicines, and getting them to the poorest parts of the world. A meeting of the capitalist class might seem an odd venue for two people so concerned about access to global medicines – but that would be to miss the way financialisation has infected international development just as much as it has the business world. Berkley and Hatchett are not scruffy charity campaigners – they are archetypal establishment figures fully at ease in the company of world leaders and billionaires. In 2009, the founder of

Google lauded Berkley as one of the hundred most influential people in the world, lavishing praise on the 'breadth of his experience and deep tenacity of his character', while Hatchett had served in senior positions in the administrations of George W. Bush and Barack Obama.[64]

They were thus representative of the thinking of the development establishment, of which the public–private philanthropic institutions each presided over were typical. Richard Hatchett runs CEPI, which we have already encountered. It was established to correct the failure of Big Pharma to invest in vaccines, albeit by supporting the very businesses responsible for that failure. Seth Berkley runs an organisation called GAVI, a twenty-year-old body set up to get vaccines to poorer parts of the world, focusing on diseases like polio, cholera and diphtheria. GAVI is backed by rich countries including Britain – but also, crucially, by the Gates Foundation. Like CEPI, and in keeping with Bill Gates's own philosophy, GAVI tries to improve the way the market works rather than change the system, working with corporations to secure better prices for Southern countries and finding ways to mitigate the risks associated with developing vaccines that are mainly going to help poorer people.

These institutions strive for a better world. But they do so with their hands tied behind their backs, because they refuse to confront the very model creating the problem. They assume that sufficient public funding will encourage big business to behave differently. And by going with the grain of the current model, they in fact contribute to the very behaviour they are trying to change.

Médecins Sans Frontières criticised GAVI for pouring money into Pfizer and GSK when it bought the pneumonia vaccines desperately needed in lower-income countries.[65] This money consumed a vast proportion of its annual budget, because the vaccines are hugely overpriced – precisely because Pfizer and GSK control their supply. Their monopolies are the reason that lower-income countries cannot get access to the vaccines on their own. But rather than challenging that system, for example by supporting cheaper manufacturers to start producing and questioning the patent system, they feed it, affirming Big Pharma's stranglehold. This in turn marginalises the very governments that need to claw back power from Big Pharma in order to create a sustainable healthcare system, instead reinforcing the power of the market – albeit a market 'corrected' for its failures. Yet Berkley and Hatchett are lauded and rewarded for their efforts.

They were right about one thing, however: if Covid-19 was about to become a pandemic, there was every chance that, left to themselves, rich nations would quickly capture any vaccines that were produced, leaving everyone else with nothing. To address this, and after securing the all-important backing of Bill Gates, Covax was launched in April 2020. In fact, Covax was one arm of a much bigger organisation looking into diagnostics, vaccines, treatments and broader healthcare; but I will focus here, for the sake of simplicity, on what became Covax's core function: distributing vaccines around the world as equitably as possible.

Covax's ambition was to deliver 2 billion vaccine doses by the end of 2021, and it was not undersold. As Berkley remarked, 'Never before has a life-saving health intervention against such an immediate global health threat been made available to people in the Global North and South simultaneously at such speed.'[66]

The idea was fairly straightforward. Fifty-one richer countries would pay for their own vaccines, but still use Covax to get better prices by buying in bulk, or simply as a fallback if their own bilateral vaccine purchases proved inadequate. At the same time, a second group of ninety-two lower-income countries would receive reduced or no-cost vaccines, enough to supply 20 per cent of their populations. The hope was that this would cover older and more vulnerable populations as well as healthcare and other frontline workers. Much of this latter mechanism was to be paid for by aid budgets and philanthropy.

So far, this all seemed like a well-intentioned plan to try to stave off calamitous vaccine inequality. But in that objective, Covax failed dramatically. Ultimately, the body delivered less than half of the 2 billion doses it aimed to get out in 2021: 907 million vaccines.[67] This was a mere 8.5 per cent of the doses delivered in the world by that point.

In fact the situation was far worse than the figure of 907 million suggests. Covax would have been an unmitigated catastrophe if it had not been for two factors. First, Covax was saved by an increase in production towards the end of 2021. A full third of the Covax doses for 2021 arrived only in December. This created its own problem, as many governments were overwhelmed by bulk orders arriving all at once. For most of 2021, no more than a trickle of vaccines was achieved.

Second, Covax was saved by donations. Half of the doses given were in fact donations (mostly from the United States – the only country to donate anything more than an embarrassingly small number of shots).[68] But donations were never supposed to be a feature of Covax, and they reduced the scheme to being the very thing it had initially tried to avoid: a charitable mechanism offering little more than crumbs from the table of those who had over-ordered. Writing in late Autumn 2021, MSF calculated that less than 2 per cent of all participating countries had been fully vaccinated using Covax doses, while eighteen countries were still awaiting any Covax doses at all.[69]

The delays, last-minute deliveries and stop-start nature of the process made it impossible for most counties to plan ahead. The *Washington Post* reported that, in October and November 2021, roughly one in five AstraZeneca doses donated through Covax were rejected, often because they were so close to expiring.[70] This in turn fuelled vaccine hesitancy among the public. One Namibian official, for example, told investigators that people in his country travelled long distances to find vaccination centres without the expected doses. 'They won't come back', he said.[71]

Most richer countries ignored Covax, but those who put their faith in it to provide vaccines often wished they had not. In July 2021, Paraguay's president, having paid $7 million for 4.3 million vaccine doses but only receiving 300,000, remarked, 'We bet on the Covax mechanism to generate equity. I cannot stay quiet; Covax didn't work.'[72]

Covax has an answer to explain these problems: vaccine nationalism. If only rich countries hadn't bought up all the doses on the market, or imposed export controls to prioritise their own populations, the situation would have been very different. 'It was a beautiful idea', one academic has said, but 'Rich countries behaved worse than anyone's worst nightmares.'[73]

There is some truth to this. The self-interest of rich countries played a disastrous role in creating vaccine inequity. And of course, no one could doubt the sheer scale of the ambition Covax set itself during the crisis. But for many experts, Covax's failure to meet these unquestionably very serious challenges was built into its 'partnership' model.

Public–private philanthropic initiatives like Covax have proliferated in the financialised era as a means of solving the world's problems. The logic goes that the problems we face are simply too great for governments to solve, especially when so much wealth is in the hands of big business and the global superrich. If we want to deal with global poverty and inequality, not to mention climate change, the state needs to harness the power of the private sector for good. Out go the old models of international cooperation between governments, and in come a set of bodies whose aim was to persuade those with money that building a better world is in their interests.

Huge sums of money have often been pumped into these initiatives by philanthropists, Bill Gates being a particularly large contributor. In keeping with what makes business leaders and philanthropists feel most at home, the old negotiating forums were replaced with very small groups of decision makers, many self-appointed, who would drive the initiatives forward. As one vaccine expert put it, 'it was just the good old boys club in the room, and they didn't bring in low- and middle-income countries, it ended up looking like what the good old boys always do: development aid'.[74] It seems almost incredible that an institution developed specifically to meet the needs of lower-income countries received almost no input from representatives of those countries. The very people who most needed a voice were also marginalised in Covax. Ultimately, it is very difficult to see this as anything other than charity, tinged with the worst colonial mind-set.

Covax clearly exposes the limitations of this form of development. This will be a vital lesson to learn, because there are powerful people who would like us to see Covax as a model for how we can deal with future pandemics and the management of global healthcare more generally. They would like us to believe fairness and justice can be achieved within a fundamentally unfair and unjust system. But the real lesson from Covax is that this is not true.

Covax worked *through* pharmaceutical corporations, reinforcing the very monopolies hindering a more distributed model of production and more equitable access to medicines. Covax refused to challenge these monopolies, which were so clearly constricting supply and keeping prices high, meekly accepting its place at the back of the queue. Covax bowed publicly to Big Pharma's demands for immunity from legal challenges, assuming the financial and legal responsibility for adverse medical reactions. Even more seriously, it put all of its faith in a very small set of manufacturers, most importantly the Serum Institute in India, which was supposed to provide the bulk of the Global South's entire supply. Relying so heavily on one source was known to represent a huge risk – and, as we shall see, once India entered its own Covid-19 crisis, the strategy failed, because India placed export bans on vaccines in order to deal with its own crisis first.

African Union special envoy Strive Masiyiwa was blunt:

> We were misled – down the garden path – we got to December believing the world was coming together around vaccines not knowing that we got corralled into a little corner while others run off and secure the supplies. That was what Covax was supposed to do for us. Covax was not supposed to purchase from one supplier in India and then tell us in June that sorry there is a problem in India.[75]

A particularly critical report by Friends of the Earth International describes Covax as trying 'to get the Covid vaccine to communities and peoples in the developing world without disrupting the global pharmaceutical market'.[76] 'Access to health care should be a declared global public good', the report says. But 'Covax narrows the response to health care interventions to the ability to purchase in this case the vaccines from the "rightful" owners. These market-based solutions undermine public acceptability of health as a global public good.'

Covax was not the only international attempt, early in the pandemic, to try to mitigate the coming scramble for vaccine access. It became the most prominent precisely because it didn't seek to change the system in any fundamental way. But another institution held out the prospect of genuinely transformational change. This body was overwhelmingly backed by the Global South – but Big Pharma was determined to ensure that it couldn't work.

For a small country, Costa Rica has an outsized role in international politics. Unusual in abandoning its standing army seventy-five years ago and investing the savings in social provision, today Costa Rica is a world leader on climate action, supplying virtually 100 per cent of its electricity by renewables. So it should perhaps come as no surprise that Costa Rica was the first country in the world to propose abandoning a business-as-usual approach to Covid-19.

On 23 March 2020, Costa Rica's centre-left president, Carolos Alvarado Quesada, submitted a proposal to the World Health Organization to

> pool rights to technologies that are useful for the detection, prevention, control and treatment of the Covid-19 pandemic. This pool, which will involve voluntary assignments, should include existing and future rights in patented inventions and designs, as well rights in regulatory test data, know-how, cell lines, copyrights and blueprints for manufacturing diagnostic tests, devices, drugs, or vaccines. It should provide for free access or licensing on reasonable and affordable terms, in every member country.[77]

The proposal was not entirely new. The Medicines Patent Pool had already been established in 2010. It was an attempt to overcome the severe problems of access to HIV drugs caused by the intellectual property system through voluntarily sharing the knowledge behind those drugs, and had since then expanded to include other essential medicines. Costa Rica now proposed applying this model to all technology useful to dealing with the pandemic.

In the weeks that followed, Costa Rica built support. In the British parliament 130 MPs from different parties called on the UK government to back the proposal, while around the world more than 500 civil society groups backed the plan, renowned heterodox economist Joseph Stiglitz remarking, 'To me it's an absolutely essential step.'[78]

In May, the proposal had been worked up into a new body, the Covid-19 Technology Access Pool (C-TAP), backed by thirty-seven countries and by the World Health Organization's director-general, Tedros Adhanom Ghebreyesus, who commented, 'Almost every day there is more news about research into vaccines, diagnostics and therapeutics. But will all people benefit from these tools? Or will they become another reason people are left behind?'

By this point, C-TAP was conceptualised as a sort of one-stop shop for Covid medicines and essential equipment such as diagnostic tests. The idea was that everything involved in making these things – the patents, but also the recipes, the know-how, the data that proved their effectiveness – would be held by C-TAP. Any country or factory interested in producing could learn what they needed to know to do so safely and effectively, with no concern that they might end up being sued.

Not only could this help massively ramp up production, it could also spur innovation. Rather than operating in a deeply secretive and competitive environment, scientists and manufacturers could learn from each other, banking progress made by others and building on it. In the words of Alvarado Quesada, 'Global solidarity will speed up science and open access to public goods so we can overcome the virus.'[79]

It all sounded very promising. There was just one problem. C-TAP was voluntary, which meant that, if it was going to work, those who now owned the patents and the know-how would have to agree to contribute them to the fund. No one was asking them to do this for free, mind you. It was always accepted that the companies contributing their know-how should be paid royalties, still to be negotiated.

But that was never going to be sufficient for Big Pharma. Albert Bourla, head of Pfizer, was first off the block to deride C-TAP: 'At this point of time, I think it's nonsense, and . . . also dangerous.'[80] Pascal Soriot, chief executive of AstraZeneca, added his voice: 'If you don't protect IP then essentially there is no incentive for anyone to innovate.'[81] Thomas Cueni, the director of the leading pharmaceutical lobbying body, the International Federation of Pharmaceutical Manufacturers and Associations, agreed, saying he was 'too busy' to attend the launch of C-TAP: 'I'm not sure, to be honest, we do need additional platforms.'[82]

And so, that was that. It was eighteen months into the pandemic – November 2021 – before C-TAP was able to sign its first licensing agreement, with the Spanish National Research Council, for a diagnostic tool.[83] This was the first transparent, global, non-exclusive licence for a Covid-19 health tool. For the rest, Big Pharma boycotted what might have been a central tool in the scale-up of Covid-19 medicines.

And so, by Summer 2020, with vaccines being rapidly developed thanks to unprecedented public funding, the world had no effective mechanism to prevent an all-out scramble for them when they arrived. This was bound to result in those with the most wealth and political clout grabbing as much of the supply as they could. Although it had been established to try to counter the inequality that the global economy would inevitably create, Covax was in reality predicated on that same logic, and would prove unable to deal with the powerful forces it thought it could persuade to behave differently. C-TAP did indeed try to do things differently; but sadly, it too relied on persuasion and voluntarism, which would prove ineffective in the face of the free-market logic that was about to dictate who received vaccines and who did not.

By Autumn 2020, the forces of the market had been unleashed.

4
The Pandemic Begins

The People's Vaccine campaign started with a letter. It was late April 2022, Ramadan, so Nabil Ahmed had a 'pre-fast breakfast' and, at quarter to six in the morning, sent a draft over to his colleagues in Oxfam and UN Aids for comments. 'I wasn't an expert on vaccines,' Ahmed tells me.[1] 'But I drafted the letter. I'm always the person that drafts the letters. I remember coming up with this term 'people's vaccine' with my colleague Anna, and we stuck that in there, and it seemed to work.'

Of course, it was not the first time that the campaigners had discussed Covid:

> As it hit Italy, Max and Anna and me thought, we've really got to get on top of this, to sound the alarm. And we wrote papers on what a pandemic might mean to healthcare, to the economies of lower income countries. But the vaccine kept coming up, and we knew it would need to be patent-free very early because Oxfam had taken on big pharma before, we knew how these companies showed themselves to be in the fights on HIV/AIDS alongside President Mandela and so many others. We knew the profound greed of monopoly power. We knew what was going to happen.

'Our fragile humanity today anxiously awaits an effective and safe vaccine to be found,' the Oxfam and UN Aids letter opens. It moves on to demand, 'The world's governments must unite behind a global guarantee that ensures that any vaccine is produced and made rapidly available universally for all people, in all countries, free of charge. The same applies for all treatments and technologies for Covid-19.' 'And then we started getting sign-ups,' Ahmed tells me.

> I remember Joe Stiglitz signing very early and he wanted to help get others. And that was repeated in all the work we did, prominent people just wanted to go out of their way to help. They knew how important this was. The first former world leader we got was Helen Clark from New Zealand, and she wanted to help and brought others in. And we pitched to *Financial Times*, May 2020, and they took it. And Cyril Ramaphosa of South Africa was really the face of it. And Winnie's influence was vital here.

Winnie is Winnie Byanyima, head of UN Aids, but so much more than a UN bureaucrat. Byanyima is a fighter in all senses of the word – a fighter against poverty, against dictatorial governments, against institutional racism and misogyny, against political corruption.[2] She fought as a refugee fleeing Uganda's political turmoil in the 1970s, as a female student in the male-dominated subject of engineering at the University of Manchester, in the underground guerrilla movement trying to depose Uganda's Milton Obote in the 1980s, and in the British feminist movement that marginalised the struggle for Third World liberation. More than anything, Byanyima is an activist, once telling a journalist while running Oxfam, 'We don't think charity is the way to solve these problems. You are not going to lift everybody out of poverty through the kindness of wealthy people.'[3]

Byanyima was central to both inspiring and pushing the People's Vaccine, and was outspoken in her support for it, saying, 'We cannot let the CEOs of a handful of pharmaceutical companies decide our future.'[4]

This was the birth of a powerful campaign idea that caught the imagination of hundreds of thousands of people across the world. It was one of the few times in my life that making a structural argument for change was easier than making a charitable argument. The idea that we could produce more vaccines but were prevented from doing so because trade rules allowed a small handful of corporations to retain control of the know-how was just obscene to most people.

'The letter sparked everything else', Ahmed told me.

> We were just overwhelmed, really. The head of the UN came out and said 'People's Vaccine', and it all just moved very fast. Probably the biggest thing I've ever done in my life was getting a large group of Nobel laureates to sign the letter to President Biden. I've worked on loads of letters . . . and you've often got to really twist arms. This was easy. The signatories themselves helped us build it.

He continued:

> We've shown we can land some massive punches. Not a knockout blow yet, but it's taught us some important lessons. It's shown us the rich world won't lead us out of neoliberalism. It must come from the Global South. They can't rely on the rich world any more than the poor can rely on the rich in this country. So it's brought back the north–south stuff. We're back to fighting colonialism. There are stirrings of a new anticolonial movement. And loads of

> people didn't understand how colonial the global economy was. You could have picked the commanders and generals of the British Empire and they'd have made the same decisions.

There are two other points about the People's Vaccine movement worth commenting on here. First, the People's Vaccine was an idea as much as it was an organisation. Max Lawson of Oxfam, chair of the coalition alongside Winnie Byanyima, used to joke, 'We haven't patented the name,' and there's a deep truth to this. People's Vaccine was not a central organisation with authorised spokespeople and lengthy signs-offs on policy. It was a network. Everyone who believed in a people's vaccine was as much a part of the movement as the professional campaigners who appeared regularly on TV.

Second, the People's Vaccine was not about a single silver-bullet solution to the health crisis that engulfed the world in 2020 – though Big Pharma often liked to pretend it was, as a way of discrediting the campaign. It was about changing unjust trade rules, which entailed not only the TRIPS waiver but a much wider questioning of the intellectual property rules that place 'property rights' over human rights. It was about replacing a market-based healthcare model that is failing most people in the world. And while it did not achieve these goals within the pandemic, it certainly began to change the story we have been told about how society should work. As Ahmed told me, 'We've pushed back on the dominant narrative of our times . . . that's huge and that's why it's united so many activists.'[5]

The TRIPS Waiver

It was not only campaigners who were concerned about the ability, or inclination, of Big Pharma and rich countries to act in the interests of the whole world. In October 2020, India and South Africa went to the World Trade Organization (WTO) with a simple proposition: that for the length of the pandemic, intellectual property rights on all medicine and equipment that could help with Covid-19 should be automatically waived. This would allow any country able to produce such medicines or equipment to do so without fear of legal action or trade sanctions.

The Peoples Vaccine came in strongly behind this demand for a waiver from the Agreement on Trade-Related Aspects of Intellectual Property Rights, or TRIPS – one of the foundational agreements of the WTO. TRIPS extended Western-style patent protections across the whole world, allowing businesses to retain patents for a minimum of twenty years, during which time they could dictate who could use their creations and what price should be charged.

For many countries, this agreement was a major obstacle to their ability to develop certain industries. India and South Africa were not asking for the abolition of TRIPS, even though there was a sound justification for such an action. They simply argued that a pandemic was an extreme and unusual situation, for which exceptional rules were required. Looking at some of the actions taken by governments around the world to deal with the pandemic – actions that in normal times would be regarded as unacceptable – they were surely right. But actions that defy the rules of the market are supposed to be the preserve of the richest; for everyone else, the rules are sacrosanct.

Numerous arguments were levelled against India and South Africa's waiver proposal, but three were especially prominent. First, it was argued that the proposal would not help to end the pandemic because waiving patents would not by itself automatically promote the sharing of the know-how and technology behind the patents. Patents govern only the legal right to use certain technologies, not the technologies themselves. This was true, and the proposers agreed. The waiver was only ever one part of the solution – necessary but not sufficient – and further action would certainly need to be taken to ensure the sharing of technology.

Second, it was argued that there were already exemptions in the TRIPS agreement allowing countries to override its provisions in certain circumstances. Governments were always free to issue so-called 'compulsory licenses', which might allow them to dismiss patents where necessary. This argument also contained a grain of truth. But the experience of many developing countries that had previously tried to override patents had included the bullying and blackmailing of governments to force them to back down. In a pandemic, this could mean lengthy legal proceedings, country after country having to fight the pharmaceutical industry one patent at a time. This legal uncertainty alone made it very difficult for companies to begin producing in this way. An automatic waiver, on the other hand, would give the certainty needed to start production that could otherwise trigger legal sanctions.

Third, it was argued that the waiver was pointless, because there was no spare capacity to produce the medicines, and everything was being done to produce vaccines as quickly as possible. There simply were no factories sitting idle that could produce the vaccines, according to the 'experts'.

This was the most disingenuous of the arguments, as it was so clearly untrue. A single company in Bangladesh had already promised that it could produce 600–800 million vaccines a year if it was given the know-how.[6] Bearing in mind that the G7 countries had still donated only 865 million doses by February 2022, this could have made an enormous difference.[7] And Bangladesh was not alone: Indonesia also said it could produce 600 million a year, while Indian activists had identified thirty-four manufacturers who could have produced the Johnson & Johnson shots.[8]

Neither was this problem restricted to Southern companies. A Danish company said it would like to help produce, but its offers were dismissed.[9] Canadian company Biolyse Pharma was also ignored, but felt so strongly that it tried to work with Bolivia to produce Johnson & Johnson's vaccine under a compulsory license.[10] But this license was refused by the Canadian government, showing just how inadequate were exemptions from TRIPS.[11]

As the pandemic wore on, it appeared that some vaccines, especially those produced using mRNA technology, were more effective in reducing hospitalisations and deaths from Covid-19. That was good news because, as we have seen, the production of mRNA vaccines did not require the same scale of production as that of traditional vaccines. That meant, according to a study by Achal Prabhala and Alain Alsalhani, that more than a hundred companies in Africa, Asia and Latin America had the potential to produce mRNA vaccines.[12] And this was just companies that had been tested, either by the WHO or because they were already exporting vaccines successfully to the EU or the United States. Furthermore, this could happen fairly quickly. As the authors of the study pointed out, 'An essential consequence of the simplicity is speed: it takes three to seven days to produce a batch of the active pharmaceutical ingredient for the Pfizer/BioNTech vaccine, as compared to one month for an equivalent batch of the AstraZeneca vaccine.'[13]

The bad news was that this vaccine technology was in the hands of just three corporations, all of them committed to turning a substantial profit. The reality was that, even by 2022, for every dose of mRNA vaccine delivered to low-income countries, fifty-six were being delivered to rich countries.[14]

The more poor countries saw a minority of rich countries buy up all the vaccines available, the more they started to back India and South Africa's proposal. By early 2021, maps circulated online showing which countries backed the proposal and which did not, showing a stark global division. The Global South – broadly speaking, the nations formerly colonised – became increasingly strident in their support for the initiative. The Global North – the former colonisers – were almost entirely opposed. And of course it was impossible to miss the fact that here was a group of countries that had access to vaccines telling countries that did not that they would not even countenance a very modest proposal that might help the latter group produce their own. Particularly strident in their opposition were Britain, Germany and Switzerland. The fact that these countries had their own home-grown pharmaceutical corporations convinced many that they were putting their own economic interests ahead of saving lives around the world.

There are two other aspects of the push for a TRIPS waiver that are worth commenting on. First, whenever the general public was asked about the proposal, in the richest countries where government resistance was highest, they were strongly supportive. A poll in May 2021 found an average of 70 per cent of the public in G7 nations wanted their governments to share vaccine know-how.[15] In Britain, a consistent opponent of the waiver, this support crossed party-political lines (73 per cent of Conservative voters, 83 per cent of Labour and 79 per cent of Liberal Democrats all in favour) as well as the highly charged Brexit division (83 per cent of Remain and 72 per cent of Leave voters). In the United States, 69 per cent of the public supported the measure, including 89 per cent of Biden and 65 per cent of Trump voters in 2020.

It seemed that, to most people, the issue was not that complicated. Especially early in the pandemic, there was certainly concern about donating vaccines. People were scared for themselves and their family, and wanted to access vaccines as soon as possible. That fear, for some though by no means all, trumped considerations of global fairness. But when it came to allowing others to produce, it was no longer a zero-sum game. The very idea that it was even possible to prevent other countries producing just seemed strange to people. For what? The profits of a few corporations? How on earth could that be placed ahead of producing as many vaccines as possible?

The second point worth noting is that some of the very countries blocking the waiver themselves indicated that they might overrule patents if it became necessary. In the early days of the pandemic, a number of countries, including Germany, Israel and Canada gave themselves express authority to override patents related to Covid-19.[16] Another arch-opponent of the TRIPS waiver, European Commission president Ursula von der Leyen, when facing off with Britain in a row about AstraZeneca vaccine supplies, threatened to invoke Article 122 of the EU Treaty, which would allow the commission to seize factories, override patents and impose export bans.[17]

This was another example of the sheer hypocrisy with which Western leaders approached the issue of vaccine access. When their own countries felt overwhelmed by the scale of the challenge, almost any policy option was on the table. But the Global South was told again and again: trust the market, your time will come.

At the start of the pandemic, it was probably utopian to think that every vaccine could be distributed on the basis of global need. After all, the vaccines were going to end up being made in specific places, in the context of the neocolonial nature of the world economy, and those places were going to be rich countries, plus a few middle-income countries like India and South Africa. It would be surprising, to say the least, if those countries decided to pool the first doses off the production line and redistribute them based on global need. More likely, the countries producing the vaccines would first meet the needs of at least their own frontline workers and vulnerable populations.

While unfair, this might not have been a disaster, providing the countries with the deepest pockets did not over-order, and providing everything possible was done to increase production as rapidly as possible. The problem was that corporate interests were now driving the agenda. Owning intellectual property in the vaccines was potentially far more important than any profits that might be made selling vaccines in the short term. There was a clear incentive to hold on to the technology and ownership rights over the vaccines at all costs.

This became clear even before the first vaccines were even rolled out. As the two front runners, Pfizer and Moderna, raced to win authorisation for their vaccine first, campaigners became alarmed that both companies had already sold huge amounts of their prospective vaccine in advance contracts. Pfizer had sold 80 per cent of the vaccines it said it would be able to produce over the following year to the richest governments in the world.[18] For Moderna, the figure was 78 per cent.[19]

Even when you add in other leading vaccine candidates that had been sold somewhat more equitably, including the Oxford/AstraZeneca vaccine, the Russian Sputnik vaccine and the Chinese Sinovac vaccine, it was still the case that more than half of all sales had gone to the wealthiest countries, whose people accounted for less than 10 per cent of the world's population.[20] While Countries like the United States, Britain and Canada had procured several times what they needed – hedging their bets to ensure they ended up with the very best candidates – most other countries had secured no vaccines at all.

The general rule was clear: the richer you were, the more likely you were to have vaccines – and, at the top end of the wealth spectrum, you'd likely end up with many more than you required. This would be a problem not only for those countries at the lower end of the spectrum: it would make ending the pandemic much harder.

Spring 2021: Donations

By early summer 2021, the G7 nations were vaccinating their citizens at a rate of 4.6 million people per day. Low-income countries were only able to manage 63,000 people per day. While the G7 was on track to have vaccinated almost all its citizens by the end of the year, low-income countries would be waiting fifty-seven years if the trend were to continue.

To compound the many problems of Covax, India had been through a catastrophic wave of Covid. The country was neither the first nor the last place to witness a terrifying collapse in its health system in this wave of mass illness; it was happening around the world. Many regions, especially in Latin America, were already devastated by the virus. But in Britain, India's crisis was the first time these horrors had become headline news, with reports of hospitals running out of oxygen and people dying in their cars in a desperate scramble for a hospital bed. No one could argue any longer that Covid-19 was worse in the West than anywhere else – or, therefore, that the West had greater need of the medicines that could help us deal with this crisis.

The Indian crisis guaranteed Covax's failure, however: the whole scheme had depended heavily on a single company, the Serum Institute, producing enough doses of the Oxford/AstraZeneca vaccine to vaccinate large parts of the Global South. But in the middle of the crisis, the Indian government simply could not countenance the export of vaccines, or anything else that might help the country dampen the Covid wave. India introduced export restrictions and mobilised the vaccines for its own urgent roll-out.

India's restrictions were not lifted for many months – a delay that damaged Covax's ability to supply anything but a trickle of vaccines until much later in the year. Such overdependence on a single producer could, of course, have been predicted, but such mistakes were baked into the Covax project, desperate as its founders were to do as little as possible to challenge the status quo.

The result was a level of inequality so great that it was even starting to worry some among the political establishment. The first concern was that leaving large parts of the world unprotected would make it much harder to end the pandemic. Studies had already suggested that many more lives would be lost to Covid if the wealthy nations took care of themselves first, and it was far better to vaccinate in a fairer way. One study predicted that, while a fair vaccination campaign could avert over 61 per cent of potential deaths, that fell to only 33 per cent under a 'West-first' approach.[21] This was even more likely if those parts of the world with the least capacity to implement social distancing and isolation measures were the ones left out.

But even for those unmoved by this fact, who simply saw some lives as worth more than others, it was still a concern that new and even more dangerous variants of the virus were more likely to emerge in unprotected areas. Short of sealing off those parts of the world that were affected, which in itself was hardly conducive to the recovery of the global economy, those variants could come back and overwhelm the protection of those of us lucky enough to have been vaccinated.

Moreover, some Western leaders were beginning to worry that most people who had been vaccinated in the Global South would have received the Chinese or Russian vaccines, rather than their Western-made counterparts. This could begin to undermine the West's so-called 'soft power'. Vaccine inequality was thus causing concern well beyond those who believe in a more equal planet. In addition, Big Pharma did itself no favours when, in April 2021, the three big Covid vaccine producers – Pfizer, Johnson & Johnson and AstraZeneca – paid out $26 billion to their shareholders: enough, as People's Vaccine put it, to pay to vaccinate at least 1.3 billion people, the equivalent of the population of Africa.[22]

The disaster in India seemed to underline the importance of doing something radically different. Already in October 2020, India and South Africa had brought their proposal to suspend patents to the WTO. In the months that followed, almost every country of the Global South came to support the resolution, either explicitly or tacitly. And almost every Northern country either explicitly or tacitly opposed it.

In May 2021, however, something big changed that picture. Joe Biden had become US president in January. While Biden was not from the Democrats' left wing, he had won by promising to heal divisions and reclaim America's role in multilateral institutions. He promised to work with his party's growing left wing, symbolised most prominently by his one-time challenger for the Democratic presidential nomination, Bernie Sanders. And he had beaten a man, Donald Trump, who had sent a shockwave through America's liberal establishment, making part of it realise that this was not a time for the timid policies of the past. To avert an even deeper crisis than the one Trump represented, change was an urgent necessity.

Against this backdrop, in May 2021 Biden's trade secretary, Katherine Tai, announced that the United States would move to support negotiations on a TRIPS waiver, remarking, 'The Administration believes strongly in intellectual property protections, but in service of ending this pandemic, supports the waiver of those protections for COVID-19 vaccines.'[23] Certainly, the waiver was less far-reaching than the one proposed by India and South Africa: it applied only to vaccines, excluding medicines and treatments that might be useful in dealing with Covid-19. Nonetheless, it was a political earthquake: the first time in decades that an American president had so blatantly defied Big Pharma or suggested that intellectual property was anything other than sacrosanct.

I remember astonished WhatsApp messages from campaigners at more conservative charities who had until then believed those of us in the People's Vaccine campaign were fighting for the unattainable, and so had not even wanted to express their support for the waiver publicly. They now found themselves more conservative in their posture than the president of the United States, and scrambled to incorporate the demand into their work. More importantly, in the wake of Biden's announcement other Western countries moved to back the waiver, or at least moderate their opposition to it.

Biden's announcement hit right at the heart of the pharmaceutical industry. Industry lobby group PhRMA publish an annual submission to the US trade representative complaining that pretty much every country in the world showed insufficient deference to the sanctity of intellectual property, and urging the US government to keep a watch on – or even institute trade sanctions against – these countries for their poor behaviour.

But the events of 2021 sent them into all-out hysteria as they complained, 'Multilateral organizations that once served as custodians of the international rules-based system increasingly are seeking to undermine and even eliminate intellectual property protections.'[24] Of particular concern was the fact that the 'WHO Director-General even publicly supported an extreme and unnecessary proposal . . . to waive entirely certain international obligations with respect to COVID-19 technologies'. Other UN agencies, they complained, had 'directed millions of dollars to programs that seek to weaken intellectual property laws and lobby governments to reject provisions in international trade agreements that would strengthen innovation incentives'. They urged the United States to provide 'leadership' to prevent international organizations 'weakening or even eliminating the intellectual property protections that drive America's innovation economy'.[25]

But it was clear to the industry that the genie was out of the bottle, and they would have to go all-out to limit the damage. They developed a number of arguments to try to dampen enthusiasm for the measure. In particular, the problem remained 'vaccine nationalism', the over-ordering of drugs by rich governments. They reassured the public: Don't worry about changing the rules. We'll all have enough doses soon. For now, the West needs to donate its vaccines to those without.

Britain, which was chairing the G7 meeting in June that year, where discussions would be dominated by the pandemic, became a particular proponent of 'donations, not structural change'.

As Britain's Covid-19 restrictions were lifting, the Cornwall G7 provided the first opportunity for us to take to the streets on the issue of vaccine inequality. Campaigners like myself travelled down to the Cornish town of Falmouth to highlight the hypocrisy of the world leaders meeting a few miles up the road. While many were still sensibly cautious about being part of a large gathering, we tried to make up in props what we lacked in numbers, and headed down with a gigantic fake syringe, puppet heads and a powerful projector to display messages on Cornwall's dramatic cliffs.

Even for a British prime minister, Boris Johnson is remarkable for his double standards. He had already been enmeshed in scandal when his in-house guru Dominic Cummings had proved unable to follow the government's own rules on isolating with Covid – yet Johnson had refused to sack Cummings despite an enormous public backlash. Later, we discovered that Downing Street had hosted a never-ending series of illegal gatherings while most British people were locked down. But that summer, Johnson decided he should take a private jet 250 miles from London to Cornwall to attend his own G7 summit, where climate change was also high on the agenda.

The issue of vaccine donations was no different. While Johnson routinely talked up Britain's generosity, by the time the G7 met Britain had not donated any vaccines at all. Nor, despite moaning about other countries using export restrictions, had it exported any itself. It had also bought many more than it required, making advance orders for 500 million doses in an attempt to hedge its bets on which vaccine would be most effective. But it was now clear that at least 270 million of these doses were effective – enough to vaccinate the British population more than twice over.[26]

Unlike most rich countries, Britain had in fact taken 500,000 Pfizer doses from Covax.[27] Britain did have a legal 'right' to these doses under the terms of Covax's contracts, which were initially supposed to ensure fair access to doses for every country. But Britain was a world leader in terms of the speed of its vaccine roll-out. Taking mRNA vaccines from a pot that was the only option for most countries, and at a time when almost none of them had any vaccines (never mind mRNA vaccines) was ethically questionable, to say the least.

Moreover, as India was entering its catastrophic wave, Britain was also taking vaccines from the Serum Institute – the company on which so many Southern countries were depending. Some 5 million doses had already been delivered to Britain as India spiralled into crisis – and the British government was putting pressure on India to deliver a second batch of 5 million.[28] Thus, by the time the G7 met, Britain had in reality taken more vaccines from supplies that could have gone to the Global South than it had donated. A few months later, it was revealed that Britain had binned 600,000 vaccine doses because they passed their expiry date.[29]

Johnson's promise to world leaders that he would lead a crusade to 'vaccinate the world' was clearly nonsense. On the eve of the G7 summit, Johnson tried to secure pledges for 1 billion donations. This was still woefully inadequate – enough to immunise only about 10 per cent of the globally unvaccinated population. But he could not even achieve this, and by the time delegates departed Cornwall, the number had fallen to 870 million, of which only about 600 million were genuinely 'new', while most of those would only arrive the following year. Without the US contribution, the numbers would have been derisory. Britain promised 100 million – only enough to provide a single dose to 1.5 per cent of the world's unvaccinated population, or a double dose to just 0.7 per cent.[30] Worse, the vast majority of those would only materialise in 2022.

The G7 was a cynical exercise, more a ploy to undermine the growing case for change than a genuine attempt to end the pandemic fairly. For that reason, it was also a turning point in global opinion – the moment at which most countries realised that both the West and the rules of the global economy had badly failed them. In the words of former British prime minister Gordon Brown, the summit would 'go down as an unforgivable moral failure'.[31]

Astra Zeneca

Of all the Western corporations that produced an effective Covid vaccine, AstraZeneca is the only one that made a meaningful contribution to the vaccination effort outside the West. The Oxford/AstraZeneca vaccine was cheap, costing only a few pounds a shot. So does AstraZeneca's approach to Covid-19 disprove the rule that the pharmaceutical industry as a whole tended to squeeze every last drop of profit out of the pandemic?

AstraZeneca is an Anglo-Swiss corporation, formed in 1999 by a merger between a very old Swiss pharmaceutical company, Astra, and a breakaway from British chemical giant ICI, Zeneca. It is a big corporation: in May 2020, it became the UK's most valuable company. Its current chief execitive, Pascal Soriot, has been credited with putting the company on a more sustainable path. In spite of his French nationality, he has become something of a British business hero, fighting off a hostile takeover of his company by Pfizer and investing in British-based research. He also likes to tell journalists he is the lowest-paid chief executive in the pharmaceutical industry.[32] By industry standards, his salary of over $15 million salary in 2020 is indeed low – though probably not a cause of much sympathy in wider society, or even in Soriot's own investor meetings.[33]

Soriot inherited a standard Big Pharma company. After years of handing the corporation's wealth to its shareholders, AstraZeneca was heading for a so-called patent cliff, its blockbuster drugs nearing the end of their monopoly periods. The company had tried to maintain profits in the usual way. In 2012, the European Court of Justice upheld a judgement that found it guilty of abusing its market position, when it misused regulations in order to keep generic competitors of Losec – a stomach ulcer treatment it produced – off the market.[34]

In 2010, AstraZeneca agreed to a $520 million settlement over allegations that the company had defrauded US government health programmes by illegally marketing an antipsychotic drug for uses for which it was not approved as safe and effective.[35] The previous year alone, the company had made nearly $5 billion from sales of the drug.[36] Also in 2010, AstraZeneca had agreed to pay a £505 million settlement to the British tax office, after a fifteen-year dispute over claims of tax dodging.[37] And in 2016 AstraZeneca lost a case in which it had attempted to prolong its monopoly on a cholesterol pill and prevent generics coming onto the market – after which it increased the price of the drug by 15 per cent, to make as much as it could before the generics hit the market.[38]

So far, so familiar. Soriot came in as CEO as a clear-sighted chief executive who recognised the situation was unsustainable.[39] He ended the shareholder giveaway, halting the company's stock-buyback programme. He also invested in new R&D pipelines to produce new blockbusters. Much of this R&D still took the form of corporate takeovers and mergers, in keeping with the financialised pharmaceutical model, though it did also mean more in-house research. He then focused AstraZeneca's operations on creating blockbuster drugs for diseases affecting richer countries.

This meant, in 2014, shutting a laboratory in India working on early research into tuberculosis, malaria and neglected tropical diseases, as well as streamlining its business operations around cancer and cardiovascular, respiratory and autoimmune diseases.[40] The decision prompted the World Lung Foundation to comment, 'Drug companies want to make drugs for chronic diseases that people in western countries are going to take for the rest of their lives' – a line echoed by Médecins Sans Frontières (MSF), which noted, 'AstraZeneca would never withdraw its R&D into these diseases if they affected rich countries or if there was more of an incentive to produce them – instead, they're going where they see the biggest profits, and it's not in these drugs.'[41]

When Covid struck, AstraZeneca hadn't been working on a related medicine. But the Jenner Institute at Oxford University had been working on vaccines and on coronaviruses, as well as malaria, tuberculosis and Ebola. The Jenner Institute had received at least £67 million from the British government for this work.[42] We have already seen, in fact, that Oxford's vaccine was developed almost entirely (between 97 and 99 per cent) through the use of public or charitable funds, judging from the information available. AstraZeneca would also later receive $1.2 billion from the US government to develop, produce and deliver vaccines.[43]

In other words, this vaccine could have been a 'people's vaccine'. Indeed, there appears to have been a push for that at Oxford, where the director of the Jenner Institute told the media, 'I personally don't believe that in a time of pandemic there should be exclusive licenses.'[44]

Here, then, was a real possibility of doing something differently. Of course, Oxford did not have the capacity to scale up enough to produce millions of vaccines. It needed a partner and entered negotiations with a number of pharmaceutical companies. According to one account, Bill Gates's team was instrumental in the final deal. Gates himself was quoted as saying, 'We went to Oxford and said: Hey, you're doing brilliant work. But . . . you really need to team up.' Gates is a well-known proponent of intellectual property rights, though he denies taking an active role in the final deal.[45] Whatever went on behind closed doors, the fact is that the situation changed dramatically after the talks with AstraZeneca. There would not now be an open license, but an exclusive license.

Of course, AstraZeneca could have made worse decisions. Soriot did try to ensure significant coverage outside the rich world, and the majority of the company's vaccines were delivered to lower-middle-income countries – though of course the bulk of this order came from one generic manufacturer in India, the Serum Institute; and even here, as we have seen, the UK was prioritised, claiming 10 million of the Serum doses. In fact, the UK's presumed prioritisation across the board within AstraZeneca's contracts – which unfortunately remain secret – caused major problems, and was at the heart of the battle with the EU that badly undermined trust in the vaccine.

It is also true that the AstraZeneca vaccine's price was low by comparison with those of other companies, but it was not without problems. In particular, stories emerged that South Africa was being charged two-and-a-half times what the EU paid, and that Uganda had been asked to pay even more, while India, in the middle of its catastrophic wave, was being charged almost four times the EU price in private hospitals that covered the needs of many Indians.[46] Meanwhile, AstraZeneca's 'no profit' pledge only lasted as long as it judged there was still a pandemic. In November 2021, the company decided this was no longer the case, and that it would start profiting from sales on new contracts.[47]

Most fundamentally, AstraZeneca refused to share the publicly created knowledge behind the vaccine – the one thing it could have done to make a greater difference. The only rationale for not sharing more openly was that it hoped at some point to profit from sitting on such knowledge. But as the pandemic wore on and the safety of AstraZeneca's vaccine was, largely unfairly, called into question, it seemed that profits would not be huge anyway. So why not drop the patents and share the know-how? Ultimately, perhaps, because that would be a step that Big Pharma is constitutionally incapable of taking.

When you examine the way the pharmaceutical industry operates, it is easy to conceive of everyone at the top as fundamentally inhumane. After all, the industry's model is based on squeezing as much profit as possible out of drugs that prevent suffering, and even death. But the industry's leaders come from a variety of backgrounds and perspectives, and, while lacking all empathy with other human beings might make it easier to do your job, most of us ultimately want to believe we are good people.

There is no reason to believe that Pascal Soriot was not genuine in prioritising the ending of a pandemic ahead of his corporation's bottom line – but the case is even more illuminating if that is true. AstraZeneca was ultimately locked in a no-win situation. Investors complained that Soriot was trying to do 'politics, rather than business', while shares tumbled in value and campaigners complained that the company was keeping vitally needed public research to itself.[48]

It seems unlikely that a Big Pharma company would go as far as AstraZeneca in future – and impossible to imagine that any could do so for more than a short time in an extreme situation. So perhaps, in this example, we have the most that could possibly be expected of the industry – and it is palpably not enough. That is not because these corporations are necessarily headed by money-obsessed sociopaths, but because this behaviour is built into the industry's structure, which dictates that a corporation simply cannot put global public health ahead of shareholder profits for long.

In February 2021, South Africa's delegate to the WTO, fed up with being lectured by countries with plenty of vaccines on order about the need to respect intellectual property, made an eloquent speech. Certainly, Covax had a laudable aim; but the claims of countries like Britain – that because they had funded the initiative, they had therefore 'done their bit' – were coming up against a hard reality:

> Irrespective of the amount of money any of the donor countries may throw at the problem, the model of donation and philanthropic expediency cannot solve the fundamental disconnect between the monopolistic model it underwrites and the very real desire of developing and least developed countries to produce for themselves. Madam Chair the problem with philanthropy is that it cannot buy equality.[49]

But these words changed nothing. The G7 had proved to countries in the Global South that a multilateral solution was unlikely to be found. Many had probably grudgingly accepted that their needs were never going to be met in the first wave of vaccinations – but they did expect that, once the West was vaccinated, supplies might be released. But as rich countries continued to buy up doses, especially of what were increasingly seen as the most effective mRNA vaccines, it was becoming obvious that 'me first' was now developing into 'me second, third and fourth'.

This particularly upset middle-income and relatively powerful countries. 'South Africa isn't used to being treated the same as a low income country', as South African campaigner Fatima Hassan told me. 'But suddenly in Covid it was clear we were all in the same boat – very low-income countries or relatively well-off countries, we were all shut out.' And as summer 2021 wore on, and negotiations at the World Trade Organization failed to make any progress, it became clear that negotiations were going nowhere. Meanwhile, deadlines set by the WHO and Covax to vaccinate a specific, often very small proportion of every country in the world, were missed in the vast majority of African countries.[50]

To get a sense of the anger felt by many in the Global South, it is instructive to notice the language used by diplomats. The head of the World Health Organization, Dr Tedros Adhanom Ghebreyesus, was appointed director-general in 2017. Dr Tedros, as he is often referred to, became something of a celebrity during the pandemic, and an outspoken critic of vaccine inequality. The former Ethiopian minister used characteristically undiplomatic language at the start of 2021: 'I need to be blunt: the world is on the brink of a catastrophic moral failure – and the price of this failure will be paid with lives and livelihoods in the world's poorest countries.'[51]

By September, as heads of government met for the UN General Assembly, Tedros's language was echoed by the UN secretary-general António Guterres, who told the Assembly:

> On the one hand, we see the vaccines developed in record time – a victory of science and human ingenuity. On the other hand, we see that triumph undone by the tragedy of a lack of political will, selfishness and mistrust . . . This is a moral indictment of the state of our world. It is an obscenity. We passed the science test. But we are getting an F in Ethics.[52]

Heads of government from across the Global South made similar points. Peru's left-wing president Pedro Castillo said, 'The inequality is abysmal and tragic . . . How will we explain to the next generation that while there was a raging pandemic in which vaccines were not available to all people, and an unprecedented climate crisis, the world invested more funding in weapons?'[53] On the far right, President Duterte of the Philippines was just as angry: 'Rich countries hoard life-saving vaccines, while poor nations wait for trickles. They now talk of booster shots, while developing countries consider half-doses just to get by. This is shocking beyond belief and must be condemned for what it is – a selfish act that can neither be justified rationally nor morally.'[54]

Something fundamental had started to shift. While early in the pandemic all but the most radical governments had assumed the international system would cater to some degree for their needs, all now realised this would not be the case. This began to change attitudes of governments who had invested faith in the multilateral system for too long. As President Museveni of Uganda told the assembly, 'We find that the actions by some to hold vaccines at the expense of poor countries, also referred to as vaccine nationalism, is wrong, but a good lesson for developing countries that don't want to innovate. It is good because it wakes up those that are asleep, waiting to be saved by others.'[55]

This fundamental loss of trust in the multilateral system would have potentially far-reaching consequences in a world already ripped apart by political, social and economic division, and facing crises even more severe and profound than Covid-19. As a crucial climate conference met, after a twelve-month postponement, in November 2022, vaccine inequality threatened to marginalise poor countries even further, when it was their voices that most needed to be heard at the summit. Many started to wonder, if the international political system and global economy could not even manage a modicum of self-sacrifice for the greater good of all of us all, what hope there was that the system could solve the existential challenges humanity now faced.

Big Pharma ramped up its PR offensive, rehearsing three arguments. The first, was that the supply problem was over. Collectively, 12 billion vaccine doses would be produced in 2021, and by early 2022 there would be a global surplus with 'sufficient vaccines produced for every adult on every continent' and by June 2022 'vaccine supplies may actually outstrip global demand.'[56] This ignored the fact that a scramble for third and fourth shots was well underway, with rich countries again at the front of the queue, despite many countries still not having sufficient doses for their first and second jabs. Adequate supply did not guarantee equal access.

It also neatly sidestepped the fact that almost half of the 12 billion would come from Chinese companies, which were increasingly responsible for inoculation of the largest part of the Global South; hardly a success of the Western pharmaceutical model.

The second argument remained that the problem was vaccine nationalism, and there was simply nothing Pharma companies could do other than urge countries to donate their excess supply. This was, then, about shifting the blame.

The third argument, and perhaps the one that caused the most anger, was to start blaming ordinary Africans for their lack of vaccines. Vaccine hesitancy was the problem, according to Pfizer CEO Albert Bourla, who proclaimed 'The percentage of hesitancy in [low-income] countries will be way, way higher than the percentage of hesitancy in Europe or in the United States or in Japan.'[57] Tom Frieden, the former director of the United States Centers for Disease Control and Prevention, described Bourla's remarks as 'shockingly irresponsible' and 'on a par with people in the Aids crisis saying Africans wouldn't be able to take antiretrovirals because they couldn't tell the time.'

Bourla seemed to have little evidence for his claim, except that countries including South Africa asked for vaccine deliveries to be temporarily paused. But the reason for this was really the deeply unequal nature of those deliveries. Having received almost no deliveries for most of the year, some countries were now receiving relatively large quantities in one go, often with very short expiry dates.[58] This would be a challenge even in a country with very developed and well-funded healthcare systems, but it was impossible in countries with poor health networks.

Of course, there was hesitancy in lower income countries, but evidence from across Africa suggested that vaccine hesitancy was much lower there than in parts of the United States.[59] A World Bank study found near universal acceptance in Ethiopia (98 per cent of people said they would take the vaccine) with high acceptance in Nigeria (86 per cent), Uganda (85 per cent), Malawi (83 per cent) and Burkina Faso (80 per cent).[60] A separate study found that people in developing countries have a much higher willingness rate (80 per cent) compared to the United States (65 per cent). But that did not seem to matter.[61]

In late November, Big Pharma's line was about to hit the reality of a new variant, known as Omicron, which would prove the strategy to date had been a disaster not simply for those in countries that couldn't get vaccines, but for everyone in the world. Before we get to that point, let's examine the corporation most criticised during the pandemic: Pfizer.

Pfizer

Of all the companies involved in the pandemic, none has brought in as much revenue from Covid-19 medicines as Pfizer. In 2021 alone, Pfizer's vaccine generated a massive $37 billion, making it easily the most lucrative medicine in any single year in history. Pfizer predicted that it would make $54 billion in 2022 from its vaccine and Covid treatment combined.[62] Together, these two medicines could double the company's already very large total pre-pandemic revenues.

Pfizer did not achieve its market position by playing nice. As the pandemic wore on, more and more media reports focused on the company, and criticism was certainly not confined to campaigners. Perhaps it was best summed up in a documentary by Tortoise media.[63] The presenter went to great pains to show that he had tried his best to be balanced and fair to the company. Nonetheless, from a wide range of interviews with government and industry insiders, 'the most generous thing any of the people I've talked to has found it in their heart to say about the way Pfizer has behaved: "They're a bunch of shitbags, they're not the only ones, but they're cleverer than the rest."'

We saw in Chapter 2 that Pfizer, with its partner Flynn, was behind a price hike of over 2,000 per cent on an anti-epilepsy drug relied upon by 48,000 NHS patients. That was by no means the only scandal that had affected the company. MSF spent years criticising Pfizer, as well as GlaxoSmithKline, for their pricing of a vitally important pneumonia vaccine. Pneumonia kills around 1 million children each year, though the disease is preventable with the use of something known as a PCV vaccine, the rights to which were owned by Pfizer and GSK. MSF campaigned against the high price of this medicine, which it claimed was sixty-eight times more expensive in 2015 than in 2001.[64] Eventually the campaign won price reductions for lower-income countries, though they were nowhere near sufficient: MSF claimed the cost remained at 'roughly US$9 for each child to be vaccinated in the poorest countries, and as much as $80 per child for middle-income countries that don't qualify'.[65] At the time of writing, 55 million children around the world still did not have access to the pneumonia vaccine, largely because of its high price.

It was little wonder that the Reputation Institute found that Pfizer had the lowest reputation of all the Big Pharma companies they looked at in June 2018.[66] Not surprisingly, when Pfizer raced to the finish line in getting its Covid vaccine authorised, many health campaigners feared what that might mean for a fair and equitable end to the pandemic.

In the Introduction, I quoted how Pfizer's CEO, Albert Bourla, clearly saw the pandemic as an opportunity to try to repair his company's battered reputation.[67] In that task, he met with some success. But he was equally clear that Pfizer would be making money, referring to the vaccine as 'a huge commercial opportunity'.[68] To justify this position, Bourla prided himself on having taken no government money for his vaccine, turning down some of the Operation Warp Speed funds that might have supported research and scale-up. Instead, the company opted for a straight sale to the US government, as well as ploughing Pfizer's own money into the vaccine's development.

But Bourla's argument was disingenuous. The vaccine, like all mRNA vaccines, was built on decades of public research. If credit for this particular vaccine should go to any single company, it would be Pfizer's partner, BioNTech – a spinoff from a German university centre that was given substantial European public funding for its development. BioNTech continues to work with Pfizer, sharing the profits of the vaccine with it.[69] It is true that Pfizer put its own money into producing the drug – up to $1 billion, according to Bourla – but it also received guaranteed government contracts from Warp Speed of nearly $2 billion in sales.[70] At most, Pfizer's investment was a small part of the picture, and was minuscule compared to the returns the corporation has seen. No wonder a former US government official involved in vaccine procurement complained, 'It's not even their vaccine.'[71]

It is not hard to see where Pfizer's profits come from. Pfizer claims that the cost price of its vaccine is just under £5 per dose. Others have suggested it could be much cheaper, some experts claiming that Pfizer's doses could be made for as little as 76p.[72] But the UK government paid £18 per shot in its first order, and £22 for its later purchase.[73] Even taking Pfizer's declared cost price at face value, that meant the NHS has paid a markup of at least £2 billion: six times the cost of the pay rise the government agreed to give nurses in 2021.[74]

Pfizer would no doubt argue that it must cover development costs, not just the cost of production alone. But if that were the case, it seems counterintuitive that prices would *increase* over time. For the EU, Pfizer raised the price by more than a quarter between its first and second set of purchases: from €15.50 to €19.50 per dose.[75] More worrying still, Pfizer's chief financial officer Frank D'Amelio is on the record as saying, 'There's a significant opportunity for those margins to improve once we get beyond the pandemic environment that we're in.'[76] As in the industry more generally, prices seem unrelated to production costs, being determined instead by whatever the firm feels it can get away with.

It has been claimed that Pfizer wanted to charge far more – certainly, it has repeatedly insisted that it is charging a special price suitable in a pandemic. Insiders have claimed that Pfizer tried to pitch its medicine to the US government for an eye-popping $100 a dose.[77] Tom Frieden, a former director of the US Centers for Disease Control and Prevention, accused the firm of 'war profiteering'.[78] Since then, Pfizer has made good on its promise, as it prepares to raise prices to between $110 and $130 a dose in the US.[79] It is unclear what economic rule justifies the quadrupling of prices for a product that is several years old, except the rule of the monopolist. People's Vaccine called the new price 'daylight robbery' that would give Pfizer a 10,000 per cent mark-up on its medicine.[80]

One investment advisor made an educated guess that Pfizer's profits were likely to be in the region of 80 per cent – well in excess of the 'high 20 percentage' profit the company claimed to be making.[81]

In order to be able to charge these prices, Pfizer has sold the vast majority of its doses to the richest countries in the world – a strategy sure to keep its profits high. Pfizer sells a tiny proportion of its vaccines to low-income countries.[82] By October 2021, Pfizer had sold a measly 1.3 per cent of its supply to Covax.[83] More Pfizer doses have gone to the Global South, but because the US government bought them in large numbers and donated them.

A string of allegations has exposed devastating costs incurred in the rest of the world by the way Pfizer's profits have been generated. Shockingly, the company stands accused of spreading disinformation about rival AstraZeneca's vaccine.[84] Pfizer funded a study claiming that vaccines like AstraZeneca's were risky for vulnerable patients and could cause cancer – a claim for which there is no evidence. This claim was then used to misinform health professionals in Canada.[85] Pfizer says the claim was made by a third party, and that it is therefore innocent of wrongdoing – but this did not explain why a member of Pfizer's board became a regular TV guest in the United States, who used his platform to discredit AstraZeneca's vaccine while talking up alternatives.[86] AstraZeneca's legal advisor accused Pfizer of spreading misinformation detrimental to public health, at a time when hesitancy around its vaccine was already high.

An even more serious allegation was that Pfizer had strung lower-income countries along, holding negotiations with Covax with seemingly little intention of selling them a reasonable number of doses.[87] The strong suspicion expressed to journalists by some insiders was that Pfizer was using the fact that it had been talking to Covax for months as a tool to ratchet up the price for richer countries. None of this was easy to prove, as Tortoise media made clear, and Pfizer denied the allegations. But stories of Pfizer's foot-dragging in its talks with poorer countries proliferate. One African negotiator claims his country was 'left treading water . . . until we were drowning'.[88] People inside Covax, the WHO and rival manufacturers simply cannot explain Pfizer's apparent stalling in any other way. Just as extraordinarily, when the company discovered that you could squeeze six good doses out of a vial of liquid rather than five, they hiked the price to Covax for exactly the same amount of liquid.[89]

What we also know of their negotiations is that they made extraordinary demands of countries. Asking for countries to waive corporate liability for rare side-effects was a relatively normal approach during Covid-19. Governments including Lebanon and the Philippines had to change their national laws to grant such immunity.[90] But Pfizer's demands were particularly extreme, specifying that liability covered not just unexpected side-effects but also negligence, fraud and malice on the part of the company itself. Pfizer quite literally sought to place itself beyond the law in the countries to which it was selling.

An investigation by the Bureau of Investigative Journalism discovered that Pfizer had demanded some countries in Latin America and Africa put up sovereign assets, such as embassy buildings and military bases, as collateral against possible future compensation cases brought against the company.[91] These demands also led to long delays – and in the case of some countries, such as Argentina and Brazil, it meant a deal could not be completed at all. In Argentina, an immunity law was even passed though congress, but it did not go far enough to satisfy the corporation. Pfizer's demands were described by a negotiator, who said their government felt like it was being 'held to ransom', as 'high-level bullying'.

This treatment was not reserved to lower-income countries. A report by Channel 4's *Dispatches* uncovered that Britain had agreed to a special investor arbitration system in its contract with Pfizer.[92] This meant that any dispute the British government might have with Pfizer would be adjudicated not in British courts but in a special tribunal, overseen by corporate lawyers. Where these special arbitration mechanisms have been used elsewhere, there has been a marked tendency for them to favour the interests of big business over those of the public.[93]

We live in an age when the power of massive corporations poses a significant threat to our democratic rights. Pfizer's story shows just what that threat looks like in practice. During a pandemic, Pfizer used people's desperation to raise this anti-democratic power to a new level. As Hassan argues, 'A private company can't have so much power.' Winnie Byanyima, head of UN Aids, said of Pfizer's chief Albert Bourla, 'He hasn't saved the world. He could have done it but he hasn't.'[94]

Moderna

Like Pfizer, Moderna sold most of its vaccine to the rich world. In September 2021, 85 per cent of Moderna's total supply had been delivered to the richest countries, with almost no doses at all going to the lowest-income countries.[95] While the company had sold a tiny 3 per cent to Covax, it had not delivered them.[96]

When less affluent countries did manage to get hold of a vaccine, it seems they often did so by paying more inflated prices. Colombia reportedly paid double what the United States was charged, and South Africa ultimately turned down a whopping $42 price tag per dose.[97] Oxfam calculated that, if Colombia vaccinated its population with Moderna's vaccine, the cost would swallow 16 per cent of the entire national budget.

Despite the enormous public funding it had received, Moderna's leadership was committed to making a profit and boosting its share price at every turn. In fact, Moderna is an outstanding example of how chasing good market news has trumped an open and honest discussion of its research. Well before Covid, one journalist looking into Moderna noted, 'Under [Stéphane] Bancel, Moderna has been loath to publish its work in *Science* or *Nature*, but enthusiastic to herald its potential on CNBC and CNN, taking part in segments on the world's most disruptive companies and the potential "cure for cancer".'[98]

Covid did nothing to dilute this focus. In May 2020 the company released a very partial set of positive results to the media, which scientists claimed were insufficient to analyse meaningfully. One former Moderna executive, speaking anonymously to CNN Business, commented, 'Issuing a press release around Phase 1 data is very unusual . . . Issuing a press release around partial data from less than half the patients is very, very unusual – practically unheard of.'[99]

The announcement had a very positive impact on Moderna's stock. Hours later, as the price shot up 30 per cent, Moderna sold 17.6 million shares to the public at its new high price, raising $1.3 billion.[100] Two Moderna executives sold off nearly $30 million in shares, and days later, Moderna's leading shareholder — a venture capital firm called Flagship Pioneering, founded by Noubar Afeyan, co-founder and chairman of Moderna — sold 1 million shares, earning $70 million.

Corporate executives at Moderna made a killing out of these news announcements, often in automated sales, in which stock is sold when a certain price is reached. Moderna's moves were in fact labelled by former Securities and Exchange Commission (SEC) officials as 'highly problematic', and worthy of investigation for potential market manipulation, while the SEC chair cautioned companies against selling stock during the pandemic, pointing out that, even if sales are legal, the optics were not good.[101]

But the profit did not seem to be enough. Rather, it was control over the know-how that seemed to be Moderna's overriding concern throughout. It is true the company made a commitment not to enforce its patents during the course of the pandemic, and later extended this commitment to lower-income countries permanently. But, in reality, this measure had more to do with public relations than any meaningful commitment to openness. In practice, Moderna refused to share its know-how or patents with the WHO, or with scientists in South Africa, who were trying to make an mRNA vaccine.[102] In fact, Moderna applied for patents in South Africa that would last until 2034, causing campaigners to worry that the company might be preparing to challenge the country if it managed to produce its own vaccine.[103]

Under intense pressure, Moderna belatedly announced plans for a production plant in Kenya, as well as a programme to 'share' mRNA technology with others.[104] But, again, these programmes seemed designed to ensure that Moderna retained full control of the technology, production and supply. The technology-sharing programme would be at Moderna's discretion, and any medicines produced would be jointly patented by Moderna. The factory would be part of Moderna's supply chain, not accountable to the needs of Africa's people. When it came to a genuinely transformative initiate like the South African hub discussed in Chapter 7, Bancel told a journalist that it was 'not a good use of our time'.[105]

Omicron

Towards the end of November 2021, a new and far more transmissible form of Covid-19 was identified in a region of South Africa, from where it very rapidly spread to Europe and across the world. Scientists speculated that Covid-19 had probably mutated in the body of an immunocompromised person, perhaps someone living with HIV, who had been unable to fight off the virus thanks to a combination of their weakened immune system and a lack of the immunity that could have been provided by vaccination. This was the moment the world had feared. And although it vindicated campaigners who had been calling for a rapid increase in the production and sharing of vaccines, this was cold comfort as everyone now faced another Christmas marked by isolation, mass hospitalisation and death.

Omicron entered the news cycle the weekend before the World Trade Organization was due to meet in Geneva. This was ironic, because the WTO summit was to have been dominated by the still unresolved matter of a TRIPS waiver. That body's failure to agree minimal flexibility in its big business–friendly rules, even temporarily during a health crisis, had now hindered the scale-up of vaccine manufacturing, resulting in a variant that would now cause the cancellation of the WTO's own summit. Just days before delegates were due to meet, Switzerland placed a travel ban on several southern African countries; within hours, the summit was indefinitely postponed.

The WTO had been formed in a different world – a moment of free-market euphoria in the mid 1990s, when some had even proclaimed 'the end of history', beyond which capitalism and liberal democracy would live in harmony for the rest of time. The dream failed definitively in 2008, as the consequences of letting the market regulate itself became clear for everyone to see – unprecedented inequality and financial collapse, ushering in a period of political instability further heightened by climate change, and now by a pandemic. But the WTO seemed stuck, unable to support the sort of resilience and economic balance that was so clearly necessary. The WTO has always had its critics, but now ever more countries were asking whether the WTO even had a long-term future.[106]

Omicron prompted a new wave of anger at the ongoing inequality in vaccine rollouts, in particular because it fuelled a new wave of vaccine purchases by rich countries that made the inequality even worse. It was revealed that in the six weeks leading up to Christmas, the most vaccinated parts of the world – the UK, the EU and United States – had received more vaccine doses than all African countries had received for the whole year.[107] Former British prime minister Gordon Brown called the inequality 'a stain on our global soul', while Amnesty International accused Big Pharma of fuelling an 'unprecedented human rights crisis'.[108]

In a sense the world got lucky with Omicron, in that the variant was far more transmissible but far less severe than previous strains – though of course that was little comfort to those who died or suffered chronic long-term symptoms as a result of the wave. But everyone now realised that there was no guarantee that this would be the last variant, and the next time a more severe strain might have even worse consequences.

Still, there was little movement at the WTO. And it was not hard to see why: Omicron was not bad news for everyone. Already, mRNA vaccines seemed to be somewhat more effective than their rivals when it came to protection from hospitalisation and death. With Omicron, this discrepancy became even clearer, putting additional pressure on supplies of the very vaccines that were already the scarcest in the Global South. In most rich countries all booster shots would now be mRNA shots. In the two last weeks of 2021 alone, Pfizer and Moderna announced seven new deals, which included a further 330 million doses being supplied to European countries in 2022.[109]

This was good news for Pfizer, BioNTech and Moderna. The week after the variant was announced, Moderna's CEO personally made more than $800 million, as Moderna's shares skyrocketed on the assumption that people would need new – and potentially regular – vaccinations.[110] This was a view pushed heavily by Stéphane Bancel in the media, when he claimed that current vaccines were likely to struggle with the variant – but that Moderna was working on alternatives. Bancel sold 10,000 shares the day after the variant was announced, cashing out more than $3 million.

The company's other shareholders did well too. Eight top Moderna and Pfizer shareholders added a combined $10 billion to their fortunes, while the world's largest investment fund, Blackrock, increased its combined share value in the two corporations by more than $2.5 billion in the week after the announcement.[111] The other largest shareholders were mostly investment and hedge funds – evidence that the real money being made by Big Pharma was channelled to the already superrich.

In the months following the outbreak of Omicron, the focus of lower-income countries' governments and campaigners started to change. While seemingly interminable conversations would continue at the WTO – and a desperately late and underwhelming compromise on the waiver even emerged – many came to the view that change would not come from trying to convince rich-world leaders that a change to the global rules was necessary. Rather, the Global South would simply have to start doing things differently – to take power back from these global monopolies on the ground. South Africa's so-called mRNA hub, backed by the WHO and formed with a pledge to share its know-how freely across the world, would become the central pillar in the fight for a different pharmaceutical system. The African continent would in fact become the central battleground between Big Pharma and a more sovereign medical R&D model.[112]

In addition to vaccines, an important aspect of the Covid-19 story is the range of anti-viral treatments. There is a range of treatments now on the market, with varying degrees of effectiveness, that have made an overall difference to the number of deaths in hospitals.[113] In fact, in the absence of access to vaccines, the supply of anti-viral treatments to low-income countries should have been prioritised, so that their pandemic efforts were receiving at least some support. Sadly, these treatments have followed a similar path to vaccines, albeit on a smaller scale. As Zain Rizvi of Public Citizen warned early on, 'The global community is sleepwalking into yet another great divergence when it comes to medical technologies.'[114]

One treatment that became well known was Remdesivir,

produced by Gilead. Like many of the vaccines, however, Remdesivir's R&D could not have happened without the support of the US government. Various agencies poured tens of millions of dollars into the drug's development and trials, first to test it against Ebola in pre-Covid times, then against Covid-19 itself.[115] The US government played a critical role in the identification and development of Remdesivir as a Covid treatment, with both money and in-kind support, after Gilead had abandoned research on the drug due to its predicted unprofitability. Despite this, Gilead sought extensive patent protection: the current patents are expected to last until 2035.[116]

One of the most shocking moments in the development of Remdesivir was when Gilead tried to obtain 'orphan drug' status for the drug.[117] This is a special status in the United States that grants additional monopoly rights, and was introduced as a means of incentivising research into medicines that might have limited markets. It is difficult to think of a disease to which orphan status should apply less than Covid-19. Even in March 2020, it was clear that Covid-19 was going to affect huge numbers of people. Under intense political pressure, Gilead eventually withdrew its application. But the company still made $5.6 billion from Remdesivir in 2021, charging between $2,300 and £3,100 per course – a huge sum, given that one paper estimated the cost of production for a course might be as little as $9.[118]

Perhaps the most effective Covid-19 treatment developed to date was another Pfizer blockbuster, Paxlovid, which can reduce the risk of hospitalisation or death by 89 per cent in high-risk patients if taken early enough.[119] In January 2022, Pfizer claimed it could make 120 million courses of Paxlovid over the course of the year, despite a predicted need for 250 million.[120] The vast majority of Pfizer's early supply contracts meant that its doses would once again be heading to Europe and North America; there were no contracts signed with African countries.[121]

But Pfizer told the public not to worry. Perhaps feeling the heat over its record on vaccines, Pfizer announced its intention to issue licenses through a patent pool to partner companies that could, it was hoped, produce more doses more cheaply. But there were a number of obstacles to this plan.

First, those generic licenses were not expected to come online until 2023.[122] Yet again, the poor would have to wait until the rich had taken what they needed. Second, Pfizer's generics licenses excluded a number of middle-income countries like Argentina, Brazil, China, Malaysia and Thailand – exactly the countries where substantial generics production capacity existed.[123] In fact, most of Latin America – one of the areas in the world hardest hit by Covid – was excluded from the open licenses, and Pfizer filed patents across almost all of the continent.[124] Third, despite these licenses, Pfizer was preparing to file patent applications in sixty-one countries, with some patent coverage in an additional eighty-seven countries. Public Citizen noted, 'Even while Pfizer was taking credit for the licensing deal, Pfizer was busy building a far-reaching patent wall to prevent generic competition.'[125]

One example shows particularly clearly that Pfizer was less than generous when it came to collaborating. To be effective, Paxlovid needs to be commenced early after infection, which can be especially difficult in lower-income countries. Desperate to find a combination that might ease this problem, experts asked for access to the drug for trials, only to be blocked by Pfizer.[126] The director of the Drugs for Neglected Diseases Initiative, Nathalie Strub-Wourgaft, remarked, 'It is difficult to understand any rationale for refusing to cooperate in the midst of a global pandemic.'[127]

Other treatments faced similar obstacles. Eli Lilly's Baricitinib, previously used to treat rheumatoid arthritis, was strongly recommended for treatment of severe and critical Covid, but its current patents in countries including South Africa, Indonesia and Brazil were not due to expire until 2029.[128] The cost of production has been estimated to be as low as $1.78 per fourteen-day treatment course, and generic versions are on sale in some countries for under $7 per course. But Eli Lilly's list price in the United States was $1,109.[129] Eli Lilly has signed some voluntary licenses with generics manufacturers in India, but severely limits where the drug can be used.

While it is certainly true that some of the deals relating to antiviral treatments are more open than those for the vaccines, perhaps as a result of the outpouring of anger across society at vaccine inequality, they do not reflect the sort of open, collaborative system that is urgently needed. There is little sign so far that access to treatments is in practice any better than to vaccines. Meanwhile, Big Pharma continues to rake in profits on medicines that, like the vaccines, have often received substantial public financing. One constant undergirds all of their strategies, on both vaccines and treatments: control of the underlying know-how, in the form of intellectual property. As Yuanqiong Hu of MSF says about Paxlovid's somewhat more open licensing, it 'keeps the decision-making power entirely in the hands of the pharmaceutical corporations'.[130] This is crucial, because it is this control that lies at the heart of Big Pharma's profits.

At the end of February 2022, British prime minister Boris Johnson scrapped all remaining restrictions that had been put in place to deal with Covid-19. Even isolating when testing positive for Covid became voluntary. Johnson said we should learn to live with the disease. Unsurprisingly, cases rocketed, and though the vast majority were relatively mild, Britain's daily death rate remained frighteningly high.

Moreover, the fact that we could even contemplate 'living with' the virus was possible only because of the development and rollout of vaccines and treatments to which many in the world still had no access. To commemorate the second anniversary of the pandemic, Oxfam crunched some numbers, putting to bed arguments that had been used to justify the inequitable distribution of vaccines in the pandemic.[131] Despite frequent claims, often repeated by people who never bothered to check international media, the pandemic had been worse in Europe and the United States than anywhere else, Oxfam found that you were more likely to die of Covid if you lived in a poorer country.

Of course, death rates in many countries were underreported, but using the number of excess deaths rather than official Covid statistics gives a very different picture of the toll. For instance, one small study found that almost one-third of bodies taken to a morgue in Lusaka in 2020 and 2021 had tested positive for Covid-19, implying that Zambia's Covid death toll was much higher than official statistics suggested.[132]

This was no surprise. After all, while nearly three-quarters of the population were fully vaccinated in rich countries, just 6 per cent of low-income countries were in the same position. The richest countries had administered six times as many booster vaccines as low-income countries had given first doses, and even disposed of nearly a quarter of a million doses, which had effectively been hoarded.

This was not just health inequality, either. Almost all of humanity – 99 per cent – were worse off as a result of the pandemic, which had pushed 160 million people into poverty; but not quite all. A new billionaire was being created every twenty-six hours, and forty of these billionaires had made their extreme wealth from vaccines, treatments, and Covid-related equipment.

This disparity had not gone unnoticed or unchallenged. The pandemic had seen the biggest, most visible and vocal global movement ever assembled against the power of the pharmaceutical industry. Former world leaders – even ones who, when in office, had been proponents of the globalisation project – had spoken out against the shocking inequity. They were joined by members of Britain's royal family, senior diplomats, the pope and the president of the United States. Even then, the coalition had not been powerful enough to force a change of direction. But the anger that had been created would not go away, and where international negotiations had failed, countries of the Global South had simply started doing things differently, challenging the pharmaceutical model in a way not seen before in the neoliberal era. These initiatives and experiments laid the groundwork for a very different global health system.[133]

5
Recolonising the Global Economy

At the heart of Big Pharma's power lie its monopolies, which are based on a set of intellectual property rules. These rules have underscored Big Pharma's transformation from a useful industry that researches important medicines into the financialised sector we see today. The story of how these rules came into being is important, because it explains so much about the nature of the global economy as a whole, and how big business came to have such enormous power over our lives. Few activists in the People's Vaccine movement understand these intellectual property rules as well as Tahir Amin.

Amin could have made a lot of money from his 1990s legal training, centred on intellectual property, if his conscience had not led him down a different path. Amin is proud of his working-class background, and living for fifteen years in New York does not seem to have made much of a dent in his Yorkshire accent. I met him in perhaps London's most famous bookshop, Foyles, and we reminisced about studying in the city in the 1990s.[1] Back then, Foyles was a ramshackle place with countless small rooms, corridors and staircases, run by the eccentric and reputedly autocratic Christina Foyle. You could spend days getting lost in there, because books were arranged by publisher with no electronic database. Finding the book you needed was a matter of pure luck. On the other hand, finding a multitude of books that deeply interested you as you tried to locate what you needed was guaranteed. Today, the shop is a neat and spacious place. It's a lot less fun, but you can find what you are looking for with ease.

To me it feels like a metaphor for London itself, which has lost so much of what made it unique and interesting, though it has certainly become an easier city to live in for those with a high enough income. The liberalisation of the City of London in the 1980s and '90s created incredible wealth, London becoming the pre-eminent home of the greed-is-good 'Yuppie' class. But it was also the home of some of the biggest ecstasy-fuelled rave clubs in the world, of squat culture, and of enormous, creative demonstrations against the rapid gentrification of the city.

It was a city at a crossroads. Margaret Thatcher had gone, but her legacy was all around us. Before Thatcher, Britain was one of the most equal and left-leaning countries in Europe. This was anathema to Thatcher, who famously insisted, 'There is no such thing as society.' The vision which drove Thatcher on, a set of ideas which would congeal into something called neoliberalism, would affect not only Britain but the entire global economy. These neoliberal ideas were at the heart of the reshaping the pharmaceutical industry into the beast that I was discussing with Amin.

But in the early nineties, when Amin and I were studying, the implications of all of this for the rest of the world were not so obvious. As a student activist, I was interested in domestic struggles, such as opposing privatisation and Britain's far right. I was far too wrapped up in the politics of my own identity to worry about what was happening around the world. Amin was studying to become a lawyer, specialising in what was then the relatively unknown and unglamorous area of intellectual property (IP). That was all about to change. 'There weren't many IP courses at the time,' Amin told me, 'but I was looking at copyright and design, and I went into private practice where I specialised in IP. It was incredible how quickly it started to be seen as the sexy area, and within ten years IP was everywhere, but back in the '90s no-one knew much about it.'

The one popular book which really shone a light on this emerging corporate worldview was Naomi Klein's highly influential 1999 work *No Logo*.[2] In it, Klein looked at the changing thinking within increasingly dominant multinational corporations. Effectively, she argued, the power of these behemoths no longer resided in their factories, their staff, or even their products per se, but rather in their brand. Klein's book had been a call to arms to a generation of young people who were growing up in a consumer culture the likes of which the world had never seen before. While an older generation of activists had been brought up on the idea that the power for change resided with the industrial workers in the factories that fuelled capitalism, in Western countries like Britain, whose post-war deindustrialisation had been zealously accelerated by Thatcher, this idea seemed dated.

Klein gave us a new way to look at the landscape. The factories still existed, but increasingly in parts of the world with which the end consumer had no relationship. Meanwhile, brand culture was exerting an increasingly powerful sway on the development of capitalism. People were now identifying more with corporate brands than with political systems, which appeared ever less able to change anything in their lives. It was the brand, rather than the individual products a company might make, that allowed corporations to out-market their competitors, to buy up the high street and drive smaller businesses under, to build the increasingly concentrated corporate sector we see today.

As we have seen, IP includes things like patents and related product data – for instance, the information that allows a company to prove its medicines are safe and effective. But it includes much else besides, including the notion of a brand. Like patents, brands are hard to quantify: they are by their nature 'intangible'. This is what Amin was working on. 'The companies were anxious about it', he tells me,

> because they saw that this thing that mattered most in terms of their profits – their brand – was really hard to define, really hard to value and protect, particularly in markets with very few rules about this sort of thing. In the past they'd have wanted to protect their factory or whatever. Now they needed to protect this. And that's why TRIPS was so important for them.

Few industries were as closely associated with the Agreement on Trade-Related Aspects of Intellectual Property Rights (TRIPS) as the pharmaceutical industry. TRIPS extended very high, US-style IP protection to the whole world. This meant, for example, every country implementing a minimum twenty-year period of protection on patents. It was perfectly in tune with the new way of thinking about a corporation's value, and it is fitting that TRIPS was one of the first agreements negotiated by the newly founded World Trade Organization (WTO).

The WTO was a linchpin of the globalisation project, replacing the much looser post-war GATT agreement that had previously governed international trade. The WTO went well beyond GATT in three major ways. First, it was a permanent new institution with enforcement powers. Whereas there was something of a 'take it or leave it' approach to GATT, allowing Southern countries in particular to ignore rules that did not suit them, the WTO rules would effectively be hardwired into international law.

Second, whereas previous thinking had been that trade liberalisation – opening up markets to international competition and cutting tariffs – could well be useful, it was still understood as a means to an end. An open trade regime was seen as an important way of encouraging growth and development, creating jobs, and sharing technology and industrial know-how. Given its importance for these goals, there was a general view that it was a good idea in principle. But there was also a recognition that obstacles to trade might help protect a country's farming sector or its emerging industries. Indeed, virtually no country on earth had developed without a heavy dose of protection from international trade, including the United States. In the WTO, any nuance on this question was abandoned. Trade liberalisation was seen effectively as an end in itself.

Finally, and perhaps most importantly, this 'free trade' agenda went way beyond most people's conception of free trade. It was not simply a question of removing taxes on traded goods, known as tariffs, but of removing *all* impediments to the free movement of goods and services. This might include all manner of regulations designed to protect consumer rights and public services, as well as those relating to the financial system. But these regulations had been vitally important under the post-war economic model, allowing governments to stabilise their economies and give countries some space to stand up to the power of international markets. Instead, the rules of the global economy now gave capital an effective right to move unimpeded around the world, transferring power strongly towards the richest, the 'owners' of the economy, at the expense of workers and citizens, while placing governments in the straightjacket of the international marketplace. This move fostered the growth of the financialised economy that helped to turn so many pharmaceutical corporations away from the R&D and production which had long been their mainstay.

It also included intangible assets, such as intellectual property, which Tahir Amin had been working on. IP includes patents (exclusive rights to use an invention), trademarks (rights to use certain words or phrases in relation to your products), copyright (protection of authorship) and trade secrets (information necessary to your production which you have a right to keep from your competitors). Protection of such intangible assets was essential, it was argued, to allow corporations and investors to move themselves and their products around the world freely. Without it, what was to stop producers in other countries simply stealing their know-how?

The inclusion of IP as a core part of the WTO also shows just how vital corporate players saw 'intangible assets' like IP as being to their newly emerging business model. As Amin told me, 'These businesses developed law, at a global level, to meet their interests and make it easier for them to make money out of these intangible assets. They couldn't wait for these rules to come in because it would mean this new form of economy would be made truly global, and really profitable.'

The political implications were enormous, given which parts of the world were rich in labour and raw materials, and which were rich in intangible assets. In a nutshell, this globalisation project was an attempt to reinvent global capitalism so as to shift wealth and power even further from labour to capital, from the Global South to the North, and from a form of decision-making in which power resided in nation states to one in which power was based on the will of the so-called free market.

~

Of course, there were patent laws before TRIPS, but in many countries they tended to be policed weakly. In particular, patents on medicines were controversial, even in countries like Britain, until well into the twentieth century. Meanwhile, in much of the Global South they did not exist until TRIPS forced those countries to adopt patent rules.

Graham Dutfield, in his history of the pharmaceutical industry, *That High Design of Purest Gold*, has detailed the history. The modern pharmaceutical industry emerged largely from the industrial dye sector in late-nineteenth-century Germany.[3] A critical moment came when dyestuff company Bayer turned to pharmaceuticals, marketing forms of painkillers, including aspirin and heroin, to which it applied the same early IP provisions it had applied to its other industrial products, even though the painkilling properties of the underlying natural products had been well known for a considerable time.

As is so often the case, the IP on these products benefited those who started manufacturing and protecting their products first. Unsurprisingly, industries in competitor countries argued for a looser set of rules that might allow them easier access to important new technologies. As incredible as it seems today, in 1919 the American Pharmaceutical Association denounced 'unfair monopolies on medicinal chemicals and dyes', arguing that patents should be 'primarily designed to benefit the public at large'.[4] The First World War gave the United States the excuse it needed to override German patents, opening up a world of technologies to its own industries. Britain passed its own prohibition on patents on chemical substances at the same time, lending support to British firms that had fallen behind in the new pharmaceutical race.[5]

Outside German industry, most opinion in the United States and Europe was still opposed to patents on medical products, seeing them as ethically wrong and counterproductive in the discovery of life-saving medicines. The British Medical Association even opposed medical researchers' cooperation with drug trials until 1950, because the resulting products might end up subject to patents, while Britain's Medical Research Council and the Royal Colleges of Physicians and Surgeons proposed an international treaty banning the patenting of medicines.[6]

But from the 1930s onwards this opinion was gradually eroded by those with an interest in patenting medicines. It was argued that certain conditions could be applied to the patent system to make it more ethical – for instance, ensuring patents were genuinely and significantly new, that they only apply to processes rather than products, and that they be tied to the production of safe and high-quality medicines. In his book, *Owning the Sun*, Alexander Zaitchik explains:

> As drug companies took their place alongside other modern research-based industries, they turned cautiously to long-taboo arguments about the uses of intellectual property. On the academic side, scientists in search of funding streams wondered if patenting and licensing models might be devised that retained the old idealism and did not open the door to unscientific avarice. Both sides settled on a similar two-pronged justification for exploring 'ethical' patenting: First, holding exclusive rights on inventions could help pay for more research and hire more scientists; second, by limiting production to trustworthy manufacturers, drug companies could wield patent monopolies in the name of public safety.[7]

Behind these arguments was a cold reality. Having 'caught up' with their German competitors, American and British companies now began to see the benefit of protecting their technologies from other potential competitors.

The People's Vaccine campaign often used the memorable words of the creator of the first polio vaccine, Jonas Salk. In 1955, as Salk's vaccine was declared safe and effective, legendary broadcaster Edward R. Murrow (a crusader against Senator Joseph McCarthy's infamous campaign of persecution against suspected communists) asked Salk who owned the patent to his new vaccine. Salk replied, 'Well, the people, I would say.' He continued 'There is no patent. Could you patent the sun?'[8]

It is an inspiring story, which proves it is perfectly possible to produce vitally important medicines without resort to patents – especially when their development is paid for by the public through government research contracts or charitable donations. But the view that patents on medicines were undesirable, though still widely shared, was being slowly cast aside. In the UK there was something of a public outcry about the fact that penicillin, which UK researchers had played an essential role in creating, had been patented by US businesses, handing control and pricing of this vital new drug to the United States. Only by 'getting there first', it was argued, could this be prevented in future.

The development of antibiotics played a huge role in fostering a stronger patent regime, which was in turn a spur to the growth of Big Pharma in 1950s. While there were still exemptions to the stringency of IP law, they did not reverse the long-term drive for more patents on medicines. In particular, the idea that IP was necessary for innovation became central to public discourse on the issue, painting a picture designed to scare the public, according to which, without the use of IP protections, the whole industry would collapse, and new medicines would cease to be developed.

Despite this move in richer countries towards the patenting of medicines, until the mid 1980s, little attention was paid in the

Global South to IP. These were not, after all, markets that mattered much to business, and the diseases they were confronted with did not feature in the setting of pharmaceutical research goals. The patenting of drugs was not permitted even by many European countries until the late twentieth century, and very few would have argued in the 1970s that developing countries needed to have the same patent laws as rich ones.[9]

It was not simply that this idea had never been considered. There was an understanding, embedded in the post-war system of regulated capitalism, that some countries required different rules from others – particularly those that needed to develop their economies. This is a common theme in the area of IP. For example, China was able to develop as successfully as it did precisely by disregarding Western IP rules, importing technologies and reverse-engineering them – sometimes by literally taking products apart, seeing how they worked, and copying them. Although giant corporations would like to convince us today that this is 'theft', the truth is that it is how almost all countries have developed.

Today, having developed a strong knowledge base of its own, China's government, like its predecessors elsewhere, is becoming much more interested in developing a stringent IP regime.[10] But what China's development path tells us is that forcing countries to reinvent the wheel – or rent the know-how necessary to build the wheel from wealthy corporations in richer countries – is economically disastrous for poorer countries. The development of higher-tech industries depends fundamentally on countries having not just an understanding of the relevant technologies, but some control over it.

In fact, in a system already heavily stacked against poorer countries, the ability to learn from other, richer countries was always seen by the development economists of the 1960s and '70s as one of the main reasons to trade. And this meant that, at a minimum, a country should have the ability to design its own patent laws for its own purposes, just as the richest countries in the world had done.

But the underlying changes in capitalism brought about by TRIPS made this impossible. If capitalism was to expand into a truly global market, countries were told, rules would need to be standardised. If that undercut the ability of some countries to develop their own technologies, and in turn their own economies, that was just too bad.

The development of TRIPS was therefore a truly audacious and hugely important move. When it was being negotiated, many of the richest countries had only recently adopted similar patent provisions themselves. According to IP expert Ellen 't Hoen, forty-nine of the ninety-eight countries signed up to the Paris Convention for the Protection of Intellectual Property excluded pharmaceutical products from patent protection, ten excluded pharmaceutical processes, and twenty-two excluded chemical processes.[11] TRIPS would change this fundamentally, and a former Big Pharma executive was central to its development.

Mocking the solemnity with which the intellectual property rules in TRIPS are now described by decision-makers, Alexander Zaitchik describes the TRIPS backstory as 'almost impossibly shallow and grubby; its founding documents younger than Justin Bieber', observing that it was 'born as a brute and profoundly undemocratic expression of concentrated corporate power'.[12] He details a process of negotiations in which former Pfizer CEO Edmund T. Pratt worked tirelessly to undermine the proponents of a healthcare system based on equality and the common ownership of knowledge. Pratt's ultimate answer was to create a global set of IP rules, and he worked with big business to build the case.

Pratt worked with pharmaceutical giants Pfizer, Johnson &

Johnson, Merck and Bristol-Myers, but also computer giants such as IBM, car companies including General Motors, agrochemical and biotech giant Monsanto and entertainment behemoth Warner, which together formed the Intellectual Property Committee.[13] Expert Susan K. Sell notes, 'If it had not been for the twelve American-based transnational corporations of the Intellectual Property Committee . . . there would be no Agreement on [TRIPS] today.'

According to Sell, central to what they achieved was a new framing of IP itself. First, they had to convince policymakers that IP really was akin to 'property' and was a 'right', because for much of history it had instead been seen as a privilege assigned to certain businesses or importers when it was in the national interest to do so. Second, they had to convince US politicians that their own financial interests in maximising IP standards globally were one and the same with those of the US government in improving its ever-worsening trade balance. Without new rules, these corporations argued, the United States was doomed to fall prey to the pirates and rogues undermining the American economy. In this way, they effectively captured US policymaking and the power of the American state to protect their commercial interests.

But how were these rules passed by a consensus-based body like the WTO, whose membership includes many of the countries that, in other forums, were arguing for a very different health system? The answer is that behind the WTO's democratic-sounding model lies brute power. Health experts in particular were shut out of 'trade' discussions, while the United States, working closely with Big Pharma lobbyists, played a role that became all too familiar at the WTO: that of isolating and bullying countries, often openly threatening them with economic consequences if they held out.[14] India and Brazil – the two Southern countries that had managed to develop impressive pharmaceutical sectors – had the most to lose, and held out the longest. But in the end they too were threatened and economically blackmailed, with the predictable result.[15]

In a broader sense, too, the Global South was not in the same state as it had been in the mid 1970s, when the Non-Aligned Movement of 'Third World' countries had worked together to defend their interests forcefully at the United Nations. The Third World debt crisis and subsequent structural-adjustment policies imposed by the Global North had undermined the economic independence of these countries. And it is important to bear in mind that this was only one WTO deal predicated on the promise of other deals, such as the scrapping of protection for food markets in the Global North, which the South saw as a reasonable quid pro quo given the importance of agriculture to their economies. The failure of the rich countries to live up to their side of the bargain in these areas would cause deep resentment in the years ahead. Moreover, the relatively unknown subject of intellectual property simply did not register strongly enough on many delegates' radars – especially since they were told that failing to join this important new body would leave them cast out of the international system.

Tahir Amin adds that the public was not properly informed of these changes when TRIPS was being negotiated 'Activists got it,' he told me, 'they said "we're being recolonised here", but mostly people didn't really see it. But now, with Covid, I think it's become obvious. Everyone in public health is talking about decolonisation. And they're right, that's exactly what it was about.'

The Fightback Begins

The United States and Big Pharma won this round: TRIPS came into force on 1 January 1995. But this would be only one battle in a much longer struggle over the globalisation project.

Towards the end of the 1990s and into the 2000s we were repeatedly told that there was no alternative to the global neoliberal project. This message was embraced not only by right-wing politicians, but by supposedly centre and centre-left leaders who would at one time have stood solidly behind the post-war economic model that neoliberalism had eroded. In fact, globalisation came to be identified most fully not with Thatcher and Reagan, but with the governments of Bill Clinton in the United States and Tony Blair in the UK.

But this vision was contested by a diversity of international movements. From landless peasants in Latin America to workers in deindustrialised parts of Europe and the United States, from environmentalists to unions organising sweatshop workers in Asia, the globalisation project galvanised coordinated opposition, some of whom came together to protest attempts to negotiate new rules, deals and treaties – sometimes completely derailing them.

One of the leading lights of the movement was Filipino writer, activist and later politician Walden Bello, who became a prominent critic of the WTO. In his best-seller *Deglobalization: Ideas for a New World Economy*, he passionately argued that the new neoliberal world order was a disaster for people around the world – but particularly in the Global South, where it was undermining any possibility of genuine development and reinforcing neocolonialism.

When I spoke to Bello in early 2022, he was on the campaign trail, standing to become vice-president of the Philippines in a close contest pitting authoritarian populist Ferdinand Marcos, son of the country's former dictator, against the liberal Leni Robredo for the presidency. Bello was standing on a third, left-wing ticket. He was not expected to win – in fact the prospect of winning filled him with horror. But he stood to open up space in the political debate in the Philippines, to show people there was an alternative between neoliberalism, organised around institutions like the World Trade Organization, and the increasingly fascistic populism of current Philippine president, the unhinged Rodrigo Duterte, and his political heir Marcos. Unless you offer a real alternative to the free market, Bello believed, people will increasingly turn to authoritarian strongmen to protect them.

The story of TRIPS 'needs to be situated in the wider context of why the World Trade Organization came into being in the first place', Bello told me:

> A large part of it was really an effort to prevent more of the sort of gains which had been made by the Global South in the 1970s and '80s. The biggest example of those gains was East Asia, of course . . . [where countries had] adopted economic planning in their trade policy, using trade policy as a mechanism for development, and it'd been successful. They were finally able to challenge the economic hegemony of the USA and the Global North . . . And so [the USA] said, 'Well, the Global South is getting away with a lot here and it's threatening our hegemony, and it's using industrial policy, and it's using our intellectual goods.' They fought back. That's what globalisation was all about, and TRIPS was a big part of that, supported by Big Pharma, the car industry, the emerging tech industry.[16]

While the movement that Bello was part of challenged the globalisation project on many fronts, one specific fight was the attempt to roll back TRIPS. Although TRIPS was adopted in 1995, there were ten years before developing countries had to implement it. Those ten years were important for the growth of the movement that opposed neoliberalism and its institutions, such as the WTO. They were also important because the HIV/Aids crisis in southern Africa had reached epidemic proportions, and it was clear that intellectual property concerns – even short of TRIPS being fully implemented around the world – were preventing it from being brought to an end. Big Pharma's legal challenge to Nelson Mandela's government in many ways marked the moment when the whole system of intellectual property was first placed in the dock in the eyes of global public opinion.

Campaigners started to push back. In 1999, the WTO's Seattle summit collapsed amid mass protests and the refusal of low-income countries to sign on to a new deal. In 2001 the WTO met again, this time in Doha, which would not permit the sort of major protests seen elsewhere. Nonetheless, a mixture of pushback from low-income countries and campaign actions across the world ensured, in the face of fierce opposition from the pharmaceutical industry and Western governments, the passage of the Doha Declaration, which reversed some of the more extreme language in the TRIPS agreement. They were helped by the fact the US government itself, in the wake of the 9/11 attacks, was at that moment considering overriding patents and issuing a compulsory licence for anthrax treatment, fearing a biological attack.[17]

At its core the Doha Declaration is a statement that nothing in TRIPS should take precedence over a government's right to implement public health measures.[18] The text clarified some of the means – identified as 'flexibilities' – that they might use. First, a government would have the right to override patents as long as it made a reasonable attempt to negotiate with the patent holder and pay compensation. Second, in a national emergency, a country could skip negotiations altogether, and produce the medicines right away. Third, there was a recognition that countries without a pharmaceutical industry were stuck. They would need to import generic medicines, but TRIPS prevented them from doing so. This required a solution. Although not spelled out, and heavily fought over in the years to come, there was eventually agreement that, after all, a country could import generic medicines against the wishes of a patent holder. This was a genuinely new right. Fourth, the transition period for the agreement as a whole would be extended for the very poorest countries.

The declaration was a victory for the Global South, less in terms of what it allowed than of what it symbolised. The new 'right' which was agreed as a result of Doha – that countries without capacity to produce their own medicines could issue compulsory licenses to import generics – was only ever used once, by Rwanda, and was found to be so cumbersome that no one bothered to attempt it again.[19] But the reframing had a concrete impact on the way in which countries agreed to implement TRIPS – for instance, it encouraged India to write a patent law that specifically laid out that country's right to oppose patents.[20] The framing around intellectual property had been reversed, and there was a recognition that no further tightening of the rules would be possible at the WTO.

Compulsory licenses were issued thirty-four times, across twenty-four countries, between 2001 and 2014.[21] Three of these were issued in rich countries. Ecuador's leftist president Rafael Correa made a particular priority of issuing compulsory licenses where public health demanded it – though WikiLeaks documents show that US embassy staff in Quito met repeatedly with Big Pharma companies, as well as staff in 'potentially sympathetic ministries', to share strategies for preventing or limiting Ecuador's compulsory licensing policy.[22]

Needless to say, the victory was indeed limited. As a result of TRIPS, it was still the case that most countries in the world needed to implement a regime in which patents were guaranteed for at least twenty years. And while there were ways for countries to override these patents, they were not at all easy, and they would be mercilessly browbeaten. The example of the US embassy in Ecuador is just one of many instances of big business and Western governments trying to close the small space that existed in TRIPS for prioritising public health. They also include GlaxoSmithKline threatening legal action and blocking supply of a generic HIV medicine to Ghana, the US government withdrawing Thai export preferences over a compulsory license on a cancer drug, and drug multinational Novartis and the US government bullying Colombia when it tried to reduce the price of a leukaemia drug.[23]

There now followed a cat-and-mouse game between Big Pharma, on the one hand, and campaigners and governments of the Global South, on the other. Backed by the United States, the EU and Japan, Big Pharma argued for rules that went beyond TRIPS to be inserted into new trade deals that rich countries signed with poorer countries. This became known as the 'TRIPS-plus' agenda, and it included even longer patent terms that went beyond the twenty-year minimum, limitations on a country's right to use 'compulsory licences' or to encourage generic competition, rules that would make it easier to apply for new patents after old ones expired, and rules that keep test data on a drug's safety or effectiveness secret for a certain number of years.

As Médecins Sans Frontières noted, 'Countries are by no means obliged by international law to do this, but many, such as Brazil, China or Central American states have had no choice but to adopt these, as part of trade agreements with the United States or the European Union. These have a disastrous impact on access to medicines.'[24]

Oxfam reported in 2002 that, one year after Doha, 'the US government, at the behest of giant pharmaceutical companies, continues to bully developing countries to introduce unnecessarily high standards of patent protection on medicines'.[25] They examined the so-called Section 301 process, through which the United States threatens trade sanctions against countries which refuse to implement 'improvements to intellectual property rights', and found that it provided a major mechanism for 'bullying' countries that refused to put the profits of Big Pharma over the healthcare of their citizens.

Oxfam highlighted the case of India, where, despite massive incidence of treatable diseases like tuberculosis and a tiny health expenditure per head, the United States was coercing the government to introduce provisions that would have hindered India's generic industry; and Guatemala, where the United States was using aid money to 'advise' the country's congress to pass a law providing for fifteen-year protection for test data – the longest such protection in the world, and three times longer than the protection period operating in the United States. And this was in spite of the fact that, at the time, Guatemala had not even reached the point where it was obliged to implement the basic TRIPS deal.

In a separate report, Oxfam showed the profoundly damaging effects of such provisions. In a study of a US–Jordan trade deal, it found TRIPS-plus provisions had contributed to a rise in the prices of medicines that was 'threatening the financial sustainability of government public health programmes', delaying the introduction of cheaper medicines – and all without any countervailing benefits:

> there has been nearly no foreign direct investment (FDI) by drug companies into Jordan since 2001 to synthesise or manufacture medicines in partnership with local generic companies . . . Patients in Jordan pay from two to ten times more for some new medicines

> compared with patients in Egypt, where new medicines are manufactured locally through licensing agreements and partnerships. The only FDI into Jordan by multinational drug companies has been to expand scientific offices, which use aggressive sales tactics to ensure that expensive patented medicines are used instead of inexpensive generics.[26]

Neither did this affect only countries of the Global South. In more recent discussions between the United States and Britain on a post-Brexit trade deal between the two countries, there were serious concerns that the US pharmaceutical lobby would undermine the NHS by compromising its ability to bargain down Big Pharma's drug prices effectively.[27] Big Pharma has long complained about the National Institute for Health and Care Excellence (NICE), which assesses new drugs based on their cost-effectiveness for the NHS. Its guidelines give real leverage to the NHS in negotiating with drug companies, because the threat that the NHS will not prescribe a certain medicine will often persuade a drug manufacturer to lower its price. President Trump made no secret of the fact that he blamed high drug prices in the United States on 'freeloading' by other countries' socialised health systems, and that he wanted to use trade deals to rectify this.

The United States also tried to embed even more stringent IP rules in multi-country trade deals like the highly controversial Transpacific Partnership (TPP) between the United States and a wide range of countries. Even though these deals did not include every country in the world, the aim was to incorporate enough countries so that any rules they agreed became global in effect, since any country wishing to engage in international trade would eventually be forced to adopt them.

~

When TRIPS was being implemented, Tahir Amin was practising law. But when he saw the impact of these laws and the way they were used, he began to question what he was doing. 'What I learnt is we would just crush people on the basis of legal suits which didn't really even make legal sense', he told me. 'Even if we weren't in the right, that didn't matter. It was purely about power. And I couldn't do it anymore. I wanted to take my practice skills and apply them to something useful.'

Amin moved to Bangalore in 2004, giving up his well-paid job in London to help the Indian government develop a health-friendly patent law. He later co-founded I-MAK, precisely to use his knowledge to reshape patent law and to help countries' use of the flexibilities in global IP law to ensure good public outcomes. 'When you practise law, you know that outcomes can be twisted – that's your job. India had some really good laws, but we were concerned that they would end up being twisted into something else. So we had to ensure [that] not only were the laws good, but that they were interpreted right, too.'

Amin is not alone. I have met dozens of campaigners in the last two years who decided to abandon lucrative careers in order to work to bring about a different system. In the campaigning world, it is often difficult to know what you have achieved in a specific piece of work. When you feel exhausted, you are haunted by the notion that things would have been just the same even if you had decided to do nothing. But campaigners like Amin have clearly made a tangible difference, which has opened up policy space for Southern governments, helped them to devise better laws and ultimately get cheaper medicines to many more people. These are life-and-death issues for so many people.

The industry desperately wanted to go further than TRIPS, and they still do. Campaigners managed to draw red lines around their agenda – for instance, stopping a big part of the Transpacific Partnership, which would have extended and expanded IP rules. But they remain far from being able to claim a victory. That will require a much more concerted effort for a longer period of time, and by more people. Covid-19 has given us the basis for such a movement. But we still have a model that is fundamentally unable to deliver the right to healthcare.

Without the WTO, things could have been very different. Historical counterfactuals are never entirely reliable; we cannot know what might have happened if the era of neoliberalism had not undermined the power of the Global South. But we do know that the globalisation project sharply changed the economic course on which many of those countries were then embarked. We know that it brutally closed down economic possibilities. And we can therefore hazard a guess at what an alternative history might have looked like. As Bello told me,

> We had a whole range of countries back in the seventies and eighties that were already developing their own pharmaceutical industries. The TRIPS agreement threatened those industries. It's terrible, because this could have created a really dynamic and different process around how medicines are developed, but it couldn't happen in the way it should have done because of these WTO rules. Under the old GATT system, I think industries would have developed in a very different way.

India was an exception. There, governments learned early on what being dependent on Big Pharma would mean.[28] With no control of the underlying technology, they would be left dependent on overpriced antibiotics – a permanent renter of high-value goods they would have to pay for through the export of low-value foods and minerals. It was a recipe for never-ending poverty.

Fortunately, in the 1950s, a more active set of UN institutions was prepared to help India's first prime minister, Jawaharlal Nehru, in his industrialisation plans, building the Hindustan Antibiotics company with an explicit commitment to public and openly shared knowledge for the production of accessible medicines.[29] By the 1980s, Nehru's daughter, now herself prime minister, Indira Ghandi, could declare, 'The idea of a better ordered world is one in which medical discoveries will be free of patents and there is no profiteering from life and death.'[30]

We all have reasons to be grateful for the development of India's pharmaceutical industry. Given the number of vaccines produced in India during Covid-19, it is clear that without that industry, which would have been much harder to construct in the TRIPS era, the pandemic and global inequality would have been even worse. When I interviewed Indian health campaigner Achal Prabhala, he told me that the Indian sector 'has certainly not been totally useless, but the thing is, because of the era of TRIPS, India moved almost entirely into manufacturing, rather than having to worry about patents. So it's still too dependent on research developed elsewhere.'

It is not difficult to imagine a different history in which this had not happened, and in which India could have benefited from technology transfer, as the United States and Britain had 100 years before. It could have been producing several times the vaccines and treatments it was able to manufacture during the Covid pandemic. It might even have helped to develop better vaccines and treatments.

A full 55 of the 120 factories that Prabhala identified as being able to produce mRNA vaccines are based in India.[31] That is a result of an era in which governments were able to design their own patent laws. In fact, virtually every country on his list developed its industry before the TRIPS-era rules, or by simply ignoring them. Prabhala told me:

> You know India's patent law was really a rewritten colonial law. They later realised that these laws were a problem and they were overturned, and this led to a huge boom in the industry. All the companies that exist now were created then. So TRIPS took us backwards. It was a historical crime. It was like being chloroformed. We need a recognition of the fact this was foisted on people who really didn't understand what was happening.[32]

6
The Hospital That Became a Trading Floor

In February 2020 a Kenyan blogger released details of a WhatsApp discussion involving management and health workers at a leading private hospital in Nairobi.[1] The conversations paint a picture of a hospital run like a hedge fund, in which doctors are forced to meet daily financial targets that override any clinical consideration. The goal: keep beds filled with paying patients, regardless of whether those patients need to be there or not.

In discussions described as 'better suited for a trading floor than a hospital management team', health workers are told to 'lock discharges' and 'increase speed' because '2 admissions against 13 discharges at this hour not good'. Staff are encouraged not to miss 'any opportunity' in 'looking for referrals', told 'this revenue is too low', and, in one 'motivational' message, are whipped up with 'It's our striking time. Let's intensify our effort . . . replace all discharges by 6pm.'

In the article, subtitled 'How Did a Hospital Dedicated to Women's Health End Up Being Managed Like a Cut-Throat Business?', journalist Morris Kiruga, known then by the pseudonym Owaahh, details how the Nairobi Women's Hospital had become a highly financialised business, employing fewer qualified health workers than it required, paying them financial rewards for each admission to the hospital, and pushing them not to discharge patients even if there was no clinical need to keep them in the hospital.

More alarmingly, Kiruga explains that what was going on at the hospital was not a one-off, but symptomatic of Kenya's highly privatised health system, in which hospitals and clinics are owned and traded on financial markets by major international investors. Most shocking of all, this particular hospital and its investors were supported by some of the biggest aid donors in the world, including Britain's Department for International Development, where this model is seen as a brave new experiment in extending healthcare to the poorest people in the world.

Big Pharma operates within a wider healthcare sector. That sector is susceptible to the same pressures as the pharmaceutical industry itself. As healthcare becomes more financialised and market-driven, so the pharmaceuticals sector and healthcare in general come to resemble each other more closely. This in turn furnishes the pharmaceutical industry with ever deeper reservoirs from which to draw its profits.

Trading in Healthcare

The Nairobi Women's Hospital was established by a young and idealistic gynaecologist, Dr Sam Thenya.[2] He was driven by a desire to treat women who had been victims of violence, and to do so for free – though, in a private health system, this of course meant their care would be subsidised by fee-paying patients or charitable funds. Although Dr Thenya did not have much money to invest in the hospital himself, he realised that, in an economy dominated by debt, you do not need your own assets. Instead, you need to attract investors who can lend you money in return for a share of your business. For investors, the hospital carried some risk, but given that the healthcare business owned real assets – in this case a hospital building – there was at least something to sell if things went wrong.

Far from going wrong, however, the hospital thrived, attracting enough funds to grow and set up several more branches across Nairobi. Importantly, the hospital seemed to be attracting a reputation for expanding healthcare to the poor in Kenya – although, as Oxfam pointed out in 2014,

> even the most basic maternity package would cost an average Kenyan woman three to six months' wages, at $463. This goes up by almost $280 if an obstetrician is involved and by more again if a caesarean section is required. The hospital claims to cater for low- and middle-income Kenyan women and their families, yet their average reported inpatient cost was $845 in 2011. Two-thirds of Kenyans would have to forgo at least their entire income for well over a year to pay such a fee.[3]

One story from this period is particularly shocking. Dr Thenya revealed in an interview in 2016 that the Kenyan president, Uhuru Kenyatta, had called him out of the blue after a member of the public had solicited the president's help in getting the body of their mother released from the hospital.[4] The president asked what Dr Thenya could do, but the doctor was adamant that the bill had to be paid before he could release the body. Kenyatta ultimately paid it himself.

After a few years at the helm, Dr Thenya sold his stake in the hospital to a private equity firm called the Abraaj Group, which became the effective owner of the Nairobi Women's Hospital. The

Group was about to become very famous in the financial press, for all the wrong reasons.

The Abraaj Group described itself as 'Dubai-based', but a large part of its operations were registered in the tax haven of the Cayman Islands. It was set up by Pakistani businessman Arif Naqvi in 2002, and became the largest private equity fund in the Middle East, investing around the world in many different sectors. Naqvi himself was committed to the idea of 'stakeholder capitalism', and was a strong proponent of using his investments to benefit the workers in the firms in which he invested, as well as the wider community. Those who listened to Naqvi clearly believed the pitch, which claimed he was on a crusade to eliminate poverty from the world.[5] His persona seemed to embody the idea that you could do this while simultaneously enjoying a luxury lifestyle.

It was no surprise that this message appealed to the likes of Bill Gates, along with a number of official development donors, including Sweden, Britain and the World Bank. Naqvi seemed like living proof that there was no contradiction between the enrichment of the world's elite and the elimination of poverty. In 2015, Abraaj became involved in healthcare, buying up hospitals in Africa and Asia. The goal was supposedly to create accessible healthcare for the poor in the regions in which the group invested. Over $500 million poured in from public and charitable sources.[6]

At a meeting in September 2017, however, some of these investors realised that something was not right. A whopping $200 million – one-fifth of the health investment fund – had not been invested at all. As the *New York Times* later reported, 'Mr. Naqvi told the angry investors that he saw the company as a vehicle to buy hospitals around the world, and that was why the fund needed the cash on hand. He also cited the regulatory delays. But the investors were not convinced, and he sent more than $100 million back to investors in December [2017].'[7]

Things went downhill from there. In June 2019, the *Financial Times* reported that Mr Naqvi had allegedly 'misappropriated more than $250m into accounts under his control or those of family members and personal associates'.[8] Naqvi was arrested in the UK in April 2019, and detained pending potential extradition to the United States. He was sentenced in absentia to three years' imprisonment in a separate fraud case in the United Arab Emirates, and Naqvi and Abraaj are both under investigation in the United States for alleged bribery in Pakistan.[9] Abraaj went under, in what has been described as the 'biggest collapse in private-equity history'.[10]

At the start of this book, I described a tendency to ascribe any behaviour in the pharmaceutical sector that generates too much adverse publicity to the failures of 'a few bad apples'. The same rule, it turns out, applied across the financialised economy. Naqvi was now entirely disgraced: a corrupt businessman who had even duped Bill Gates, the most generous, socially conscious billionaire the world has ever known. But this is to miss the real lesson of the story. As Abraaj collapsed, its healthcare assets, including the Nairobi Women's Hospital, were bought out by another private-equity firm, TPG Capital, which still owns them today. They will continue to invest in this sector with partners including the Bill & Melinda Gates Foundation, the World Bank, and the British government, with the supposed aim of increasing healthcare coverage to the poor.[11]

But, as Morris Kiruga makes clear in his investigation, the problem did not start or end with corruption in one private-equity fund. Rather, it is hard-wired into the business model. As Kigura says, when TPG took over the Nairobi Women's Hospital, 'These high finance events and deals all took place outside of Kenya', with no democratic accountability to the patients in whose name the elite investors were supposedly acting.[12]

The need to please investors and generate returns means that businesses must perform in something of a beauty pageant to attract the grossly undertaxed wealth of the global elite. Businesses must prove that they are a better bet than anyone else investors might choose to entrust their wealth to. They must therefore adopt the interests of high finance, cutting costs and increasing revenues as rapidly as possible.

It was this imperative that hospital treatment was priced well beyond the means of poor Kenyans, driving health workers to act according to the dictates of the market during every waking hour. It was this imperative that impelled management to reduce their highly qualified staff, coming to depend instead on staff incentivised to put generating revenue ahead of clinical need. In a nutshell, it was the system itself that was at fault, not bad apples within it.

We cannot hope to understand the inequality that characterised the Covid-19 pandemic without examining the wider healthcare system. Financialisation is a bad enough model when applied to a car company; its effects are much worse when applied to the research, development and production of essential medicines. But when it is applied in frontline health services, catastrophe ensues. Sadly, however, the Kenyan experience is not unusual. Indeed, for many people who profess to care genuinely about eliminating poverty, this model is seen as the way of the future. It is a model that turns the whole of the healthcare system into a mirror-image of the pharmaceutical sector.

This vision of healthcare would once have been regarded as counterproductive to the goal of achieving better health – a little like patenting medical products. This idea was overcome in a process that paralleled financialisation and gave birth to the neoliberal world order. It began in the 1970s, with the undermining of the Non-Aligned Movement, an international grouping of countries that looked to neither the United States nor the Soviet Union, but stood together to support its own 'Third World' development. Indeed, the term 'Third World', today regarded as derogatory and outdated, was first used as an adaptation of 'third estate' – the ordinary class of people in late-eighteenth-century France who had created the revolution in their own interests.[13] The Third World, it was implied, was the revolutionary subject of the post-war world.

The Non-Aligned Movement reached its zenith in 1974, when Third World countries developed a proposal for a radically different set of rules to guide the international economy. What became known as the New International Economic Order was passed by a majority at the United Nations general assembly. This programme was a blueprint for fair trade relations and constraints on financial and corporate power. Essentially, it sought to end the economic dependence of most of the world on the former colonial powers, and to allow the Third World to complete its liberation from empire.

The New International Economic Order had nothing to say about healthcare specifically. But at the United Nations the World Health Organization developed its own version of the policy. The WHO was at this time run by an inspirational figure, Halfdan Mahler, who believed that everyone in the world could and should have access to quality healthcare. He argued passionately for a generational push for 'primary health care' – by which he meant not basic healthcare, but universally accessible healthcare, including the full participation of communities and individuals in decisions about their health.

Then as now, this was a revolutionary approach, because it involved the empowerment of communities and individuals over their own lives. Up to this point, healthcare had been, as it so often is today, something *done to* the patient by the professional – just as development in general is done to the poor world by the rich world. One example of this was the focus on trying to eradicate certain diseases purely through top-down medical interventions that entirely ignored the social and economic conditions of those being treated or inoculated. Certainly, it might, for example, be easier to provide vaccines than running water, food supplies, education or democratic rights; but this approach was at best severely limited, and at worst counterproductive. But this top-down, 'expert-knows-best' approach to healthcare was clearly something that benefited the pharmaceutical industry, as well as the wider healthcare industry.

Under Mahler, the WHO wanted something very different. Just as the New International Economic Order tried to put Third World countries in charge of their own economic destiny, so the WHO tried to put ordinary people in control of their own health and well-being. Making medicines available was an important part of this effort, but Mahler's conception of primary healthcare also required that everyone had the rights to food, sanitation and mental well-being upon which that healthcare depended. Years later, he remarked:

> if we could imagine a tabula rasa in health without having to deal with the constraints – tyranny if you wish – of the existing medical consumer industry, we would hardly go about dealing with health as we do now in the beginning of the 21st century . . . It is, therefore, high time that we realize, in concept and in practice, that a knowledge of a strategy of initiating social change is as potent a tool in promoting health, as knowledge of medical technology.[14]

If the 1974 UN General Assembly was the high point of the Third World's economic struggle, 1978 provided a similar moment in the struggle for universal healthcare. A major international conference was called in Alma-Ata, capital of the Kazakh Soviet Socialist Republic, to give life to Mahler's vision for the WHO. The result was the Alma-Ata Declaration – a manifesto for primary healthcare, which became a beacon for health activists around the world that resonates right up to the present. The Declaration urged governments and health workers to protect and promote the health of all the people of the world. By healthcare, it meant 'a state of complete physical, mental and social wellbeing, and not merely the absence of disease or infirmity', and it clearly stated that healthcare was 'a fundamental human right'. This went way beyond access to medicines, also including health education, the promotion of decent food and nutrition, an adequate supply of safe water and basic sanitation, and family planning. It even referred to 'a fuller and better use of the world's resources, a considerable part of which is now spent on armaments and military conflicts'.

To Western countries, however, Alma Ata, like the New International Economic Order, was a dangerous trend that threatened to undermine the excessive power still enjoyed by rich countries. More than anything, it was a call to equality. Particularly irritating was that Mahler criticised Western corporations. Big Pharma was subjected to criticism for marketing drugs to the countries of the Global South in a way they were not able to get away with in the Global North. In 1978, the WHO went further, urging countries to adopt a newly developed list of 'essential medicines' that they should make all efforts to obtain, including by reducing drug prices and using generic versions – a move parts of the pharmaceutical industry regarded as 'completely unacceptable.'[15]

Big Pharma was particularly alarmed by Mahler's approach to Nestlé's deeply controversial marketing of baby-milk formula in developing countries, whereby the WHO devised a new code to try to control the industry's behaviour. The fact that Mahler was starting to talk about corporations like Nestlé provoked a concern, quoted from a CIA report in Nitsan Cherov's account of the period, 'that politicization has now spread from the General Assembly to the international technical and specialized organizations'.[16] One US representative to the United Nations wrote, 'It appears that the infant formula drive was just the opening skirmish in a much larger campaign', while Cherov quotes a pharmaceutical industry journal warning of 'a coming WHO effort to impose unacceptable controls over all pharmaceutical commerce in the Third World'.[17]

The increasingly powerful neoliberals were especially alarmed at this vision of healthcare. For them, publicly provided healthcare was anathema. Healthcare was not a right, they believed. Rather, backed by the rapidly growing healthcare industry, they argued that healthcare should be provided by the market, which would afford a more efficient and targeted health service, not dependent on high rates of taxation but on customers paying for what they used.

In countries where public healthcare already exists, it is famously difficult to take away. In Britain, no government, however neoliberal, would dare to argue for the abolition of the NHS, even as successive governments run it down slowly, subjecting it to successive cuts and reorganisations, and opening it up to private competition and nonsensical 'internal markets'. Once the possibility of public healthcare is on the table, it generally requires an enormous crisis to get people to accept something different.

Thus, manufacturing crises became a common part of the neoliberal playbook. In the 1980s, the spark for much of the world was the so-called Third World debt crisis, which was used to undermine the political power of developing countries at the UN and destroy the dream of the New International Economic Order. The banks, which had recklessly lent to Third World countries in the 1970s, were effectively bailed out by the International Monetary Fund and the World Bank – public institutions both run from Washington, DC. These institutions became the biggest lenders to many countries, using the leverage this gave them to impose 'structural adjustment' programmes on dozens of indebted countries in Africa, Asia and Latin America. These policies would have devastating consequences, in particular halting in its tracks the drive for universal healthcare.

The theory behind structural adjustment ran like this: indebted countries needed to start saving money so that they could repay their debts, and this saving required a very different set of economic policies to the ones being pursued. Austerity was crucial: the liberal public spending of the 1970s and early 1980s had to go. That meant dramatic reductions in spending on things like healthcare. In country after country – from Zimbabwe to Nicaragua and the Philippines – healthcare spending was slashed in the late 1980s.

The other pillars of structural adjustment were no better. Privatisation saw utilities and companies sold off at fire-sale prices while the liberalisation of trade wiped out small farmers and fledgling producers. It was no wonder that structural adjustment failed catastrophically in its stated objectives. Far from falling, debt levels ballooned. Countries went backwards in terms of basic human development – something previously thought near impossible outside a context of all-out war or total social collapse, bringing a sharp halt to the hopeful postcolonial creation of health services.[18]

An important indicator of basic health services is the number of doctors a country employs. At the start of Covid-19, Britain had thirty-two doctors per 10,000 people.[19] That was fairly low for a developed country – a result of attempts to run down Britain's NHS by successive governments. Germany had forty-five, and Norway fifty-two doctors per 10,000. Even relatively rich developing countries have a small fraction of that number: eight doctors per 10,000 people in South Africa, seven in India. But Sierra Leone fares much worse. That country, which was told by the IMF in the mid 1990s to reduce public-sector employment by 28 per cent and limit wages, today has just 0.7 doctors per 10,000 people. While low-income countries have average per capita health spending of around $41, high-income countries spend $2,937.

None of this is necessary. As the doctor and campaigner Dorothy Logie puts it,

> Many African countries had successful primary health care in the 1970s and impressive achievements in literacy, child mortality, and life expectancy. But throughout the 1980s these achievements were eroded as money was diverted from social spending to debt servicing . . . The bank's policies are so driven by monetarist ideology that the living standards of millions take second place to chasing some economic nirvana. Is it right that a bank should dictate global health strategy to such an extent?[20]

It is easy to see who lost out from the policies of structural adjustment – millions of people across the Global South whose lives were cut short, livelihoods stolen and rights denied. But there were winners, too. Big businesses were suddenly given cheaper and easier access to economies of the Global South – and the healthcare industry, in particular, received an enormous boost from the destruction of public healthcare.

The IMF and the World Bank did not say countries shouldn't have healthcare, only that poorer countries wouldn't be able to fund all-singing, all-dancing health systems. They therefore needed to focus first of all on the very poor, and not try to provide healthcare for everyone. Secondly, governments should limit their financial exposure by making patients pay something, supporting the introduction of 'user fees' to access health services.

Thirdly, governments were told to work with the private sector as much as possible. Business, it was argued, would provide healthcare more efficiently and cheaply than the public sector. In order to pique the interest of business in the first place, countries would need to become more attractive places to invest. This meant giving up on any attempt to control the domestic economy. The most important job of governments, as neoliberals had always held, was to make things easier for business. All good things would follow.

Governments in richer countries had a role to play, too: using aid spending to encourage the private sector to invest in poorer countries, 'de-risking' investment, creating new ways for countries to borrow money, fostering public–private partnerships, and advising countries to create 'business-friendly environments'. This strategy would allow countries to 'turn billions into trillions' – billions of dollars of public money leveraging trillions of dollars of private money.[21]

In reality, the idea that private investment would make up for a deficit in public funding was always nonsense. The private sector invests because it wants to make a return. If the public sector wants to make it easier for business to profit, business is unlikely to turn that offer down, but will still extract all it can – and when that extraction is coming from health services, it will come at the expense of people's healthcare.

There is no better symbol of the folly of this approach than the privately run Queen Mamohato Memorial Hospital in Lesotho. Opened in 2011 to replace Lesotho's national hospital, and backed by the World Bank – which said it would cost no more than the old hospital – it ended up nearly bankrupting Lesotho's health budget, as public money was turned into a long-term income stream for investors, delivering a 25 per cent return on their investment.[22]

Countries in the Global South have been treated like guinea pigs for a free-market model that rich-country governments were unable to get away with applying in their own countries. Those rich governments even portrayed themselves as saviours when they used newly enlarged aid budgets to restructure healthcare systems, making them 'affordable' and 'sustainable'. These state donors were joined by a new group of players: phenomenally wealthy individuals who poured their wealth into fighting poverty by unleashing market forces in healthcare.

The Fall of the WHO . . . and the Rise of Gates

This was the genesis of the public–private–philanthropic system which, as we have seen, performed so badly during the Covid-19 pandemic: a counter-revolution in which the UN was marginalised. Nitsan Chorev documents this process in *The World Health Organization between North and South*. First, US president Reagan withheld funding from the body, and his administration made clear the agency 'should not be involved in efforts to regulate or control the commercial practices of private industry, even when the products may relate to concerns about health'.[23] In other words: lay off Big Pharma.

More generally, rich countries forced a no-growth policy on the WHO, and increasingly earmarked their donations for whatever special projects they supported. Using somewhat undiplomatic language, Mahler made clear to member states, 'For more than a year now your Organization [has been] held financial hostage . . . What crime has WHO committed against those who are withholding mandatory contribution?' Today, these voluntary, earmarked contributions account for more than 80 per cent of the WHO's budget; in the words of *Nature* magazine, the agency lives 'hand-to-mouth'.[24]

At the same time, there was an all-out campaign to undermine the WHO's political legitimacy, transferring competence for healthcare to the World Bank, which had a radically different approach to the issue. David Legge, a leading light in the People's Health Movement, told me that the Bank's approach to healthcare was guided by 'a competitive market in health insurance, the privatisation of public-sector healthcare, and only a minimum safety net for the poor'.[25] In this, the Bank was in tune with the increasingly important big philanthropists, whose intervention in the field would alter global healthcare in profound ways. No one would symbolise this new wave better than Bill Gates.

'Concise, urgent and powerful' is how the *Guardian* describes Bill Gates's new book, *How to Prevent the Next Pandemic*. 'Bill Gates strides into the boardroom of Bafta in central London, pumps my hand and the clock starts ticking', says another awed journalist, rather breathlessly, of meeting the great man. He does not even seem fazed that his forty-five-minute meeting is cut a few minutes short.[26] Gates, after all, has a lot to do, and little time to be held to account.

Bill Gates's stranglehold on global health policy is a problem. I do not doubt the efficacy of many of the medicines Gates provides to the Global South. Why his Foundation uses some medicines rather than others has been questioned, and that is only right given the sheer scale of the operations concerned. But I have not seen any evidence that suggests he does not genuinely want to prevent and cure disease. I also don't believe his primary motivation is making money from this work. His investments are so gigantic that he makes money from virtually everything – but that is not a very likely reason for him to spend so much of his own money on charity work.

Despite this, it is a problem that one of the world's richest men, by virtue of his wealth, can become the most powerful voice in global healthcare. It is a problem that an ultra-rich white American man has more power over the healthcare of people in parts of Africa, Asia and Latin America than the governments of those citizens – and that his money has subverted the role of what should be the most important voice in global healthcare, the WHO. Gates's money effectively silences civil-society activists, and softens up the media that should be holding him to account.[27] By all of these means, Gates has managed to divert us away from asking why a supposedly democratic society has allowed one man to accrue so much wealth and power.

The philanthropist revolution did not start with Gates. Academic Susan K. Sell believes we are really living in an age of monopolies, and 'really have not seen this kind of economic concentration since the age of robber baron capitalism at the end of the nineteenth century'.[28] 'Robber barons' was the name given to a set of American businessmen who managed to monopolise new technologies in the first era of globalisation. We still know some of their names: Rockefeller, J. P. Morgan, Vanderbilt and Carnegie. Like Gates, some of these robber barons placed large fortunes into foundations that are still important today. As John D. Rockefeller's Standard Oil corporation was forcibly broken up, Rockefeller used his wealth to set up the foundation, handily protecting his fortune from inheritance tax, as well as building his prestige.[29] By the late 1970s, these foundations were well-established and powerful bodies in their own right.

The global economy has returned us to an age of robber barons. Our food is increasingly produced by a handful of massive, increasingly concentrated corporations that can dictate prices and terms to hundreds of millions of farmers. Our communications are mediated by a handful of Big Tech corporations that are reaching into parts of our lives corporations have never before been able to access – indeed, into our minds. Then as now, it is these monopolies that are at the heart of global inequality, undermining our democracy. And very often the establishment of foundations by the owners of monopolies has reinforced the monopoly mind-set, as they have come to acquire vast power over the development of other countries.

It is hardly surprising that Gates's views were formed by his own business experience, particularly his unwavering support of the intellectual property system. Gates's wealth came from Microsoft, a company that has argued for high levels of IP protection, and has been almost a textbook example of monopolistic behaviour.[30] This has been reinforced by the fact that Gates appoints so many senior pharmaceutical industry executives – leading, in the words of one detailed report, to a 'revolving door between the Gates Foundation and pharmaceutical corporations'.[31] It also explains why he sees no problem with having pharmaceutical industry representatives directly involved the decision-making processes of bodies like GAVI, which grants vast sums of money to that very industry. Max Lawson of Oxfam calls this 'a clear conflict of interest', drawing a link with the fact that GAVI massively overpays for its vaccines, effectively giving a huge subsidy to the industry.[32]

Much philanthropic power is now exercised precisely through a suite of public–private–philanthropic entities like GAVI. These bodies define the problem, set the priorities, undertake the research, fix the budgets, and decide what they will spend the money on and who will receive it. Big Pharma, like healthcare business more generally, is a partner to be supported. In this way, the wealthiest dictate the priorities of the poorest. It is less a conspiracy than a confluence of interests, producing a model with very little accountability.

We have some idea of the types of healthcare facilities Gates has invested in from the Kenyan example, and we will see more later in the chapter. These investments bring in further support from official development institutions that are often in awe of Gates. We have also seen how strongly the Gates Foundation shaped the way the world dealt with the Covid-19 pandemic; Gates is personally waging a battle to shape how we deal with the next one.[33]

More generally, the influence of these foundations has helped to reconstruct healthcare so that it once again became dominated by top-down, expert-led, tech-dominated interventions, wherever possible working with the businesses that 'understood' the world of healthcare best. Rather than the philanthropists being accountable to governments, or to the people who elected those governments, governments came to be accountable to the philanthropists – and the managers, businessmen and experts who sit on their boards. 'Can you deliver?', governments are asked. 'If not, we'll find another way of providing healthcare to your people.'

It is hard to imagine a more colonial model for delivering healthcare. Poverty alleviation is something to be done to the poor by the rich by employing clever people and new technologies. There are no politics, no histories, no acts of exploitation behind this poverty – just technical and logistical questions to be overcome. As Oxfam remarks in its report 'Public Good or Private Wealth?', Gates, the

World Bank and official donors push 'targeted' benefits to the poor, 'ignoring post-war history' in favour of 'exporting 19th century style "poor relief" to developing countries'.[34]

But in recent years there has been a change. By the time the financial crisis hit in 2008, it was clear to a large number of people that inequality was a real matter of concern, and could not be disentangled from poverty. In fact, extreme wealth was driven precisely by exploitation, of both people and the planet, and by the ruthless advance of market logic into ever more areas of life. Clearly, the problem is not the poor, but big business and the superrich.

If this is true, how could giving more power to them, even through the vehicle of their philanthropy, be the solution? For as much as he has given away, Bill Gates has found it literally impossible to reduce his wealth at a faster rate than he accumulates it.[35] In the first year of the pandemic, he added $24 billion to his fortune.[36] As Linsey McGoey, an academic at the University of Essex, noted, 'We have seen an incredible enrichment of the wealthiest individuals on a global level, and there is a direct correlation between increased wealth accumulation, regressive tax measures, and funding towards philanthropic activities. Philanthropy may be growing, but only in the context of rampant inequality.'[37]

Aiding Whom?

Despite all the evidence, the obsession with supporting a highly financialised health sector continues. The Nairobi Women's Hospital is only the tip of the iceberg. The British government's aid programme has seen over £500 million ploughed into private healthcare in recent years.[38] This money flows through an agency called British International Investment (once known as the Colonial Development Corporation, then the CDC Group), which is wholly owned by the British government. This department specialises in promoting 'private sector led development', which includes handing millions of pounds to financial funds to invest on its behalf. These funds have supported a chain of gyms in Brazil that runs one of the most expensive fitness centers in Sao Paulo, a cosmetic surgery clinic in India, which offers liposuction for between £950 to £3,800 and male nose surgery from £800 to £1,100, and a hospital in Harare that attracts the country's political elite.[39]

This is a model replicated at an international level by the private-sector arm of the World Bank, which has teamed up with the Gates Foundation in the Health in Africa initiative to mobilise $1 billion in equity investments and loans to finance the growth of private-sector participation in healthcare in sub-Saharan Africa. One of the initiative's first investments was in a fund managed by the Abraaj Group.[40] Oxfam commented that the scheme's 'investments to date have, in practice, predominantly been in expensive, high-end, urban hospitals offering tertiary care to African countries' wealthiest citizens and expatriates.'[41]

The mental gymnastics required to sell this as a genuine form of development is certainly impressive. In reality, it represents the worst form of trickle-down economics: an idea that, for most economists, was discredited in the 1980s, and which asserts that any form of economic growth – any addition to the wealth of those at the top – will eventually be good for the poor too, to whom it will 'trickle down'.

If Covid-19 highlighted the problems of Big Pharma, it also proved the disaster of market-based healthcare. In 2022 I spoke to Dr T. Sundararaman – known by friends as Sundar.[42] He is a leading light in the inspirational People's Health Movement in India. 'The private hospitals in India went through three phases', he told me:

> In the first phase many shut shop and ran. They were too scared and said 'don't come'. The public hospitals, despite all our criticisms of the public doctor in India, stayed on the job. Nobody left. There was a very public character that came out in them.
>
> In the second phase they opened up for non-Covid care only, and charged exorbitant amounts for it. In the third phase, they opened up for Covid care but some were giving completely inappropriate care and many were extortionate. There were exceptions, but they really were the exceptions . . . And many hospitals rejected very sick patients – cherry-picking patients who might well have got better themselves. And governments were quite helpless in the face of this.

This is a story heard many times during Covid-19. Just as the market failed disastrously during the pandemic as a whole, so the marketised hospitals failed in their basic duty of treating people.

One Indian hospital funded by British development funds, Vikram hospital, came under criticism after refusing to treat Covid-19 patients referred to it by local government.[43] It was later threatened with legal proceedings by the government. Other hospitals in Bangladesh and Pakistan, similarly supported with British development money, were accused of overcharging patients through the pandemic. These included Evercare hospitals in Dhaka and Lahore – the second of which lists its price for a hospital room with a ventilator as approximately £350 a day: over four times the average monthly wage.[44]

These episodes form part of a grim story of the failure of the privatised healthcare model in low-income countries throughout the pandemic. One heart-rending study, from Maharashtra state – one of the worst-hit areas of India – detailed some other cases.[45] The report makes clear that there are 'examples where private doctors and hospitals have played an exemplary role', but they are few and far between.

One case the report details concerns Altaf Javed, a thirty-year-old shop owner taken into hospital with what his brother thought were fairly mild symptoms. 'We were taken aback when the doctor said his condition was serious and he had to be admitted immediately as he seemed to have COVID-19. Confused and anxious, we agreed immediately and he was admitted in the general ward. Even before his admission, we were given a long list of medicines, which came up to almost Rs 30,000!! [£308].' But the treatment was so poor that Javed pleaded to be taken to a different hospital:

> When we reached the hospital, we told them Altaf's condition was serious and he needed immediate attention. But we were told upfront that if we didn't have the money, we should not even bother coming to the hospital, saying their minimum package [cost] Rs 1,00,000 [£1,029] for three days. The management made it clear that we had to pay an advance deposit of Rs 50,000 [$514] for ICU admission for Altaf. Right away, they gave us a list of medicines that came up to Rs 56,000 [£576] in the hospital medical store.

The family did all they could to raise the money, but realised they would not be able to keep him there for long. When they told the hospital they would need to discharge Javed and bring him home, they were told they would have to raise further funds to discharge him.

Before he could be discharged, Javed died: 'Ironically, we never got a confirmed COVID-19 report – Altaf passed away before we got the test results. We were never given any of his hospital records and files. The hospital bill had come to Rs 1,68,000 [$1,729] for two days.'

The report contains dozens of similar stories. So serious was the overcharging that the Supreme Court of India became involved. One newspaper report that looked in to the prices of Covid care in Dehli found that the total bill for care came to 'more than what at least 94% of the people in the country earn in a year', and asked, 'Is it time to take over private hospitals?'[46]

While India received a lot of global attention for its terrible suffering in the pandemic, such stories are common around the world. One academic paper listed 'hospital closures, furloughing of staff, refusals of treatment, and attempts to profit by gouging patients' as commonplace in private hospitals across low- and middle-income countries 'in a form of disaster capitalism'.[47] In Egypt, an MP accused some private hospitals of massively inflating prices on blood plasma.[48] In South Africa, the government had to condemn private healthcare workers who refused to treat Covid patients. In Kenya, the government said it had received 'numerous complaints' of overcharging, including the equivalent of over £50 for protective gloves.[49] In Peru, private providers managed to extract a massive $15,000 per Covid patient from stretched government health budgets.[50]

Some countries did manage to control the greed of the private sector. Dr Sundar told me that, in India,

> some of the better states requisitioned private beds. They reimbursed the private hospital, but at a rate they fixed. There were no negotiations. That worked, but it was small-scale. But by and large, the opposite thing happened – it was the public hospitals that became Covid hospitals, and in turn this meant the poorer part of the population who needed those hospitals for non-Covid treatment was pushed out to fend for themselves, at times literally onto the street.

Owain David Williams, in an excellent study of the subject, also pulls out positive examples.[51] Malaysia and Thailand forced private providers to treat Covid patients at fixed government rates, while Egypt set a price cap on Covid treatment – though howls of protest from the private sector led to a quick increase in the cap.

Nevertheless, the World Bank did not step back from its obsession with private-sector suppliers, and the majority of its emergency Covid-19 lending targeted the private sector. And similar policies have been eagerly encouraged by the Gates Foundation and by the UK and US governments, which are increasingly unabashed that aid provides opportunities for their own businesses.[52]

The answer to these problems is so obvious that only a deep ideological commitment to the market and the private sector could blind you to it. In the countries where it has been tried, public universal healthcare has worked not only to give everyone access to care, but also to reduce poverty and inequality. The care must be universal, because only then does the whole of society share an interest in it. The alternative – state-provided or state-funded healthcare only for the poor – means that care inevitably becomes a second-class service that is vulnerable to erosion over time.

Such systems are not the preserve of Western countries. Sri Lanka has provided free, universal healthcare since the 1930s. Its achievement should be studied by any government coming to power in a Southern country. Sri Lanka added twelve years to life expectancy in just seven years from 1945, and its low rates of maternal and child mortality rival those of its rich neighbours. A Sri Lankan woman can expect to live almost as long as a German woman, despite having an income ten times smaller.[53] In fact, a World Bank paper, presumably commissioned to establish how this unthinkable experiment can have worked against all 'common wisdom', finds that 'Sri Lanka represents the global frontier for indicators such as infant mortality: no country with a similar income level has better outcomes'.[54] Malaria, polio, tetanus and measles were found to have been eradicated, or at levels of near-eradication. Even more puzzling to the World Bank was the fact that this 'excellent performance has been achieved despite (or perhaps because of) the fact that few major reforms have been undertaken over many decades'. In particular, there was seemingly no effort made to target or subsidise 'the poorest'; but because the system was universal and funded by general taxation, it in fact serves the poor much better than any number of other World Bank experiments.

Incredibly, Sri Lanka's health system achieves better outcomes than almost any other country in its income bracket – and at lower cost. Unfortunately, the neoliberal era has taken its toll, with the entry of more private providers intended to improve the system but having exactly the opposite effect. Public investment has declined, and understaffing and long waiting lists have become more prevalent.[55]

The state of Kerala in India has also garnered acclaim for its health system, helping this fairly poor state to achieve health outcomes similar to those of the United States, despite a per capita income 99 per cent lower and annual spending on health of just $28 per person.[56] Kerala has made healthcare a high priority, dedicating high rates of government spending to it – though, again, the private sector has boomed in recent times. Cuba, too, is famous for its health outcomes, with lower rates of infant mortality than the United States. Former UN chief Ban Ki-moon has described its system as 'rooted in primary health care, which has yielded outstanding results – lower infant mortality, higher life expectancies, universal coverage. This is a model for many countries around the world.'[57]

One interesting recent case is that of Thailand, where a universal health system was introduced by populist prime minister Thaksin Shinawatra in 2002. Today, over 80 per cent of healthcare is delivered by the state, funded by taxation and free to everyone.[58] The result has been a massive increase in numbers of healthcare staff, a rapidly falling maternal mortality rate, and increasing life expectancy. Thailand's system is seen by many as a model for other counties to emulate. Now that universal healthcare exists there, it will be extremely hard to take away.

The radical idea of primary healthcare is based on principles of holistic care – exactly the opposite to the so-called 'vertical', top-down approach of Bill Gates, which seeks to wipe out a specific disease. It is true that, if you are looking for quick and measurable results, wiping out a single disease with a single medicine might be the simplest way to achieve that. But doing so also misses the bigger picture. Disease and illness are clearly about much more than a lack of access to medicines. Lifestyle and education – sanitation, high-quality food, housing and employment – are central to tackling ill health. We wiped out many diseases in Europe not simply by giving people medicines – in fact, by and large they played a minor role. More important was the effort to develop a holistic approach to healthcare and social deprivation in general. Universal healthcare can play a vital role in that larger transformation; technology-driven attempts to wipe out single diseases, much less so.

If this all seems obvious, why are we still so far away from universal healthcare in most countries? The power and influence of the 'market knows best' players in the development field, like Gates and the British government, are clearly a part of the picture. But we are also now battling the gigantic, multi-trillion-dollar healthcare industry, which is bigger even than the pharmaceutical industry – and, as we have seen, increasingly financialised. Moreover, it has large areas of common interest with other monopoly industries, most importantly Big Tech.

In 2017 I worked with the *Guardian* on an article about Big Tech corporations eyeing up healthcare and education in Africa as the next frontier for profit making.[59] You can imagine how it might work: faced with underfunded public hospitals and overpriced private hospitals, Big Tech could provide medical advice through your mobile phone or a shared computer. The piece revealed that Apple's then boss unveiled that he was putting healthcare at the centre of all the company's smartphone developments: 'A smartphone can be your personal doctor, monitoring your health minute by minute, accessing test results and providing medical information.' Amazon has already begun to extend its virtual private employee healthcare programme to employees of other companies.[60] It does not require a huge leap of imagination to see this as a blueprint for healthcare in poorer countries.

Perhaps this sounds like a reasonable stopgap solution for people who are unable to access healthcare. But the problem is that such stopgaps tend to become permanent. As with private healthcare in general, it simply lets the public sector off the hook permanently, often undermining even what little provision there is. It becomes the future of healthcare. And when monopolies also own our health information, we need to be very worried indeed, because this is lucrative personal data that can be sold to insurance companies, pharmaceutical corporations and the healthcare industry, greatly enhancing the power of all three.

Building Hope

For many of those fighting for a different health system, there is no distinction between being a health worker and being a political activist. This is a way of thinking that is baked into the People's Health Movement – an inspirational network of health-worker activists spanning the world.

Dr Sundar has been one of the leading figures in the movement since its inception. As he told me,

> It was about empowering people, giving them the information and tools to understand their health rights and to fight for them. It was big. In 2000 we brought out a huge rally of people, which became people's health movement in India. We'd been promised health for all by 2000 by the WHO. Governments had come together to agree this, but the promise hadn't been fulfilled. They wanted to forget, but we the people hadn't forgotten. So we brought together this movement . . . to fight for primary healthcare.[61]

The People's Health Movement takes the WHO's Alma-Ata Declaration as it's starting point. The global health crisis is not simply a consequence of insufficient medicines or the depredations of Big Pharma. It is a social, political and environmental crisis. It results from inequitable access to water, housing, sanitation, education and employment, as well as universal public health services themselves. Fighting for a better future is just as much a question of defeating a trade agreement that threatens good-quality food production as it is of building hospitals.

Such ambitious goals might seem overwhelming. But, as many people have told me during my research for this book, life as an underpaid and poorly supported health worker also often feels overwhelming, even meaningless, in the absence of efforts to engage in attempts to achieve structural change. The important thing, which is at the heart of the People's Health Movement, is to bring these two realities together to build genuine power.

The People's Health Movement also exists in developed countries. In Britain, groups like Medact and Health Poverty Action bring health practitioners and activists together into a movement for change. Beyond this, a less formal health movement extends more broadly into society. Today, those standing up against the many attempts at partial privatisation of the NHS, including of course the many nurses and doctors who are actively working to preserve our socialised healthcare system, are part of the same struggle. So too are those in the United States campaigning against the corporate vultures preying on their healthcare system.

This movement has secured important victories – but they can never be permanently banked. The struggle is never-ending. There is an old phrase attributed to the British politician most associated with the creation of the NHS – Labour left-winger Nye Bevan – who was said to have told people, 'The NHS will last as long as there's folk with faith left to fight for it.' This ongoing struggle is true for the economy more generally. Which aspects of our economy are abandoned to the market, and under what conditions, are political decisions – the product of political struggle. Capitalism is not all-or-nothing, a system that either exists or does not. It is a constant battleground.

7
A New Hope

Season of Death

You cannot explain the strength of the People's Vaccine movement without understanding something about the HIV/Aids crisis of the late 1990s. It was a crisis that unmasked more explicitly and publicly than anything before the extremes to which the pharmaceutical industry would go in order to preserve their monopolies. Some of those involved remain active today, playing a leading role in the campaign against Covid-19 vaccine inequality.

One of those campaigners is Fatima Hassan, a South African who was deeply affected by the Aids epidemic in her country. Hassan finished law school just as South Africa was transitioning to democracy. She told me growing up in an apartheid state meant that activism was 'in my blood, I think'.[1] She was interested in labour law, but soon realised she couldn't join a private law practice, where she would have been representing employers, and instead took a post at the Aids Law Project. The three-month post became a ten-year job.

'The stigma around living with HIV then was terrible', she told me, 'and it wasn't only about the poor – we advised rich and middle-class people too who were living with HIV. We were trying to get very basic rights for people – the right to have a home and a job, to go to school, to dignity, to not be forced into testing without consent.' But, having won some of these rights, the campaigners realised there was another major problem facing those with HIV: they could not get lifesaving drugs, known as antiretrovirals, because they were too expensive.

In 1998, Simon Nkoli died. He had been one of Africa's first publicly HIV-positive gay men, and his death sparked the formation of a group called the Treatment Action Campaign, a coming together of anti-apartheid, LGBT and HIV activists. The group set out to fight for access to the drugs Big Pharma was refusing to license to generic manufacturers or sell at an affordable price. Hassan explained the importance of this movement:

> So many of my clients and many of my friends died prematurely because they could not get tested and treated in time. For a while, it was a season of death – unnecessarily so. But it's in this period that I met so many people who now also work on Covid-19 access issues, because we're dealing with the same companies, the same arguments, the same rich north governments. The disease is different, of course. You know, the stigma around HIV was just terrible. So that's different, but much of the politics around access and IP barriers is exactly the same.

Of course, HIV was not only devastating communities across southern Africa. In the West, where it had become a major crisis for gay and bisexual men, a new wave of activists battled against their marginalisation, and for the drugs that those living with the disease needed. Most prominent was the Aids Coalition to Unleash Power, or ACT UP. Inaugurated in New York but with chapters rapidly springing up across the United States and beyond, the network became best known for its creative direct actions against pharmaceutical corporations and their investors.

Gregg Gonsalves was a prominent ACT UP activist in New York. Like Hassan, he went on to become a key campaigner against Covid-19 vaccine inequality. He told me how his HIV activism had led to his awakening to the deep iniquities in the global economy.[2] Gonsalves was initially focused on understanding how the disease worked, and 'getting pills into people's hands'. But that changed – partly as a result of the internet, partly through a transformational conference in Durban, South Africa, in 2000. It was there, he told me, that he and others 'started realising that we'd won access to the drugs *we* needed, but most countries hadn't . . . our attention was now turned to the global political economy'. Many anti-apartheid campaigners in Durban were active in raising the alarm about the role racism played in the way the pharmaceutical system worked.

By this time, 28 million people were living with HIV in sub-Saharan Africa as a whole, and more than 2 million Africans were dying of the disease each year. South Africa was hit particularly hard. Over 4.5 million people were infected with HIV, and 1,700 new people were being diagnosed every day, of whom 200 were new-born babies.[3] So serious was the epidemic that life expectancy in South Africa fell from sixty-three in 1990 to fifty-three in 2004.[4]

What was particularly shocking was that, by the early 2000s, HIV had become a treatable illness, thanks in part to the work of groups like ACT UP. Antiretrovirals could massively prolong the life of someone infected with HIV, reduce suffering, and prevent mother-to-child transmission. But in South Africa, where that treatment regime was priced at $10,000 per person per year, it was out of reach of all but the very wealthiest. Generic versions of the medicine were being produced by developing countries like Thailand and Brazil for a fraction of the price. This had allowed Brazil to provide antiretrovirals for free, halving the death toll from Aids.[5] But South Africa was prevented from importing them by its tight patent law, which was fully compliant with TRIPS.

In fact, South Africa's entire healthcare system was deeply unequal, having emerged from the system of apartheid. Nelson Mandela's government had a radically different vision of healthcare, but it was not going to be built overnight. One element in realising this vision was the Medicines Act, passed by the government in 1997, which sought to promote more affordable medicines. Among other things, it would have allowed the government to use 'parallel importation' – importing generic medicines from countries with production capacity – as well as making it easier to issue compulsory licenses and rendering the pricing of medicines more transparent.

This did not please the pharmaceutical industry at all, and the Medicines Act became entangled in legal challenges that culminated in thirty-nine of the world's largest pharmaceutical companies, including GlaxoSmithKline, Merck, Bristol-Myers Squibb and Roche suing the South African government. As Oxfam pointed out at the time, these companies enjoyed global sales of well over three times the South African government's national budget, and profits amounting to twice the sum that the government spent on education, health and welfare combined.[6]

While this case was proceeding, the international pharmaceutical companies embarked on a PR drive, using every argument, however offensive, against their opponents. 'It played on all manner of racist ideas', Hassan told me. 'You know at one point a representative from the United States government even said that most Africans didn't have watches and couldn't tell the time, so there was no point giving us antiretrovirals as we wouldn't be able to take them on time.'

The case dragged on for three years, during which the government was unable to implement the Medicines Act and tens of thousands of people died unnecessarily from Aids-related illness. The corporations claimed that the Medicines Act deprived them of their right to property and contravened WTO rules. South Africa argued that it had a constitutional duty to protect and improve the health of its citizens, which should override such rules. Big Pharma also used its power to mobilise the support of the United States and European governments. In the United States, Bill Clinton's government dutifully placed South Africa on a sanctions watch list after lobbying by the PhRMA group.[7] Britain's European Commissioner, Leon Brittan, joined the Americans, writing to the South African government in an attempt to persuade it to back down.

But the case was not intended to endear the pharmaceutical industry to the general public. In South Africa, the Treatment Action Campaign, or TAC, brought Big Pharma's behaviour to global public attention. TAC worked by creating a movement of activists, many of whom were living with HIV themselves. It was made up of many inspirational figures, but one notably came to international prominence – Zackie Achmat. Not only was Achmat a brilliant and persuasive speaker; he voluntarily took action that threatened his life, refusing to take antiretrovirals even though he was able to access them from abroad, in order to bring attention to the plight of HIV sufferers in South Africa.

The work of TAC and its allies brought international attention to South Africa. As a result, Bill Clinton withdrew the threat of trade sanctions, and eventually the pharma corporations dropped their legal case, their collective reputation in tatters. Moreover, outrage about the situation in southern Africa helped pave the way for the WTO's Doha Declaration.[8]

The impact of TAC is difficult to overstate. Not only did it eventually ensure that HIV patients had access to medicines; at a time when healthcare was being heavily pushed as something for the private sector and 'market mechanisms' to deal with, campaigning around HIV/Aids proved that sufficient activism could effectively push back against this agenda. As leading TAC activist Mark Heywood has written, 'the AIDS activist movement was so effective that, tantalisingly, it suggested a possible change to the paradigm of public health responses to disease in general'.[9] This was not a result of well-intentioned or far-sighted policymakers. 'None of these gains would have been possible without civil society activism', says Heywood. 'It is seldom emphasised in telling the story about AIDS that the first generation of AIDS activists were ordinary people taking control of their own lives and bodies.'

Placing HIV-positive people at the heart of the campaign proved so important because it changed attitudes about the virus, without which fighting for access to decent healthcare would have been impossible, while in turn generating new waves of activists and supporters. The empowerment of those suffering with HIV was vital in allowing people who were being marginalised and demonised to begin to argue their case with experts from a position of confidence and equality.

According to Diarmaid McDonald, who runs Just Treatment – a patient campaign group that challenges the pharmaceutical industry's control and pricing of drugs – activists today can learn important lessons from the Treatment Action Campaign.[10] McDonald believes that TAC and other movements were fundamental to changing the situation around HIV and Aids. But he also thinks the power of that movement was undermined by what, in some ways, became an 'Aids industry', consisting of massive NGOs that attracted vast sums of money to deal with HIV/Aids, but no longer derived their power from the activism of those living with HIV. It was this legitimacy that had enabled the movement to challenge, and ultimately defeat, Big Pharma. 'Today there are no patients in the room when you have big NGO conferences about access to medicines', McDonald told me. In fact, today patients are too often encouraged to side with Big Pharma when those corporations set up their own 'astroturf' campaign groups specifically designed to transfer blame for lack of access onto governments: 'We need to do better. And patients must be at the centre of it.'

For South Africans, beating back Big Pharma was not the end of the road. When Nelson Mandela left office he was replaced by Thabo Mbeki, who became personally convinced that HIV was not the cause of Aids, and that antiretroviral medicines were therefore of no help. The attention of activists turned to fighting their own government. 'We were fighting on two fronts', as Fatima Hassan put it. On the one hand, activists needed to support their government in international forums where it was being bullied by rich governments and corporations. Other the other, they needed to criticise and challenge it at home.

They played a similar role in Covid-19. In fact, Hassan does not believe the push of Southern governments for Covid-19 vaccine equity would have happened without activists and the lessons of the HIV movement. Even the TRIPS waiver itself came from the movements: 'Governments wouldn't have come up with this on their own. We had to push, we had to come up with options. At times, we had to let them take the credit too.'

We should not imagine that Southern governments are uniformly ready and waiting to do the right thing. The fight described here is not simply one between the Global North and the Global South, but is taking place within each country as well.

For many, the Covid-19 campaign had many similarities with the Aids fight, representing a continuation of the same battle. Though this time Southern governments understood the need for vaccines, they nonetheless made mistakes. Hassan believes they had far too much faith, first of all, in initiatives like COVAX, and then in the belief that rich governments would back a TRIPS waiver because it was such a moderate demand. 'They took too long to realise that the West wasn't going to play fair', says Hassan.

Decolonisation

While Aids was a particularly extreme example, campaigners and social movements have repeatedly demonstrated how the pharmaceutical industry at best ignored most countries in the world, and at worst used them as a testing ground for new medicines, using techniques they could never get away with in the West. They also stand accused of overly medicalising social problems, heavily promoting drugs when a more holistic method of eradicating illness and disease, focused on decent sanitation, housing and employment, might be more appropriate. Big Pharma finds a hearing within contemporary aid programmes, whether they are driven by Western states, private foundations or even large NGOs.

This represents a modern form of colonial thinking. This point is well made by Els Torreele, a long-time healthcare activist, who served for a period as director of Médecins Sans Frontières's Access Campaign.[11] Torreele left her research work when she recognised that, far from working to improve healthcare, she was in fact screening for breakthroughs that would be used or ignored according to the interests of the pharmaceutical industry. 'We would not be able to weigh in on how our results were used', she told me. This meant she had no control over what would be used, how it would be used, or how much would be charged for it.

In essence, this meant that the industry framed the central questions facing researchers – most importantly, what they should work on – because those researchers would only research something that had a chance of being picked up. This in turn dictated a focus on what Big Pharma thought it could make money from.

Torreele gives me an example of research she has undertaken on parasites. Initially she reviewed the research that had been undertaken, and found a huge amount of research effectively sitting on the shelves of pharma companies, which was very promising. 'But it had ended up going nowhere because no company thought there was profit in it', she told me. 'Patents reward novelty and inventiveness and industrial applicability – there is no link with medical benefits, and for me this is the fundamental problem. The pharmaceutical industry is driven by incentives which have nothing to do with medical benefit.' The result is a plethora of new medicines that may be novel enough to attract patents, but are useless in improving health outcomes.

For Torreelle, the progress made in access to medicines like the HIV drugs is still too small: 'It's still playing by the rules of the game, a game in which companies are fully in control of who gets to live, at what price.' There remains a need for something far more transformational, which genuinely reclaims medical innovation for the cause of public health. And this means a model in which the health needs of the Global South are no longer adjudicated by the wealthy in the Global North – a model in which local doctors and researchers do not have their options determined by international donors. In other words, there is a need not only to de-financialise the pharmaceutical industry, but also to decolonise the global medical research model.

This same point was made to me by Catherine Kyobutungi, a Ugandan epidemiologist who now runs the African Population and Health Research Centre.[12] Kyobutungi started her career as a doctor in rural Uganda. She worked hard for three years, but ultimately quit because 'the system is so broken'. She went into research, but found it equally frustrating, because the priorities were set by organisations in rich countries. So she then went into campaigning around the need to decolonise medicines.

Kyobutungi recognises that, while inventing a new medicine might not be easy, it seems easier in our political economy than changing the deeper social determinants of healthcare – ending hunger or redistributing land. This is why the field of healthcare has been increasingly narrowed down to pharmaceutical corporations making drugs, and international donors and healthcare corporations distributing those drugs. We have ceased even to ask about the deeper changes needed. 'I know it's hard,' Kyobutungi tells me, 'but does that mean we don't even try? That's what it feels like – that it's so hard we won't even try any more. So we just give people pills.'

Perhaps this is no surprise. Many governments and philanthropists in the Global North, who often fund such healthcare programmes, are outright opposed to the wider transformation of society, given the threat it represents to their interests. But there are also narrower problems to confront. Kyobutungi explains the trend in development thinking towards measurable results in a fixed time period, which tends to favour the distribution of a certain number of vaccines over broader, and probably less tangible social change, even if that social change could have a far larger impact on people's health. It is also true that these donors support research and development that reinforces their own thinking. 'Researchers look into, for instance, HIV because that gets funded, and then that becomes *the* problem. And we treat HIV. And this fuels more research into HIV', she tells me.

> The whole story of 'global healthcare' assumes that one part of the world – the Global South – has problems, and one part of the world – the Global North – has solutions . . . But that's not what we want or need. We want to define the problems ourselves. And for us, you can't cure disease only with medicines. You need food, housing, employment, and so on. We need to break out of the colonial mind-set.

For Kyobutungi, the answer is that African governments must think bigger. That is difficult, particularly because too many have become so heavily reliant on foreign investment and aid. Even on the narrow subject of medicines, they will need to develop their own systems not simply to manufacture more medicines, but to research and develop different types of medicine, and to make sure doing so becomes sustainable.

Kyobutungi is just one of many activists working to decolonise Africa's health systems. That involves pushing back against not only former colonial powers and big corporations, but against their own governments. Tian Johnson heads the African Alliance in South Africa. Johnson, a queer African activist, has worked on HIV and human rights for nearly twenty years. Among other things, he has explored the inequitable access to a new wave of HIV-prevention drugs, colloquially known as PrEP.[13] In 2017, a campaign group Johnson convened issued a statement declaring that 'PrEP should be provided by trial sites to participants who want it', because '[o]ur lives, the lives of those we love and the lives of those around us literally depend on it,' also noting that 'it is on the back of black African women that live in some of the world's most unequal societies that we claim the scientific successes that we claim here today'.

Although not widely known about beyond the most at-risk groups, PrEP renders transmission of HIV nearly impossible. After a fight, PrEP was eventually offered to at-risk groups on the NHS in Britain. The NHS was initially, and rightly, concerned about the cost of the drug, though it is now able to purchase a generic version. However, for most people in the Global South – including countries where HIV transmission is still a huge problem, including South Africa – access to PrEP is still a distant dream.

Today, new longer-lasting, injectable versions of PrEP are coming online. They are believed to be more effective than oral PrEP, and only require one dose every few months.[14] But these medicines are even further out of reach for the majority than the pills. Injectables could be a game-changer for people in many countries, eradicating new HIV infections. The same drugs can also provide better treatment and suppression of HIV in positive patients. The drugs in question are made by a company called ViiV, which is itself owned mostly by British Big Pharma giant GlaxoSmithKline. ViiV sells its drug at around $23,000 per person per year in the United States.[15] It says that its lowest 'not-for-profit' price is between $240 and $270 per patient per year – but experts have said it could be made for as little as $20.

In the words of UN experts, we know what action the world should take to prevent HIV transmission: make such medicine 'free to all who choose it'.[16] Indeed, ambitious international goals have been set to ensure access to PrEP. But, as the same UN experts point out, 'One key structural barrier that jeopardizes widespread access is the fact that production of these medicines is so far monopolized by a tiny number of companies based in a tiny number of countries, keeping prices high and limiting (and concentrating) supply.'[17]

We can end the Aids pandemic, according to these experts. But we cannot do so with the model currently in place. That model means that, here and now, many people are contracting HIV and dying of Aids unnecessarily.

Johnson believes this behaviour is not only obscene, but is directly fuelling suspicion of medicines in countries like South Africa, undermining work by activists to convince people to take life-saving drugs. Johnson says that countries like South Africa are still treated like 'research subjects' by Big Pharma. 'It doesn't help when vaccine trials are so clearly run in the interest of Big Pharma', Johnson tells me, 'with no guarantee of post-trial access to the results of that research by the communities that made it possible. When all is said and done, we don't even get the drugs our participation has made possible.'

This is a shockingly common story. During the Covid-19 pandemic, medicines were trialled in countries that ultimately did not receive the final drug. Canada's *Star* reported on a young musician called Siwela, who signed up to a vaccine trial when Covid hit. His regular income, based on tourism, had dried up, and the expenses paid by the trial provided him and his family with a lifeline.[18] As part of the trial, Siwela learned how important the vaccines were. But then came the sense of betrayal as he 'would go on to watch as his neighbours were left waiting for vaccines, even as they were given out to protect others around the world'. 'Vaccine was tested here in South Africa but being sold to other countries', Siwela told the Star. 'That's the saddest part . . . That's why people feel like we were used.'

Johnson suggests such feelings are far from uncommon. The pandemic offered an opportunity to resolve mistrust, and to help inform and encourage sceptics about the importance of medicines. But when trials failed to improve access to medicines, when vaccines were exported out of South Africa to a much better-provisioned Europe, and when South Africa was charged twice the price the EU paid for vaccines, trust was undermined and hesitancy exacerbated. Such mistrust will go on to inform future health crises, making the work of groups like African Alliance harder. For Johnson, intellectual property is only part of the problem. The bigger story concerns the way the industry works and treats Africa: 'It distances people from the science and behaves as if people have no agency . . . Communities are consistently treated as a sideshow, as non-essential.'

The solution is the decolonisation of the model. This must come from the Global South itself, which is why Johnson and many fellow campaigners do most of their work in Africa, informing communities and mobilising people to take control of their own healthcare and make demands of their own governments. Some of the hardest work, for Johnson, is 'holding our own accountable' and pushing for a leadership able to take transformative steps forward.

Tian Johnson is right that the job of decolonising medicines, let alone wider healthcare, is huge. But I remain hopeful that Covid has set in motion some changes that could make a radical difference. Fabrizio Chiodo is a scientist from Italy who works with the Finlay Institute. He was working on synthetic vaccines before the pandemic, and came to believe in their importance for building a very distinctive kind of public-health system. For all the problems of Big Pharma's control and profiteering during the pandemic, he believes some of the vaccine development in the Global South, particularly Cuba, points the way to that new model.

Chiodo describes vaccines as a 'tool against Big Pharma' precisely because of the difficulty of profiting from one-off vaccinations.[19] This is why countries like Italy, Denmark and the Netherlands have traditionally made public vaccines. He concedes that Covid-19 has shown that vaccines can, in fact, be very profitable. If anything, it has given the corporations concerned a financial interest in not producing more effective vaccines. If Covid boosters can become a regular process, needed in the same way as treatments for chronic conditions, this would provide an endless income stream. The answer, Chiodo believes, is more effective vaccines that will challenge Big Pharma's wealth.

Cuba has, incredibly, produced five Covid-19 vaccine candidates, three of them authorised and two others going through trials, and has used them to inoculate a greater proportion of their population than any other country in the world.[20] This success is built on a medical research system that would be impressive even in a relatively rich country, never mind a poor country that has faced a decades-long embargo.

The reason is political. After the revolution, Cuba's new leaders recognised that the country would be blocked from new technologies. The government would have to make huge investments, or Cuba would be left without medicines. This left a tremendous legacy of very strong biotech research, and today Cuba produces 80 per cent of its own vaccines. 'When the virus arrived, they were set up to go', Chiodo tells me. But he is also at pains to explain that this is not the result of a huge, centrally planned bureaucracy: 'Actually, the vaccines were produced by different institutes. So you have competition within the public system. But you also have the ability to cooperate, collaborate and plan.'

While some view Cuba's vaccine as less innovative and effective than the new mRNA vaccines, Chiodo disagrees. It is not that he thinks Pfizer's vaccine is not effective, only that it is far from a complete solution. Not only is it expensive and difficult to store; many are worried about giving it to children. Cuba's vaccine is different. At $1 per dose, it is cheap. It is also easily stored, and completely safe for children – which is why Cuba has vaccinated more people than anywhere else. For Chiodo, this shows how distinctive Cuba's approach has been. Rather than accepting that children are unlikely to suffer too badly from Covid, Cuba recognised that children can get the disease badly, and can of course carry it.

So why has this thinking not been emulated everywhere? For Chiodo, this question goes to the heart of the problem. Cuba used a longstanding technology which is difficult for corporations to monopolise and profit from. The problem, he suggests, is that corporations were not simply looking for an *effective* vaccine, but a *profitable* one. 'How can massive drug companies, like Sanofi and GSK for instance, fail to make a vaccine when Cuba succeeds?', he asks. 'I think because Cuba wasn't interested in making a profit. They wanted something cheap, but effective. So they used a more reliable technology.' It is fitting that Abdala and Soberana – two of the vaccines Cuba has produced – are named after a poem written by a hero of Cuban independence and the Spanish word for 'sovereign'.

Cuban vaccines have been used outside the country, but not as widely as might be expected – though the country has shared its know-how with a number of others, including Vietnam and Mexico. But there is a deeper problem for which Chiodo blames a colonial mind-set that looks to Western technology and corporations as superior. It is a way of thinking that is hardwired even into international institutions like the WHO, which, while accepting the high level of scientific understanding embedded in Cuba's medical system, still tends to prioritise Western medicines. This bias may be bad for all of us, given the groundbreaking nature of research in Cuba and other countries of the Global South – and not just on Covid. As Chiodo tells me, 'Cuba has a vaccine against two lung cancers while they're only just studying this in the USA.'

Cuba is not the only country in the Global South to have developed a vaccine. In fact, Covid sparked a proliferation of vaccine research. Indian health campaigner Achal Prabhala noted that if it were not for vaccines from the Global South, the inequality would have been much worse: 'In the first wave, the Chinese vaccines, Sinopharm and Sinovac, reached a huge number of people globally, more than Pfizer or Astra Zeneca.'[21] In 2021, Sinovac and Sinopharm delivered 4.4 billion doses – each producing more than any other company in the world.[22]

China took a very different approach from that of the United States and Europe. First, it invested heavily, like Cuba, in already proven vaccine technology, rather than taking the huge gamble on mRNA technology.[23] While the US strategy paid off well, with mRNA vaccines showing high effectiveness against specific variants, scientists are divided on whether this success will be replicated long term. It might be that vaccines based on older technology will give a lower level of protection, but will be effective against a broader range of variants, though the jury is still out on this. While mRNA vaccines may certainly prove a good bet for countries with less advanced infrastructure in long term, being potentially easier to make more quickly and on a smaller scale, traditional vaccines are currently easier to store. They may also be cheaper – though it is important to say that China's successful vaccines were in fact quite costly. It should also be noted that China is now looking at developing mRNA vaccines, though it did not develop them in the first wave of Covid-19.

Beyond the technology, another very distinctive aspect of the Chinese approach was that, having suppressed Covid-19 fairly successfully in the lockdown through its 'zero Covid' policies, it did not have the same urgent need for domestic supply – though this approach came back to bite the country in late 2022 when low levels of immunisation met a rapid reopening of the economy. China rather used its vaccine supply to build its diplomatic power and prestige – a strategy of vaccine diplomacy, rather than vaccine nationalism.[24] This was extremely important for the majority of 'left-behind' countries.

China also exported huge amounts of protective equipment and testing kits, and sent medical staff to countries it worked with.[25] But China went beyond the donation model, providing a more sustainable solution for the countries it partnered with. China's vaccines are not patent-free – nor has China participated in the WHO's patent-sharing C-TAP body. But China has not insisted on the sanctity of intellectual property in the same way that the West has. By and large, China was much better at helping countries produce vaccines independently, so that they could build self-sufficiency, and even actively encouraged other countries to become vaccine suppliers themselves.[26] For instance, Sinovac shared technology and trained Egyptian scientists so that they could not only produce their vaccine, but also become a regional production hub and begin exporting to other countries, which Egypt has done.[27] The facilities are now exploring the possibility of producing vaccines for other diseases. In Chile, Sinovac has also invested in long-term R&D capacity.[28]

From the perspective of campaigners, these deals are far from perfect. China's companies are not acting altruistically; they have made a lot of money from vaccine production, while China clearly values the diplomatic leverage it gains from vaccine partnerships. Nonetheless, China has shown that it is possible to run a very successful medical R&D system without making the property rights of the corporations involved the most important aspect of its strategy. This is, without question, a positive thing for those countries in the Global South that China has worked with. It might even be that China's success spurred President Biden to back a TRIPS waiver, and to donate relatively large amounts of vaccines in 2021.

One last point to note is that China's vaccines were not all developed by centrally planned public institutions. In fact, Sinovac is a private company. As Achal Prabhala asked, 'Why does a private vaccine coming out of China seem to us as a "state vaccine" but a state vaccine which comes out of USA is a "private vaccine"?' This highlights an obvious bias in how we think about medicine production. In the West, there was very little information on vaccines produced in the Global South, and consequently a general indifference towards these life-saving medicines.

But Prabhala sees real hope in the story of vaccine production in the Global South during Covid-19: 'These vaccines are all individual and different in terms of how they're made and what they do best. But what's really exciting is this is the first time I've known so many good vaccines come out of the Global South.' It might have been born of necessity, but the confidence that these successful vaccines have given to Southern governments could prove one of the most important and exciting developments in international medicine production.

There are many other vaccines, but perhaps one of the more interesting ones was not made in the Global South at all – though it is being exclusively used there. It is in fact an American vaccine, made on an entirely different basis to those produced by Big Pharma. It is now being rolled out in India and provides a real insight into how a different system might operate.

Dr Peter Hotez runs a vaccine research centre at the Texas Children's Hospital. In that role, he and his fellow scientists 'make vaccines for diseases that the pharma companies won't make, for parasitic infections such as Chagas disease and schistosomiasis'.[29] Everything the scientists do is aimed at making medicines that can be cheaply and easily produced in settings without access to advanced levels of medical technology. As Hotez says, rich countries have 'never had any interest in that'.

When the pandemic struck, the scientists looked into using their expertise to make a Covid vaccine. They explicitly set out to 'make a vaccine for the world', and received almost no external support from US schemes like Operation Warp Speed. But with just a few million dollars from philanthropists, they did it anyway. Hotez has said, 'If we had even a fraction of the support that, say, Moderna or the other pharma companies had gotten, who knows? We might have been able to have the whole world vaccinated by now.'[30]

Nonetheless, they have managed to secure an agreement with an Indian company to pump out a hundred million doses per month, and agreements with Indonesia, Bangladesh and Botswana to produce more.[31] If they are able to reach their target of 3 per cent of global Covid vaccines, that would compare with some of the Big Pharma corporations like Moderna. As Hotez said, President Biden 'boasted that, a couple of weeks ago, right before the new year . . . he donated 275 million doses to 110 countries. Well, heck.

I mean, we have already matched that with our research institute in Texas, and we're about to exceed it.'[32]

Hotez believes his vaccine, like the Cuban one, is a good option for vaccinating children. It is a great irony that children in the Global South have had a pathway to vaccination with an American vaccine that Americans themselves cannot access. He describes his approach in an interview with Democracy Now:

> what we do is we license the technology, and we provide the prototype, production cell bank, no strings attached, no patent. We help in the co-development. And then the countries themselves and those companies own it . . . We're hands-off. We don't try to meddle into their business. You know, very much we are a believer in this concept of decolonization.[33]

Covid has thrown up several ways of researching and making vaccines. This is positive. Either implicitly or explicitly, these initiatives challenge Big Pharma's obsession with total control of the field. But I will turn finally to South Africa, and perhaps the most exciting development of all to emerge from the pandemic. Like all such examples to date, it shows that it is perfectly possible to make major scientific breakthroughs without Big Pharma.

'What happens next with the hub is very significant. It looks like they've really done it. You can ask as nicely as you want, but at the end of the day, if you don't want to be dependent on Northern charity or on the marketplace, you have to do it yourself.'

I am speaking again to South African activist Fatima Hassan. Often when you are campaigning, you don't get what you want. You might get a more moderate version of what you have demanded. You might get a lot of hot air concealing the fact you have won nothing at all – rather like the eventual WTO deal on TRIPS agreed in 2022. Or, you might not even get that far, failing to make any breakthrough at all. But now and again you will help put something in motion that will initiate a transformation that goes beyond anything you expected.

It is far too early to assess long-term effects of vaccine inequality and the global People's Vaccine campaign. But in mid 2021, with that inequality reaching its deepest point, and campaigners getting mainstream media coverage on a nearly daily basis, the South African government, in partnership with the WHO, launched an initiative to start doing things differently. It was the seed of something that, campaigners like Hassan hope, could grow into a radically different model for researching and producing medicines.

The mRNA Hub was officially launched by the WHO in July 2021. The concept was simple: to help countries in the Global South reach the stage where they could produce their own mRNA vaccines, and then share the associated knowledge openly. Initially they asked the companies that currently control mRNA vaccine technology – Pfizer, BioNTech and Moderna – to share their know-how. The corporations were already producing vaccines, and no one was suggesting they should stop doing so.

But the companies' interest was less in making money from individual sales than in controlling a technology that could be used to create major money spinners for years to come. Vaccines for other diseases were already in development.[34] Why would these corporations share know-how that could transform our medical landscape and save countless lives, when monopolising it could allow them to make a killing for decades into the future? The corporations refused to help – a posture they maintain to this day.[35]

The scientists and officials involved in the mRNA Hub, driven by a campaign-like zeal to do something about vaccine inequality, were undeterred. They said that, if the corporations refused to help, they would simply work out how to make an mRNA vaccine on their own, taking a leaf out of the book of every country that has successfully developed its economy in the last 200 years.[36] Within just a few months, they declared a breakthrough: they had worked out how they could produce it.

While mRNA is not a silver bullet for treating and inoculating against disease, it *is* an important technology, holding out the promise of new ways to prevent HIV infections, TB, certain types of cancer and more besides. What's more, it could, in theory, provide a way to deal with rapidly mutating diseases and to produce small amounts of vaccines quickly – something which could be well suited to travelling clinics serving rural areas poorly served by medical infrastructure. Yes, mRNA helped make a few corporations a huge amount of money, but the underlying technology is likely to be very important in the future of medicine.

Of course, the mRNA Hub's breakthrough was not the end of the road. Scaling up production was a whole new challenge, as was testing and trialling the vaccine. But this endeavour showed that it was only a matter of time. And this is where the truly radical aspect of the Hub's work comes into play. Because once it had developed the know-how to make mRNA vaccines, the Hub started to share that information with those who could make safe and effective use of it. Firstly, scientists from Argentina and Brazil – two countries that had said Pfizer's bullying had left them unable to sign contracts with the company – travelled to Cape Town to receive training in how to make mRNA vaccines. More countries were added to the list – most recently Ukraine, in the midst of its brutal invasion by Russia. At the time of writing, the know-how was being actively shared with fifteen countries.[37] The project is also complemented by the creation of a WHO training hub in South Korea, to help low- and middle-income countries produce their own biological medicines, including insulin and cancer treatments.

This is a potentially momentous development. It is beginning to remake the system of pharmaceutical research and development from the ground up, giving countries across the Global South an alternative to relying on Big Pharma. No patents have been broken in the research phase, but, as one expert told me on WhatsApp, 'they're just sort of behaving as if patents didn't exist'. The implications for the future of the industry are profound.

As Hassan told me, Big Pharma did not think Africa could generate the complex knowledge to figure out mRNA technology and produce vaccines.

> I think they believed [their own rhetoric] actually, they thought it would take forever because they really do think Africans can't do this. Well, they were and are in for a shock. We will do whatever it takes – including patent defiance – to protect the work and knowledge generated by the Hub and its ability to manufacture for the Global South. We will then be able to turn round and say: We did this ourselves.

In a piece that includes a vivid description of the project for Canada's *Star*, Alex Boyd summed up the almost post-liberation sense of optimism and energy around the Hub.[38] The facility is run by a company called Afrigen, headed by Petro Terblanche, and staffed by youthful and passionate scientists doing their ground-breaking work while the facility is literally being built around them. 'If all goes to plan', Boyd wrote, the Hub 'could upend global vaccine production . . . For a growing number of people in

Africa, it's not just that donations are taking too long to arrive, it's that they have to ask for them at all.'

As the Hub's chief scientist put it, 'We didn't have help from the major COVID-vaccine producers, so we did it ourselves to show the world that it can be done, and be done here, on the African continent.'[39]

But Hassan points out that, for all the optimism, the battle is by no means over. There are many outstanding issues, not least the broad patents Moderna has filed in South Africa that may be used to challenge the Hub's work. Hassan and her colleagues have been calling on Moderna to drop these patents, and for the South African government to take executive action to ensure the Hub's work is not hobbled, as well as seeking assurances on its freedom to operate. She believes Big Pharma will do everything it can to undermine the project, and history suggests she is right.

The Hub's early success fired the starting gun for a battle that would rage across the African continent – a battle for the future of the region's pharmaceutical sector. To reclaim ground from the Hub, Big Pharma started signing deals with African countries and announcing its own plans to start production there.

Some vaccines were already being partially produced on the continent, though this production was limited to what is known as 'fill and finish' – basically, putting vaccines into bottles and packaging them. In March, Moderna went a step further, announcing that it would build a new production facility in Kenya.[40] But perhaps the most eye-catching initiative was that of BioNTech, which promised to ship fully staffed and operational prefab laboratories that it dubbed 'BioNTtainers' to Rwanda and Senegal.[41] These facilities – forty-foot containers resembling the new low-production-cost 'Boxpark' shopping centres that have popped up around London in recent years – would be shipped to target locations, where European staff would start producing vaccines.

The central problem with all of these schemes is control. None of the schemes genuinely transfers technical know-how. In the worst cases, African manufacturers are only able to perform the cheapest and simplest aspects of the process. But even in the best case, African countries are playing host to multinational corporations based elsewhere, with no ability to use the technology independently. This is the extended-supply-chain model of globalisation, in which value is held in the West even if countries of the Global South are allowed to perform certain parts of the process.

As Achal Prabhala says of the BioNTtainers, a 'major problem with the BioNTech exercise is that it is proprietary. Effectively, it's a splashier way by which a multinational company sets up manufacturing outposts around the world.'[42] The heart of the model is not transferring technology, but maintaining exclusive control over it. Prabhala calls it the 'Apple' model of vaccines, because BioNTech can maintain proprietary control over the vaccine platform throughout the process. 'What we need with mRNA is something more like the Android model', he explains, 'where multiple manufacturers can utilise the same mRNA platform independently.'

It could certainly be argued that even these corporate-backed developments are in some ways a sign of success. Before the pandemic, Big Pharma had little interest in Africa. Its move to open factories on the continent at least adds to the infrastructure available – except, that is, when these initiatives seem directly designed to undercut the transformational work of the mRNA Hub. Just before BioNTech's announcement, an article in the *British Medical Journal* reported that a foundation working with BioNTech had informed the South African government that the mRNA Hub's intention 'of copying the manufacturing process of

Moderna's COVID-19 vaccine should be terminated immediately', adding, 'the sustainability outlook for this project of the WHO Vaccine Technology Transfer Hub is not favourable'.[43] In another document, the foundation urges decision makers to set up an easier regulatory pathway to ease approval of BioNTech's containers.

Patent expert Ellen 't Hoen noted, 'If you run a not-for-profit foundation and you go around trying to stop people from developing lifesaving vaccines, then I don't know what your agenda is but it smells really bad.'[44]

Developing the capacity to research and develop medicines in different parts of the world will be central to building a new pharmaceutical model. Creating new factories and labs to produce the final medicines will also be important. And governments will need to accept that the free hand of the market will not keep these factories operational at all times without planning and intervention. Right now, there are factories in Africa and elsewhere that geared themselves up to produce Covid-19 vaccines, only to find insufficient orders when public interest waned.

There are many possible ways to remedy this situation. The WHO and international purchasing bodies must start prioritising approvals and orders from producers in the Global South, not Western-based Big Pharma companies. Governments of lower-income countries need to improve their ability to generate demand for essential medicines, allaying scepticism where it is prevalent. And governments need to work together more effectively to plan and coordinate medicine demand and supply, including by being prepared to support or run operations directly.

This might not be easy, but if it has become clear to so many governments in the Global South that they must not again be left dependent on international markets or Western largesse, then they need to develop the will to change the model – and that means investment. Unless lower-income countries can take control of the technology behind the medicines they need, building their ability to research and develop medicines as well as produce them, it will be impossible to break the current monopolistic system.

Moreover, the pandemic has shown us that little will be gained by debating on the floor of institutions like the WTO. Governments simply need to start doing things differently.

8
Reach for the Moon

Mariana Mazzucato is on a mission to challenge neoliberalism – but her starting point is not one of moral disgust at the effect of our economic system. Rather, she believes it is based on a lie, and she dissects that lie books like *The Entrepreneurial State*.[1]

Neoliberalism preaches that real value in society emanates from the brilliance and creativity of the individual entrepreneur. The heavy hand of the state will only hinder that brilliance – through regulations, taxation, or any other attempt to ensure the entrepreneur serves the public good. Much better for all of us, neoliberals argue, is to get out of entrepreneurs' way and allow them to be rewarded for their work.

For Mazzucato, this is not how things work at all. If we really peel back the layers of our financialised economy, she says, we find instead that the biggest risks, the largest investments and the most entrepreneurial activity are in fact undertaken by the state – that despised figure of neoliberal doctrine. What is more, powerful states know this; that is why, as we saw during the pandemic, they would not dream of leaving really important matters to the market.

To illustrate her point, Mazzucato takes an iconic consumer product of the neoliberal age – the iPhone – and demonstrates how it is really built upon the risk taking and ingenuity of the state. Mazzucato looks at twelve technologies that the iPhone is based on – from the microprocessors, memory chips, hard drives, displays and lithium-based batteries to the networks, software, HTML coding, GPS, touchscreens, and even Siri – and shows the crucial role played by the state in creating each of these technologies.[2]

So the state does in fact intervene, invest and assume risk. But we are left with a problem. The doctrine of neoliberalism means that governments behave as if they are embarrassed about their role in the economy. Politicians who spend their lives preaching the virtue of the individual do everything to conceal the role played by the public sector. When they intervene, they do so in order to 'correct the market' – or more likely to clean up its mess – and then get out of the way as quickly as possible. What do we, the public, get out of this? Some important technologies, of course – but technologies whose ownership is subsequently transferred to big business, and then rented back to us at whatever cost the market allows. Far from reinvesting its profits back into research, the private sector stashes them in the banks of the superrich, and then waits for the public to help them 'invent' the next blockbuster.

The development of Covid-19 vaccines is a wonderful illustration of how all of this works in practice, and it shows why this model is such a problem. Simply allowing the private sector to extract all the rewards of research it does not conduct means that we, as a society, are not being properly compensated for our collective contribution. But the problem for the economy as a whole goes deeper than this. We have a situation in which governments, despite underwriting so much economic development, are failing to set the terms of that development, and are thus failing to ensure the public interest is placed at the heart of the economy. What is more, they are not even incentivising the private sector to engage in new research and innovation, but simply allowing big business and financial interests to fleece us of publicly created value. Our economy is thereby becoming less productive, less able to produce the technologies we need – in short, more hollowed out.

From Mazzucato's point of view, governments should end the pretence that the market is the source of all prosperity and progress, and embrace the role they play. Rather than pretending they are merely correcting market failures, they should proudly claim their role of setting clear missions based on public need. Rather than diverting talent into the finance sector, they should encourage the best and brightest to do the work that the rest of us need to be done. If they took the bull by the horns, set the terms of the debate, and used their power and resource to leverage a virtuous circle of research spending and innovation, we might find that few of humanity's problems were really beyond us.

Mazzucato cites the example of John F. Kennedy's mission to put a man on the moon – proof that if you have a clear enough goal and a nearly endless supply of money, you can make the impossible become a reality in surprisingly short order. Today, instead of a space race, let us consider the need for a green revolution, or for a new wave of life-saving drugs.

In 2018, Mazzucato worked with campaigners, including some in my organisation, on a report called 'The Peoples' Prescription'.[3] In it, Mazzucato argued that, just as during the moon mission, we need a 'combination of top-down direction-setting and bottom-up experimentation and exploration' to stimulate health innovation and move the pharmaceutical sector 'from one based on profit maximisation towards one based on public value maximisation'.

'The Peoples' Prescription' argued that governments must adopt a clear mission for improving health, set its direction, nurture collaboration with the business, public and charitable sectors, and use its powers – starting with procurement budgets – to foster experimentation. Public resources should not be handed over for free. They must carry with them conditions, requiring firms that benefit from public investment to reinvest their profits back into innovation, to share any technological knowledge created with others, and to make any resulting products as accessible and affordable as possible. Taxpayers must stop paying twice for medicines developed with public funds.

One way to achieve this would be to rethink patents. For Mazzucato, patents do not represent innovation; while they might play a role in encouraging innovation within the right framework, they more often achieve the very opposite, as we have seen. The patent system is in severe need of reform – at a minimum, they should be shorter and more narrowly drawn. But even without that reform, governments with sufficient political will can make changes immediately – for instance, by requiring a 'golden share' of patents developed with public funding. This would help the public sector to earn a better level of royalties, which could in turn be reinvested. Much more importantly, however, it would give us control over the knowledge produced, all without falling foul of international law. In fact, the United States already has the power to license a third party to produce a patented medicine developed with public funding, if it is not available to the public on reasonable terms – though that power has never been used.

Others want to go further, scrapping patents for certain medicines altogether. One alternative that has been regularly floated is using prize money as an incentive, rather than patents. Bernie Sanders proposed a Medical Innovation Prize Fund – a government-created fund to reward researchers, whether profit making or not, who reach predefined health objectives. Some might question whether this would be sufficient to compensate for the loss of patent income. But the amount Sanders suggested is not small: a fixed percentage of GDP, which in 2016 would have amounted to $102 billion. Other proposals have suggested applying such funds to 'blockbuster' diseases like cancer – through the creation, for example, of a cancer innovation fund.

Reforming the way our drugs are made would provide a blueprint for reforming the wider economy. 'The Peoples' Prescription' proposed limiting share buy-backs that extract value out of healthcare systems, tying executive compensation to real advances in treatment rather than stock price increases; giving taxpayers and patients a voice on corporate boards; and amending the legal duties of company directors so that they are obliged to serve a broader interest than the narrow concerns of shareholders. Some of these concepts were written into a proposed Senate bill presented by Elizabeth Warren, the 'Accountable Capitalism Act'. Others have been adopted on both the left and right of British politics.

Every speech by a political leader to their party conference is important. Although such speeches are nominally crafted to shore up the party faithful, in reality they speak to the media and the nation beyond. It represented business as usual, therefore, that, when Jeremy Corbyn addressed the Labour Party conference in Brighton in September 2019, he was effectively making an election pitch. 'Yesterday, here in Brighton, I met Luis Walker, a wonderful nine-year-old boy. A bright, bubbly, lovely boy,' Corbyn told delegates:

> Luis is living with cystic fibrosis. Every day he needs four hours of treatment and is often in hospital, which obviously keeps him from school and his friends – the normal life of a nine-year-old. Luis's

> life could be very different with the aid of a medicine called Orkambi. But Luis is denied the medicine he needs because its manufacturer refuses to sell the drug to the NHS at an affordable price. Luis, and tens of thousands of others suffering from illnesses such as cystic fibrosis, hepatitis C, or breast cancer, are being denied life-saving medicines by a system that puts profits for shareholders before people's lives.[4]

Cystic fibrosis is a genetic disease that causes a build-up of mucus in the lungs, impairing the ability to breathe, as well as wreaking havoc with the digestive system. Over time, it can cause a series of secondary complications and will shorten a patient's life dramatically without treatment. There is no cure, but there is a new class of medicines that can help transform patients' health. One such treatment, made by a company called Vertex, is known as Orkambi. But the price tag – over £100,000 per year per patient – was deemed too expensive by the National Institute for Health and Care Excellence, the body that assesses the cost effectiveness of medicines; and so Orkambi was not available on the NHS.

Diarmaid McDonald was just starting the patient campaign group, Just Treatment, when he heard about the problems people like Luis were having getting hold of the Orkambi:

> We were just starting to analyse which drugs were effective but weren't available on the NHS, and right in the middle of doing this, we got an email from a mum whose daughter could have benefited from Orkambi. She'd been fighting for over two years to get access to it, asking nicely, pleading with the NHS and the government, going public. Nothing had worked. But she'd seen what we'd done in terms of getting access for a breast cancer drug. And she wanted to know if we could do the same.[5]

McDonald worked with a small group of parents whose children needed Orkambi. The parents had already been running impressive campaigns, and McDonald joined with other health campaigners to take them to the next level: developing a really clear message for the public and building trust with the families. The most difficult task, he told me, was dispelling the misinformation that this was the fault of NHS bureaucrats refusing to supply the medicine, and the fear that going public would make accessing the drug even less likely. This concern is common in the world of medicines campaigns. In fact, many 'patient advocacy' groups represent the interests of the pharmaceutical corporations, using patients to stir public sentiment in order to pressure the NHS into backing down and providing new medicines, even when they are massively overpriced.

One of the parents involved found that the drug was being made generically in Argentina, where Vertex had not filed patents. It was still expensive, but only one-fifth of what Vertex was charging. McDonald accompanied some of the parents, flying to Buenos Aires to buy the drug, and they flew home with it in their bags. The publicity was enormous. The scandal of Orkambi's prices became front-page news. Luis Walker and his mother appeared on breakfast chat shows, and campaigners were able to focus on the core issue: the effects of the monopoly power wielded by Vertex, which held patients' lives to ransom, and the government's responsibility to act.

'The government, under pressure from its MPs, said it was considering its "moral obligation" to break the patent', McDonald told me. 'Orkambi became an important symbol of the problems of the pharmaceutical industry. But what happened with Labour went beyond that victory.' It moved towards system change.

The experience of meeting Luis Walker and his inspirational mother Christina, combined with their admiration of Mazzucato's work, convinced Corbyn and his shadow chancellor and long-time political soulmate John McDonnell to make pharmaceutical reform a major plank of the 2019 conference. Months away from an election, Vertex, the producer of Orkambi, was faced with the possibility of a government that would simply override its patents. Vertex caved in, agreeing a deal to supply Orkambi to the NHS at a fraction of the price it had demanded previously.[6]

But for Labour, this was only the first step in a programme to restructure the way the sector could work, all put together a year before we had even heard of Covid-19. Orkambi was only one drug – and most countries still had not been afforded compassionate access to it. As McDonald told me, only 12 per cent of patients around the world have access to Vertex's latest cystic fibrosis drug, because so many countries cannot afford its prices. But that does not prevent the company from registering patents, including in South Africa and India, where the company has almost no sales. 'They are using the IP systems in the Global South to protect their sales in the West – at the cost of lives around the world. So it's the same old story – money and control. And we need something to change that. That's what the Labour policy could have done.'

Corbyn and McDonnell were also inspired by personal experience. Corbyn's friend Mike Marqusee, a writer and activist, had died of cancer in 2015. Marqusee's last work is a tribute to Britain's NHS and an attack on all the forces working to undermine it.[7] While he expressed his gratitude to 'doctors, nurses, technicians, receptionists, cleaners, and porters [and] scientists – going back generations', this gratitude did not extend to the US corporation, Celgene, that owned the drug he was being given – a version of the 1950s medicine thalidomide with a few very small modifications. The drug was protected by a thicket of patents – even encompassing the safety protocol to stop pregnant women from taking it

– which were used to prevent other companies making it more cheaply.[8] In fact, the cost of this very old drug just continued to rise, while the producer was accused of making it nearly impossible for competitors to get the drug samples they needed for comparison tests, and making 'pay-to-delay' deals with generic manufactures to suppress competition. As Marqusee wrote, the corporation 'uses its monopoly to charge the NHS extortionate rates for its product . . . In effect companies like Celgene are hostage-takers: pay the ransom, they demand, or someone dies. The ruthlessness is breathtaking, but it is accepted as a corporate behavioural norm.'

Like Mazzucato, John McDonnell saw pharmaceutical reform as part of a much bigger economic programme: the transformation of neoliberal capitalism:

> I was thinking through how we overcome the form of economic thinking that has dominated our economy for years, in order to meet people's needs. And it seemed to me that the way Big Pharma operates was such a good example of where this thinking leads you, largely because they're dealing with life and death. They don't cooperate, they compete. It just doesn't make sense. Really, it became increasingly clear that if you want to meet people's medical needs, you need some form of democratic control over the pharmaceutical sector in this country. Then you can deal with the long-term problems we're confronting. And beyond that, you need to help others in the world who want to do the same.[9]

His reform programme was not simply a pet project but part of a bigger drive to rewire the economy as a whole. It remains the most comprehensive proposal to reform the pharmaceutical system by any Western political party in many decades: in effect, the de-financialisation of the pharmaceutical industry and the removal of its monopoly power, including greater use of compulsory licenses, review of UK patent criteria, refusal to put any TRIPS-plus provisions into trade deals, a pledge of stricter public-interest conditions on research, use of public royalties to finance innovation, deterrence of pharmaceutical lobbying, use of aid money to facilitate technology transfer within the Global South, and the establishment of prize funds as an alternative to patents in encouraging research – in the case of antibiotics, for example. The programme also pledged to create a democratically owned pharmaceutical company to save the NHS billions of pounds a year.

The Antibiotic Apocalypse

Labour's programme was never implemented; the party lost the 2019 election. But Mazzucato's ideas are spreading far more widely across the political spectrum, especially as the realisation grows that the current pharmaceutical system is bad for almost all of us.

Lord Jim O'Neill is often referred to as a plain-speaking Yorkshireman. In 2019, he certainly used plain English to tell Big Pharma what he thought of them. That year, after spending five years running a taskforce exploring the problem of increasingly ineffective antibiotics, he lost patience with the industry: 'If pharmaceutical companies delivered just a tenth of the commitment that comes from their words, we might actually get somewhere. It leads me to think that some of the more radical ways of changing the risk/reward incentive and social circumstances of it now need to be explored more.'[10] O'Neill put a radical proposal on the table: 'If you're not going to do it yourself, we're going to turn certain parts of your business into being a utility.'[11]

O'Neill is an unlikely pharmaceutical reformer. He spent years at the infamous 'vampire squid' investment bank Goldman Sachs, latterly chairing its asset-management division. He coined the term BRICs to refer to the four emerging economies of Brazil, Russia, India and China, and later the term MINT, identifying the rising powers Mexico, Indonesia, Nigeria and Turkey. From there, O'Neill became a Conservative member of the House of Lords and a government minister. It was Prime Minister David Cameron who appointed O'Neill to look into antibiotics, after Cameron became alarmed at the rise of antimicrobial resistance. He warned that this was an immediate threat that, if not addressed, risked an 'unthinkable scenario' potentially casting us 'back into the dark ages of medicine.' In this role, O'Neill became increasingly concerned not only about the risk antimicrobial resistance posed to human beings and the economy, but at the failure of the big players in the pharmaceutical industry to respond to the threat.

Antibiotics were discovered by accident in 1928 by Dr Alexander Fleming, who returned from holiday to find mould growing on a Petri dish containing bacteria. Noting that the mould seemed to be preventing the bacteria from growing, Fleming deduced that it must be producing an antibacterial chemical. He named the substance penicillin. It took more than a decade for others to become sufficiently interested to fathom how to mass-produce the antibiotic. But by the end of the Second World War, penicillin was on the road to becoming the wonder drug of its age.

It is hard to overstate the impact antibiotics have had on the way we practise medicine. Before the era of antibiotics, something as simple as a small cut on your finger might, if you were unlucky enough, prove fatal. Even routine operations could be deadly. A world without antibiotics means diseases that we currently view as little more than a nuisance – such as gonorrhoea – would be serious, life-changing infections. A whole range of vital interventions, from caesarean sections to cancer treatments, would pose a serious threat to life. It is no exaggeration to say we have built our medical system around antibiotics.

Over time, however, bacteria develop resistance to antibiotics. Sadly, we have not done enough to limit our use of these vital medicines, often giving them out to deal with infections that our bodies would have eliminated on their own. Worse still, antibiotics have become a staple of industrial agriculture, since routinely feeding healthy animals with antibiotics was found to promote rapid growth and allow animals to be kept in closely confined and unhygienic conditions without falling ill. While efforts have been made to scale back the use of antibiotics in agriculture in Europe, they remain far from sufficient, while industrial farming in the United States continues to make extensive use of the medicines.

But, apart from overuse, there is a further problem. The success of penicillin sparked a golden age of antibiotic discovery, with many new classes of the medicine identified in a short time. But from the 1970s, new discoveries became less easy, and no new classes of antibiotics have been discovered since the 1980s. That is largely because the 'low-hanging fruit' had been harvested, and new discoveries have proved harder and more expensive. As a result, Big Pharma has withdrawn from the field. It was simply unprofitable to pour ever more funding into the search for drugs that, for as long as a patent is likely to last, would be used only as a last resort. In 1980, twenty-five large drug companies had antibiotic discovery programmes; today, only three remain.[12] None of this has been helped by the endless mergers and consolidations in the sector, driven by the imperative of maximising shareholder returns.

O'Neill's work explored the whole gamut of measures needed to reduce antibiotic resistance, as well as how to find new or alternative medicines that could replace them. Failure really was not an option, as the modelling he commissioned in 2014 made clear. By 2050, 10 million people a year were predicted to die of antibiotic-resistant infections – more people than currently die from cancer.[13] Already, these 'superbugs' were leading to 700,000 deaths each year. But five years later, nothing seemed to have changed. If anything, things seemed to be getting worse, with Novartis, Sanofi and AstraZeneca all pulling out of research after 2014.[14]

It is not that no research was being done. In fact, O'Neill's work had helped encourage early-stage discovery – overwhelmingly in small pharma companies, but also some public institutions. But while that early research was producing some results, it was simply not enough – and such useful discoveries as were being made were not being taken up. A WHO study reported, 'Private investment . . . has further decreased, with large pharmaceutical companies and private venture capital investors abandoning the area.'[15] As one WHO advisor noted, 'The pipeline is insufficient to counter the rising resistance in these priority bacteria.'[16]

O'Neill was astonished. After all, this was not some disaster unfolding far away: the impact of antibiotic resistance was already being felt, albeit most heavily in parts of the Global South. But even here, in the West, nearly 2.5 million people would be dying from superbugs by 2050.[17]

And so, in a press conference in 2019, he said that it was time to think the unthinkable. Accusing Big Pharma of talking 'incredible nonsense' about their commitment to antibiotics, he effectively called for the nationalisation of part of the industry. He later recalled, 'If you had asked me three years ago, I would have thought that would have been a bit crazy. But nearly three years after our review came out, there's endless talk but there's no progress in waking up the pharmaceutical industry to want to do this. So, by default, I find my mind thinking why not explore the idea of some public utility that's got public-purpose ownership of it, just take it away from them and take it over.'[18]

On the back of O'Neill's work, even the pro-pharma British government began to realise change was necessary. In 2020, the UK announced a new scheme to pay for new antibiotics – one that O'Neill and others had suggested.[19] Known as the 'Netflix model', it allows governments to pay for something akin to a subscription service. Rather than paying per pill, which obviously provides perverse incentives when it comes to drugs that should be strictly limited, payment is made for access to a new *type* of drug, regardless of how much is used. This is not nationalisation in any sense, but is nonetheless a model that has the capacity to upend incentives in the pharmaceutical industry. Moreover, if joined by other countries, paying on the basis of their wealth, it could theoretically mobilise enough funds to deal with long-term international health needs, effectively giving some direction to pharma companies about what to research and produce.[20]

The disquiet, even in some conservative circles, about rising antibiotic resistance suggests a deeper recognition that the current pharmaceutical model is not working for the vast majority, and that it is likely things will get worse. In 2018, investment giant Goldman Sachs asked a provocative question: 'Is curing patients a sustainable business model?'[21] It was referring to the growth of gene therapy, which holds out the promise of giving patients a 'one-shot cure' for all manner of conditions. The company took one example: hepatitis C. Gilead sells a product that can cure this disease, but the pool of patients suffering from it is finite. And the more of them you treat, the fewer people transmit the disease, and so the fewer patients there will be in the future. The more effective the drug companies are in their task of finding effective treatments, the smaller the market they enjoy. It is no surprise that this system is simply not producing the medicines we need. The profits pharmaceutical companies demand are inconsistent with producing drugs at a price we can afford.

Goldman Sachs made clear that the lack of sustainable profits does not apply to all diseases. Cancer, they point out, 'poses less risk to the sustainability of a franchise', since the treatment of more people for cancer does not prevent others getting it. In fact, longer lives guarantee more need for cancer treatment. But even here there is a problem. Billy Kenber shows how research costs for new drugs have been rising for decades.[22] It is true that these costs are exaggerated by the industry. It is also true that some of the drugs concerned are not hugely useful. The perverse incentives of the IP system mean that corporations are investing in drugs that make, at best, a very marginal difference, but which they know they will be able to sell almost regardless of price. Beneath the profiteering and opacity, however, medical breakthroughs do seem to have become more difficult and expensive to achieve. This is not a reason to accept Big Pharma's argument that they should simply be allowed to charge higher prices for longer periods of time. If the industry's purpose has come to be the production of drugs that make little difference at prices we cannot afford, this only shows even more convincingly that this sector is not structured to meet the challenges we face.

Perhaps that is why, in 2017, Andrew Witty, former head of GlaxoSmithKline, called for the replacement of the patent system with prizes as a way of funding research into rare diseases. 'The system is broken,' wrote the Dutch ministers of health and trade in

2017. 'Patent and intellectual property exclusivities are the only cornerstone of the current model. Companies can ask the price they like. This will no longer do. We need to develop alternative business models.'[23]

And there are indeed examples of things being done differently.[24] In Brazil, state-owned pharmaceutical companies compete with private companies, twenty state-owned laboratories manufacturing 80 per cent of vaccines and 30 per cent of the medicines procured by the public health system, which helps the state to provide free antiretrovirals. Brazil is also a good example of how regulation can help pay for research. It runs a system that mandates companies to reinvest a share of their profits into public R&D funds.[25] A hospital in Amsterdam is producing its own cost-price version of a medicine that treats a rare metabolic disorder – a response to the manufacturer's more than fivefold price hike for the medicine.[26]

But it is perhaps in the United States, of all Western countries, where there is most hope of change. As we have seen, there is enormous leeway in the United States for exploitation and overpricing, in spite of the vast sums of public money that are ploughed into medical research. But although change in the United States starts from a low base, the size of the national economy and the fact US politicians can normally be relied upon to represent the industry means that any change there is very significant.

President Biden's 2022 State of the Union address contained a passage that almost appears to have been inspired by Jeremy Corbyn's 2019 speech:

> First – cut the cost of prescription drugs. Just look at insulin. One in ten Americans has diabetes. In Virginia, I met a 13-year-old boy named Joshua Davis. He and his Dad both have Type 1 diabetes,

> which means they need insulin every day. Insulin costs about $10 a vial to make. But drug companies charge families like Joshua and his Dad up to 30 times more. I spoke with Joshua's mom. Imagine what it's like to look at your child who needs insulin and have no idea how you're going to pay for it. What it does to your dignity, your ability to look your child in the eye, to be the parent you expect to be. Joshua is here with us tonight. Yesterday was his birthday. Happy birthday, buddy.
>
> For Joshua, and for the 200,000 other young people with Type 1 diabetes, let's cap the cost of insulin at $35 a month so everyone can afford it.[27]

Peter Maybarduk is an expert on the problems of the US pharmaceutical industry.[28] Based in Washington, DC, Maybarduk was involved, when he was a student, in the 'battle of Seattle', which brought the WTO to a decade-long stalemate, before going to work for Ralph Nader, founder of Public Citizen and one-time US presidential candidate. He was hired to help middle-income countries like Ecuador and Nicaragua issue successful compulsory licenses for medicines they needed. And he was inspired to continue the work when he found that this was a way to generate meaningful change. 'I saw that it only really takes a handful of people to overturn a patent', he told me. 'And that can save many thousands of lives.'

As important as these changes are, however, they are still one-off events. How do you change the model itself? This structural change, Maybarduk says, is very challenging in a country where Big Pharma has roughly two lobbyists for every member of Congress, as well as huge power at state level, and has successfully woven a narrative that it represents the embodiment of innovation. Maybarduk admits that his international focus has partly been a result of thinking 'we just can't win in the US'. It was a view reinforced when Big Pharma secured the world's longest exclusive rights for biological medicines, tacked onto the Obamacare reforms that were supposed to make healthcare more equal.

But then things started to change. When a deeply controversial trade deal called the Transpacific Partnership (TPP) was being discussed, campaigners noted that it contained significant TRIPS-plus provisions, which tried to create a much tougher international standard even than TRIPS. While this was not the only thing people disliked about the TPP, it was a significant part of the campaign against it around the world. In the Global South, campaigners started to fight back against Big Pharma's provisions, helping spark dissent in the United States as well. By 2016, no presidential candidate would touch the agreement. It was effectively dead in the United States, while the pharma provisions were removed from it by the countries that went ahead with the deal.

For Maybarduk, this change was sparked by a combination of the sky-high prices of drugs in the United States – from Gilead's hepatitis C medicine to the price hikes for insulin – and the opioid crisis, which has affected the American psyche profoundly. 'Today everyone hates pharma, and you have that combined with the sort of populism in our political culture now.'

So what do these recent changes amount to? Even having a US president who is critical of Big Pharma in a major speech is unusual. We know Biden deeply angered the industry by his backing of a TRIPS waiver in the pandemic. But he then went further, proposing a plan to give the federal government the authority to negotiate the price of some medicines – a key power the absence of which had allowed Big Pharma to charge federal insurers whatever they could get away with. Although this was a power most European governments already enjoyed, in the US context this was a major step forward.

The initial proposals were scuppered when Republicans teamed up with a handful of right-wing Democrats to block them, in a moment that spoke to the ongoing hold of the pharmaceutical industry over leading politicians. One obstructive Democrat senator who disavowed her party's platform on the issue has taken over $500,000 from the pharmaceutical and healthcare industries over the years.[29] Together with two colleagues, also in receipt of large amounts of pharma lobbying money, these Democrats managed to water down, though not completely derail, Biden's proposals, which were finally passed as part of his mammoth Covid-19 recovery plan.[30]

Even so, the significance of this move can be seen in the response of Big Pharma. So concerned was the industry that their lobbying grew to outstrip all other industries in the first half of 2022, one leading senator saying that pharma companies had been 'throwing everything but the kitchen sink against this'.[31] A representative of major lobbyist PhRMA sent a chilling message to members of Congress saying that, if they had voted for the bill, they would not 'get a free pass', and warning darkly, 'Few associations have all the tools of modern political advocacy at their disposal in the way PhRMA does.'

At the state level, meanwhile, governments have gone further. Price-hikes on insulin in the United States has forced one in four diabetics to ration their medication. Insulin is available for as little as $32 a vial in Canada, but can cost $300 a vial in the United States.[32] To address this problem, California, Michigan and Maine have all started looking into the public manufacturing of insulin. In Michigan, the proposal was introduced by a Republican. And California has allocated $100 million for the state government to make insulin through a public enterprise at close to cost price, and available to all. The 'People's Insulin' movement could, in the words of science writer Leigh Philips, go far beyond cheap insulin, and begin to 'pry open the door to a revival of large-scale, long-term public investment, economic planning, and social democracy in the twenty-first century'.[33] Interestingly, it's already having an effect on the bigger players, with Ely Lilly promising to slash the costs of its own product by 70 per cent.[34]

According to Maybarduk, 'The really big thing, and you can't overstate how big it is, Pharma has stopped winning. And instead of [our] losing to them, they're in danger of losing to us.' And this is starting to have an impact on the international picture too. One month after I spoke to Maybarduk, Biden made a new pledge. He said a series of technologies developed by the US government would be shared with C-TAP, the patent pool set up by the WHO to help disseminate Covid technologies freely. Maybarduk described the pledge, which amounts to sharing technology rather than just doses, as 'the difference between charity and justice'.[35] He told me, 'There's now widespread popular opposition to the monopoly control of drugs globally. It's really all to play for.'

These seeds of change have implications beyond the pharmaceutical industry. In short, the state is back. No one can deny the level of state intervention and planning during the financial crisis or the Covid-19 pandemic. Heads of state including Modi in India, Trump in the United States, and Johnson in the UK have shown that the use of public funds and state intervention in the economy are not restricted to governments of the left. As market failures have become more common, right-wing governments have used the power of the state to maintain political legitimacy. It is also the case that they can actively use that same power to hand even more power and wealth to private businesses and rich investors. As notions of market infallibility break down, it is important not to see state action as being necessarily progressive in nature.

To this end, we need to build movements behind alternative economic visions. In the United States there is a burgeoning 'anti-trust' movement, building on an early-twentieth-century tradition that eventually saw successive US governments break apart the massive financial, oil, railroad and other monopolies that had become dominant, exploiting and extracting value from American workers, farmers and consumers alike. It is a movement that has a good fit with the fight against Big Pharma.

According to reformers like Zephyr Teachout, if we see corruption as the use of public power for private ends, monopolies are inherently corrupt, as well as having a corrupting effect on academics, scientists, the media and politicians.[36] Yet these monopolies are actively encouraged by the economic rules that have been entrenched over the last forty years. In the last decade, half a million corporate mergers have taken place, allowing corporations to build up an enormous power base that puts them in control of huge swathes of our economy. The main effect of this is massive inequality – and not only economic inequality. In the United States this process of monopolisation has severely eroded black-owned businesses and the free press, instilling fear in small producers, workers and journalists.

Needless to say, this process is profoundly anti-democratic. This is why activists like Teachout see the anti-monopoly movement as a struggle for democracy. This approach has been taken up by parts of the Democratic Party, and is finding its way into the thinking of the White House, where Joe Biden appointed antitrust journalist Lina Khan to chair one of the world's most powerful regulators, the US Federal Trade Commission. According to Nicholas Shaxson and Michelle Meager, this is not a one-off event but part of an exciting new mobilisation that 'has seen the US suddenly streak far ahead of the UK and Europe when it comes to tackling the democracy-warping powers of the world's biggest multinationals. If these gains can be consolidated and extended, and expanded outside the US, it is no exaggeration to say that this could transform our societies and economies for the better.'[37]

In a sweeping executive order in which Biden promised to implement 'full and aggressive enforcement of our antitrust laws', the president commented, 'We're now 40 years into the experiment of letting giant corporations accumulate more and more power . . . I believe that experiment failed.'[38] The headline rule he was introducing allowed the importation of prescription drugs from Canada, in a clear attempt to force down the price of pharmaceuticals in the United States.

This anti-monopoly drive includes a radically new approach to trade laws. In addition to Biden's support for the TRIPS waiver, he has taken a fundamentally different approach to trade than Obama or Clinton, putting workers' rights at the heart of trade policy and proclaiming a desire to reduce vulnerability in a trade system that has been shown to be acutely vulnerable to shocks.

Journalist and writer Barry Lynn, another antitrust campaigner, sums up this vulnerability well: 'Nations are fighting over how to secure vaccines, how to divvy up the production of semiconductors, how to respond to China's mercantilism and militarism, how to manage technology and information monopolists such as Facebook and Google, and even how to share the metals necessary to build the batteries for electric cars.'[39] Lynn is not a protectionist, but recognises that a result of these problems 'has been a surge in calls for governments to introduce protectionist measures, closely manage domestic industries, and pursue new visions of autarky'. Instead, he posits, 'Washington can start by acknowledging that most of the current problems can be traced to a single source: the concentration of control over production and communications in the hands of a few corporations and countries.'

The world trade system needs to be rewired, removing the pro-monopoly, 'free market' utopianism of the Clinton era and replacing it with one that 'break[s] concentrations of power within the international economic system', including by 'eliminat[ing] most of the patent rights of dominant corporations, as it did between the late 1930s and the early 1980s'. That production does not all need to be 'brought home', but it seems reasonable to expect a greater degree of self-sufficiency. Left-wing Democratic Senator Elizabeth Warren certainly agrees with this, and has twice introduced legislation that would boost US-based drug manufacturing. Her July 2020 bill would have raised $1 billion to dramatically upgrade America's national capacity to manufacture important medicines. The change that can reasonably be expected under Biden is more limited; and steps forward are often followed by at least half a step backwards. But what does seem clear is that we have begun to take some cautious steps down a new road.

There are other traditions that can help us refocus our economy, including the idea of the commons. This refers to a very old concept related to the way in which land was owned in England in the Middle Ages. The commons was land that ordinary people had a right to use for sustaining themselves – grazing animals or collecting food, for instance. In recent years the discussion around the commons has broadened. There is a live discussion around the idea of an 'urban commons' – community-owned land that can provide a haven from the over-privatised and marketised spaces that many of our cities have become. On a small scale, this may amount to something like a community garden, but it might also include cooperative services, resource sharing, or even more participatory control over local authority budgets.

Knowledge is particularly conducive to operation as a commons, because it cannot be depleted. When it comes to agriculture, for example, one person's use of firewood prevents its use by others. But with knowledge this does not apply. However much I might use it, there is never any less knowledge for everyone else to use. There are concrete examples of knowledge commons, especially online – most obviously Wikipedia, and open-source software such as the Linux operating system.

A commons-based system is not without rules. If it was, it could quickly end up being depleted, overgrown, or taken and enclosed by a private party. Commons need to be cared for and renewed. The enormous community that Wikipedia depends upon, and the rules that maintain its quality, are an example of such a model. But these rules have a different purpose from the rules of neoliberal capitalism. In fact, many of the rules are precisely concerned with preventing the encroachment of private interests.

In 2020, Duncan McCann wrote a report outlining how intellectual property might be managed as a commons.[40] Like Mazzucato, McCann begins with the irony that, while the Britain's public sector spends over £14.4 billion every year, directly and indirectly, on research and development to meet the challenges we face as a society – often 'challenges that the market is either the primary driver of, or unable to address . . . the state does not recoup anything directly for that investment. The state is left to cross its fingers and hope that it receives a satisfactory return on its investment.'

To redress this problem, McCann proposes the creation of a 'Public IP Commons'. This would mean that the public retained ownership of any IP that had resulted from public research, and that IP being managed in the public interest, to prevent its being taken and effectively privatised by those with the most resources. The body managing the IP would license it out for use on different terms depending on who wanted to use it. For example, a charity or non-profit organisation might be granted a long or perpetual license at little or no cost. A start-up could be given a short lease, with a fee that increased according to its profitability. A bigger company would pay a bigger fee – to be reinvested in research – or be compelled to grant the public an equity share in any product that resulted from the knowledge it had used. The overall purpose would be to maximise the use of knowledge by society at large.

This may seem like a radical proposal, but McCann points out that similar arrangements are common in the private sector, where the work that one is paid to do becomes the employer's property. It could be positive for small pharma companies, which carry out much of the research work that takes place under the current system. Currently, success is defined for such companies in terms of any breakthrough they make being bought up by one of the big players. A commons strategy could ensure a far more balanced, diverse and vibrant sector.

Economist Joseph Stiglitz teamed up with Dean Baker and Arjun Jayadev to argue that 'economic institutions and laws created in the twentieth century, to manage the growth of currently advanced industrialised economies, will be increasingly inadequate to govern global economic activity. Nowhere is this more evident than in the area of intellectual property rights.'[41] Like Mazzucato, they see the intellectual property regime as not simply unfair, but antithetical to innovation, and argue that, in a knowledge economy, we need to share knowledge as widely as possible, and that challenging patents therefore becomes a public good. They give an example of the US Supreme Court ruling against a patent on a gene related to breast cancer, which unleashed a wave of research that had previously been stifled, facilitating the production of better and cheaper tests for breast cancer.

This argument extends well beyond pharmaceuticals. It is only necessary to consider the knowledge required to mitigate climate change, where there is a clear and urgent imperative to learn and share – especially with the countries suffering the worst effects of climate change despite being the least responsible for it. Allowing millions of people to go without medicines simply because the patent holder has no interest in selling to the country where they happen to live is clearly a symptom of a profoundly broken system. Just as concerning, though, is that our system inhibits innovation, knowledge sharing and the development of countries in the Global South, instead perpetuating their impoverishment.

The key message here is simple: take all steps to limit the privatisation and monopolisation of knowledge. At the most basic level, stop giving it away. Given how much medical research is generated with public funds, this alone might make a huge difference. Much of this could also be achieved unilaterally, but we do also need to tackle the global rules that inhibit actions of this sort. While countries like India have pushed for many years for a discussion of intellectual property at UN climate change conferences, rich countries have always refused to engage in that conversation.

Clearly, we have the potential to create a pharmaceutical system fit for the twenty-first century. Elements of such a system would include a research system that uses funding, legislation and public ownership to prioritise the public interest; a patent system based on the dispersal of knowledge and collaboration as widely as possible; a manufacturing system that is internationally dispersed and free from monopoly power. Moreover, these ideas can also be applied to the wider economy – in de-financialising our economies and undermining private monopolies everywhere.

And as we saw throughout the Covid-19 pandemic, some politicians even in major developed countries have started to see the light. After all, they rightly ask: Why should the public contribute tax money to the development of most of the drugs we use while our citizens then cannot afford those same drugs? Why do we remain dependent on a pharmaceutical industry that has slashed investment in the actual production of medicines, therefore rendering ourselves unable to deal with epidemics that might become more frequent in future decades?

The systemic change we need is by no means guaranteed, however. While we reach for the moon, Big Pharma still retains massive power. But there are signs of hope. There is a growing understanding, on the right as well as the left, that handing every decision to the market has failed us, though there is an intense battle over what should replace the neoliberal model. There are more specific sources of hope, too. First, the US government's growing antagonism towards Big Pharma, as well as towards corporate monopolies and free-trade in general. Fatima Hassan told me that, in her experience, this was unprecedented: 'If Biden really takes them on, and he might, this is a game-changer. The US government has seen itself as subservient to this industry up until now.' It will not happen without a struggle, but it is no longer completely out of reach.

Second, there is no forward momentum among the international institutions responsible for handing Big Pharma its power. The WTO is able to make only the weakest of deals and has lost its formal enforcement mechanism. Biden shows little appetite for re-empowering the body. Meanwhile, many deep and far-reaching trade deals that presented such a threat a decade ago have been beaten back, with little to replace them. Following the pandemic, the notion that we need more local, resilient forms of economy now has much greater support. As Matt Kavanagh, director of Georgetown University's Global Health Policy and Politics initiative, says, 'I think there's a real threat to the legitimacy of the World Trade Organization and the TRIPS agreement overall . . . There's a very significant chance that in the years to come after Covid-19, there will be a lessening of commitment to actually engage the WTO.'[42] The challenge will be finding agreement on a model to replace it; at a time when international cooperation is desperately needed, we must not confine ourselves to removing a set of rules and institutions, but also build support to develop a basis for real cooperation. Without this, hyper-globalisation might just as easily be replaced by authoritarianism and widening conflict.

Third, governments of the Global South have received a clear wake-up call: neither the West nor big business will save you in a crisis. There is a renewed energy for South–South cooperation, best encapsulated in the development of the mRNA Hub. But the challenge will need to go much deeper than that. Governments of low-income countries will need to be courageous, united and far-sighted if they are to overcome the prevailing system; given the current composition of the governments of some of the largest of those countries, this represents a challenge, to say the least.

The final piece of the pandemic story that can give us some hope comes from the growing backlash against inequality. For most of my adult life, criticising a billionaire philanthropist like Bill Gates would have brought an immediate accusation of ingratitude. Surely, people who give away vast sums of their wealth are to be praised! Today, after living with the consequences of this system, people feel differently. That is largely the result of a huge amount of work on inequality by NGOs like Oxfam, as well as campaigners in the tax justice movement and the grassroots movements like Occupy and the campaigns that succeeded it. There is a growing belief that global health policy should not be dictated by the world's richest men – in fact the recipients of this largesse are often the most critical, albeit also fearful. The more the world's superrich throw their weight around, the more social networks they purchase, the more they launch themselves into space from a planet on which their own workers need to take two or three jobs to make ends meet, the worse this mood will become.

This is positive development, firstly because such inequality is inseparable from poverty. One person's wealth is another's exploitation. But it is also positive because the idea that the philanthropist knows best should have been put behind us long ago. It is incompatible with the idea that living a good life should be based on a set of rights we can all enjoy, and at odds with democracy itself.

Of course, this is all still a site of huge struggle and contradiction. Els Torreele cautions against excessive optimism, telling me, 'The global health architecture has been a total failure in driving health equity during the pandemic, but for some reason they've managed to portray this as a success.' She points out that high-level discussions are currently focused on creating a 'Covax 2.0', cementing the public–private–philanthropic model as a permanent means of confronting pandemics. Those driving such a solution – mostly powerful white men based in the developed world – believe the only problem with the way the world dealt with the pandemic was that it was not fast enough. But, as Torreele tells me, speed was not the problem: we have never seen such rapid vaccine development. The problem was equity, and a greater speed of response will not resolve that. In fact, it may simply accelerate the problem.

The future has not been written. Only serious public mobilisation can hope to dislodge the status quo, nurturing positive developments and taking them further. Thus, there is no reason to be complacent, but there are reasons to be hopeful. Fatima Hassan says that, during the HIV/Aids crisis, huge mobilisation did eventually manage to get medicines to those who needed them, but that nothing changed in terms of the wider model. This time, 'there's a much greater understanding that there's something fundamentally wrong when pharmaceutical CEOs can decide on supplies, and delivery dates and which places are allowed to benefit; on who gets to live and who doesn't. The conversation is very different this time.'

Tahir Amin agrees:

> A lot of people actually feel defeated today. It's like the financial crisis, where people feel the system proved its own failings on a big scale, but capitalism came back stronger than it was before. But I think change takes longer; it will happen. This is a monumental moment, and even if capitalism's hold on this looks strong now, it will change. Yes, there are things to worry about, like the tech industry's interest in healthcare. But really the big question is: Do governments have the courage to really take this to where it needs to go? How can we pressure them to make sure they do?[43]

Notes

Introduction: Bad Apples

1 David Crow, 'Pfizer Chief Albert Bourla: "We Are the Most Efficient Vaccine Machine" ', *Financial Times*, 13 August 2021.

2 Justin McCarthy, 'Big Pharma Sinks to the Bottom of US Industry Rankings', *Gallup*, 3 September 2019; Charlotte Hu, 'These Are the Most – and Least – Reputable Drug Companies in the US', *Business Insider*, 19 June 2018.

3 Hannah Kuchler, Donato Paolo Mancini and David Pilling, 'The Inside Story of the Pfizer Vaccine: "A Once-in-an-Epoch Windfall" ', *Financial Times*, 30 November 2021.

4 Crow, 'Pfizer Chief Albert Bourla: "We Are the Most Efficient Vaccine Machine" '.

5 Anjalee Khemlani, 'Pfizer: "No Issues" in Testing for COVID-19 Kid Vaccine as Delta Variant Rises', *Yahoo News*, 28 July 2021.

6 Crow, 'Pfizer Chief Albert Bourla: "We Are the Most Efficient Vaccine Machine" '.

7 Kuchler et al., 'Inside Story of the Pfizer Vaccine'.

8 Rohit Malpani and Alex Maitland, 'Dose of Reality: How Rich Countries and Pharmaceutical Corporations Are Breaking Their Vaccine Promises', *People's Vaccine*, 21 October 2021, at peoplesvaccine.org.

9 'Pfizer, BioNTech and Moderna making $1,000 Profit Every Second While World's Poorest Countries Remain Largely Unvaccinated', *People's Vaccine*, 16 November 2021, at peoplesvaccine.org.

10 *People's Vaccine*, 'COVID Vaccines Create 9 New Billionaires with Combined Wealth Greater than Cost of Vaccinating World's Poorest Countries', 20 May 2021, at peoplesvaccine.org.
11 Ceri Thomas, 'Pfizer's War', *Tortoise Media*, 27 September 2021, at tortoisemedia.com.
12 Kuchler et al., 'Inside Story of the Pfizer Vaccine'.
13 Madlen Davies, Rosa Furneaux, Iván Ruiz, Jill Langlois, ' "Held to Ransom": Pfizer Demands Governments Gamble with State Assets to Secure Vaccine Deal', *Bureau of Investigative Journalism*, 23 February 2021, at thebureauinvestigates.com.
14 Thomas, 'Pfizer's war'.
15 Kuchler et al., 'Inside Story of the Pfizer Vaccine'.
16 Thomas, 'Pfizer's War'.
17 Kuchler et al., 'Inside Story of the Pfizer Vaccine'.
18 'Moderna Vaccine Belongs to the People', *Public Citizen*, 16 November 2020; *People's Vaccine*, 'COVID Vaccines Create 9 New Billionaires'.
19 Nurith Aizenman, 'Moderna Won't Share Its Vaccine Recipe', *NPR*, 19 October 2021.
20 Rebecca Robbins and Benjamin Mueller, 'Covid Vaccines Produced in Africa Are Being Exported to Europe', *New York Times*, 16 August 2021.
21 Manas Mishra and Michael Erman, 'Gilead Asks FDA to Take Back Lucrative Orphan Drug Status on Possible Coronavirus Treatment', Reuters, 25 March 2020.
22 See, for example, Billy Kenber, *Sick Money: The Truth About the Global Pharmaceutical Industry* (Edinburgh: Canongate, 2021).
23 'Public Accounts Committee (Reports) Volume 650', *Hansard*, 30 Novmber 1961.
24 Bethany McLean, 'Everything You Know About Martin Shkreli Is Wrong – or Is It?', *Vanity Fair*, 18 December 2015.
25 Dan Diamond 'Martin Shkreli Admits He Messed Up: He Should've Raised Prices Even Higher', *Forbes*, 3 December 2015.
26 Matthew Herper, 'Solving Pharma's Shkreli Problem', *Forbes*, 20 January 2016.
27 Eliana Dockterman, 'Former Drug CEO Martin Shkreli Is Getting New Lawyers', *Time*, 19 January 2016; Kate Gibson, 'Martin Shkreli: I Should've "Raised Prices Higher" ', *CBS*, 4 December 2015.
28 McLean, 'Everything You Know About Martin Shkreli Is Wrong'.
29 Alexander Zaitchik, 'Long, Strange TRIPS: The Grubby History of How Vaccines Became Intellectual Property', *New Republic*, 1 June 2021.

30 'South Africa vs. the Drug Giants: A Challenge to Affordable Medicines', Oxfam, February 2001, at oxfamilibrary.openrepository.com.

31 Ed Vulliamy, 'How Drug Giants Let Millions Die of Aids', *Guardian*, 19 December 1999.

32 Ibid.

1. A History of Scandal

1 Joanna Walters, 'I Don't Know How They Live with Themselves – Artist Nan Goldin Takes On the Billionaire Family Behind OxyContin', *Guardian*, 22 January 2018.

2 Nan Goldin, *Artforum*, January 2018.

3 Ibid.

4 Walters, 'I Don't Know How They Live with Themselves'.

5 Alex Morrell, 'The OxyContin Clan: The $14 Billion Newcomer to Forbes 2015 List of Richest US Families', *Forbes*, 1 July 2015.

6 Ibid.

7 Patrick Radden Keefe, 'The Family that Built an Empire of Pain', *New Yorker*, 23 October 2017.

8 Ibid.

9 Peter Fuhrman, 'Roche Kicks Its Valium Dependence', *Forbes*, 21 March 1994.

10 Editorial, 'Senate Panel Is Told of Dangers of Valium Abuse', *New York Times,* 11 September 1979.

11 Keefe, 'Family that Built an Empire of Pain'.

12 Chris McGreal, 'Rudy Giuliani Won Deal for OxyContin Maker to Continue Sales of Drug behind Opioid Deaths', *Guardian*, 22 May 2018.

13 Centers for Disease Control and Prevention, 'Prescription Opioid Overdose Death Maps', at cdc.gov.

14 Katherine Ellen Foley, 'John Oliver Blames "Reckless, Greedy" American Drug Companies for the Country's Deadly Opioid Crisis', *Quartz*, 24 October 2016, at qz.com.

15 Art Van Zee, 'The Promotion and Marketing of OxyContin: Commercial Triumph, Public Health Tragedy', *American Journal of Public Health*, February 2009.

16 '28 ODs in 4 Hours: How the Heroin Epidemic Choked a W.Va. City', *CBS News*, 4 September 2016.

17 McGreal, 'Rudy Giuliani Won Deal for OxyContin Maker'.

18 Stanford–Lancet Commission, 'Responding to the Opioid Crisis in North America and Beyond', *Lancet* 399: 10,324 (5 February 2005).

19 Morrell, 'The OxyContin Clan'.

20 Katherine Ellen Foley, 'Big Pharma Is Taking Advantage of Patent Law to Keep OxyContin from Ever Dying', *Quartz*, 18 November 2017, at qz.com.

21 Zach Coleman, 'China Rises as Key Market for Leading Opioid Producer', *Nikkei Asia*, 15 January 2019.

22 Erika Kinetz, 'Fake Doctors, Misleading Claims Drive OxyContin China Sales', *AP*, 20 November 2019.

23 Harriet Ryan, Lisa Girion and Scott Glover, 'OxyContin Goes Global – "We're Only Just Getting Started" ', *Los Angeles Times*, 18 December 2016.

24 Stanford–Lancet Commission, 'Responding to the Opioid Crisis'.

25 Ibid.

26 Jessica Glenza, 'Opioid Overdose Deaths to "Grow Exponentially" without Action – Study', *Guardian*, 2 February 2022; Ryan et al., 'OxyContin Goes Global'.

27 Ryan et al., 'OxyContin Goes Global'.

28 Berkeley Lovelace, Jr., 'Purdue Pharma Chair: Best Way to Fight Opioid Crisis is for OxyContin Maker to Stay in Business', *CNBC*, 16 September 2019.

29 Kristina Sgueglia and Allen Kim, 'Tufts University to Remove Sackler Name from Buildings and Programs', *CNN*, 6 December 2019.

30 Geoff Mulvihill, 'Judge Rejects Purdue Pharma's Sweeping Opioid Settlement', *AP*, 17 December 2021.

31 Stanford–Lancet Commission, 'Responding to the Opioid Crisis'

32 Billy Kenber, *Sick Money* (Edinburgh: Canongate, 2021).

33 For more on this, see Chapter 2, below.

34 Author interview with Diarmaid MacDonald, 27 January 2022.

35 Stanford–Lancet Commission, 'Responding to the Opioid Crisis'.

36 Glenza, 'Opioid Overdose Deaths to "Grow Exponentially"'.

37 Lev Facher, 'More than Two-Thirds of Congress Cashed a Pharma Campaign Check in 2020, New STAT Analysis Shows', *StatNews*, 9 June 2021, at statnews.com.

38 'Big Pharma's Lobbying Firepower in Brussels: At Least €36 Million a Year (and Likely Far More)', *Corporate Europe Observatory*, 31 May 2021.

39 Stanford–Lancet Commission, 'Responding to the Opioid Crisis'.

40 Pew Prescription Project, 'Persuading the Prescribers: Pharmaceutical Industry Marketing and Its Influence on Physicians and Patients', 11 November 2013, at pewtrusts.org.

41 Sarah Boseley, 'Drug Companies Pay Doctors £40m for Travel and Expenses', *Guardian*, 5 April 2013.

42 Ray Moynihan and David Henry, 'Selling Sickness: The Pharmaceutical Industry and Disease Mongering, *British Medical Journal*, 13 April 2002.

43 Dominique Tobbell, *Pills, Power, and Policy: The Struggle for Drug Reform in Cold War America and Its Consequences* (Oakland, CA: University of California Press, 2011), p. 84.

44 Jay Hancock, 'Talk About Déjà Vu: Senators Set to Re-Enact Drug Price Hearing of 60 Years Ago', *Kaiser Health News*, 22 February 2019.

45 Tobbell, *Pills, Power, and Policy*, p. 92.

46 Keefe, 'Family that Built an Empire of Pain'.

47 T. Joseph Mattingly II, 'Kennedy, Kefauver, And Castro: A Historical Lesson on the Politics of Drug Pricing Reform', *Health Affairs*, 1 November 2021.

48 Ibid.

49 Author interview with Tahir Amin, 6 February 2022.

50 Colleen V. Chien, 'The Inequalities of Innovation', Santa Clara University School of Law, *72 Emory Law. Journal 1 (2022)*, 16 June 2022.

51 Ellen 't Hoen, 'Private Patents and Public Health: Changing Intellectual Property Rules for Access to Medicines', Health Action International, 2016, at haiweb.org.

52 C. T. Taylor, Z. A. Silberston and Aubrey Silberston, *The Economic Impact of the Patent System: A Study of the British Experience* (Cambridge: Cambridge University Press, 1973).

53 Hansard, vol. 293 cc1127–31, 'The Pharmaceutical Industry: The Sainsbury Report', 24 June 1968.

54 Hansard, vol 341 cc786–91, 'Tranquillisers: Monopolies Commission Report', 12 April 1973.

55 Tobbell, *Pills, Power, and Policy*, p. 9.

56 Nancy Olivieri, 'How John le Carré Changed My Life', *Toronto Star*, 22 December 2020.

57 David Healy, 'Repetition Compulsion to the Death or Beyond?', 29 March 2020, at davidhealy.org.

58 Jon Thompson, Patricia Baird and Jocelyn Downie, 'Report of the Committee of Inquiry on the Case Involving Dr Nancy Olivieri, the

Hospital for Sick Children, the University of Toronto and Apotex Inc.', Canadian Association of University Teachers, 2001.

59 Arthur Schafer, 'Institutional Conflict of Interest: Attempting to Crack the Deferiprone Mystery, *Journal of Medical Ethics*, 8 January 2020.

60 Arthur Schafer, 'Biomedical Conflicts of Interest: A Defence of the Sequestration Thesis – Learning from the Cases of Nancy Olivieri and David Healy', *Journal of Medical Ethics* 30: 1, 2004, 8–24.

61 Anne Kingston and Michael Friscolanti, 'The Other Side of Barry Sherman', *Macleans*, 5 April 2018, at macleans.ca.

62 Shafer, 'Biomedical Conflicts of Interest'.

63 Nancy Olivieri, 'Nothing Is Right about the Approval of Aducanumab – and Nothing's New', *British Medical Journal*, 4 November 2021.

64 Ibid.

65 C. Michael White, 'Why Is the FDA Funded in Part by the Companies It Regulates?', *University of Connecticut School of Pharmacy*, 21 May 2021.

66 Caroline Chen, 'FDA Repays Industry by Rushing Risky Drugs to Market', *ProPublica*, 26 June 2018.

67 Dianna Melrose, *Bitter Pills: Medicines and the Third World Poor* (London: Oxfam, 1982).

68 Melrose, 'Bitter Pills', p. 27.

69 Melrose, 'Bitter Pills', p. 1.

70 Melrose, 'Bitter Pills', p. 67.

71 *The Mark Thomas Comedy Product*, Series 6, Episode 2: 'Drug Dumping', 3 April 2002 (Vera Productions).

72 Joe Stephens, 'Where Profits and Lives Hang in Balance', *Washington Post*, 17 December 2000.

73 *Dying for Drugs*, dir. Brian Woods (2005).

74 Stephens, 'Where Profits and Lives Hang in Balance'.

75 Jeanne Lenzer, 'Secret Report Surfaces Showing that Pfizer Was at Fault in Nigerian Drug Tests', *British Medical Journal*, 27 May 2006.

76 David Smith, 'Pfizer Pays Out to Nigerian Families of Meningitis Drug Trial Victims', *Guardian*, 12 August 2011.

77 Lenzer, 'Secret Report Surfaces Showing that Pfizer Was at Fault'.

78 Ibrahim Garba and Danielle Paquette, 'In This Nigerian City, Pfizer Fears Loom Over the Vaccine Rollout', *Washington Post* 20 March 2021.

79 Stephens, 'Where Profits and Lives Hang in Balance'.

80 Tobbell, *Pills, Power, and Policy*, p. 187.

81 Thomas Hanna, Miriam Brett and Dana Brown, 'Democratising Knowledge: Transforming Intellectual Property and R&D', CommonWealth, 19 September 2020, at common-wealth.co.uk.

82 Stanford–Lancet Commission, 'Responding to the Opioid Crisis'.

83 Stanford–Lancet Commission, 'Responding to the Opioid Crisis'.

84 Author interview with Diarmaid MacDonald.

2. A Hedge Fund with a Pharmaceutical Firm Attached

1 David Teather, 'Ambition Topples the "Genius" Who Transformed Porsche's Fortunes', *Guardian*, 23 June 2009.

2 Blake Hounshell, 'Porsche Makes More Money from Options Trading than from Cars', *Foreign Policy*, 14 November 2007.

3 Emily Hughes, 'Fast Bucks: How Porsche Made Billions', *BBC News*, 22 January 2009.

4 Rohin Dhar, 'Porsche: The Hedge Fund That Also Made Cars', *Priceonomics*, 24 October 2014.

5 Ibid.

6 Siobhán Dowling, 'Wiedeking Is to Blame for the Porsche Disaster', *Spiegel International*, 24 July 2009.

7 My ideas on financialisation are heavily influenced by Emma Dowling and David Harvie, e.g. 'Harnessing the Social: State, Crisis and (Big) Society', *Sociology* 48: 5, 2014, 869–86.

8 Frances Thomson and Sahil Dutta, 'Financialisation: A Primer', Transnational Institute, 13 October 2018, at tni.org.

9 Vitor Gaspar, Paulo Medas and Roberto Perrelli, 'Global Debt Reaches a Record $226 Trillion', IMF Blog, 15 December 2021, at imf.org.

10 See, for example, Maurizio Lazzarato, *The Making of the Indebted Man*, (Cambridge, MA: MIT Press, 2012).

11 Andrew Baker, Colin Haslam, Adam Leaver, Richard Murphy, Leonard Seabrooke, Saila Stausholm and Duncan Wigan, 'Against Hollow Firms: Repurposing The Corporation For A More Resilient Economy', Centre for Research on Accounting and Finance in Context, University of Sheffield, 2020.

12 Colin Haslam, Adam Leaver, Richard Murphy and Nick Tsitsianis, 'Assessing the Impact of Shareholder Primacy and Value Extraction', Productivity Insights Network Blog, 2021, at productivityinsightsnetwork.co.uk.

13 My calculations.

14 Rodrigo Fernandez and Tobias J. Klinge, 'Private Gains We Can Ill Afford: The Financialisation of Big Pharma', SOMO, April 2020, at somo.nl.

15 Ken Garber, 'The Cancer Drug that Almost Wasn't', *Science*, 22 August 2014.

16 Derek Lowe, 'The Palbociclib Saga: Or Why We Need a Lot of Drug Companies', *Science*, 22 August 2014.

17 Fernandez et al., 'Private Gains We Can Ill Afford'.

18 I-MAK, 'Overpatented, Overpriced: How Excessive Pharmaceutical Patenting Is Extending Monopolies and Driving Up Drug Prices', August 2018, at i-mak.org.

19 Luke Goldstein, 'Rollups: The Emerging Magic Mushroom Monopoly', *American Prospect*, 10 January 2022.

20 Ibid.

21 Baker et al., 'Against Hollow Firms'.

22 Ibid.

23 Adam Leaver and Richard Murphy, 'Financial Engineering and the Productivity Crisis', Productivity Insights Network, 2020, at productivityinsightsnetwork.co.uk.

24 Tom Dickinson, 'Katie Porter Delivers Another Knockout Punch', *Rolling Stone*, 19 May 2021.

25 Eric Sagonowsky, 'AbbVie, Already Famous for Its Humira Strategy, Forms Another "Patent Wall" Around Imbruvica', *Fierce Pharma*, 21 July 2020, at fiercepharma.com.

26 I-MAK, 'Overpatented, Overpriced'.

27 Leo Ewbank, Kane Sullivan, Helen McKenna and David Omojomolo 'The Rising Cost of Medicines to the NHS: What's the Story?', King's Fund, 26 April 2018, at kingsfund.org.uk.

28 Morten Thaysen, 'Rising Drug Prices Are Now More than Twice the Entire NHS Deficit', Global Justice Now, 18 May 2017, at globaljustice.org.uk.

29 Digital NHS, 'Prescribing Costs in Hospitals and the Community 2019–2020', 12 November 2020, at digital.nhs.uk.

30 Karen Davis, Kristof Stremikis, David Squires and Cathy Schoen, 'Mirror, Mirror on the Wall: How the Performance of the US Health Care System Compares Internationally', Commonwealth Fund, June 2014, at commonwealthfund.org.

31 Press Release, 'Prescription Drug Prices in the United States Are 2.56 Times Those in Other Countries', Rand Corporation, 28 January 2021.

32 Staff Report, 'Drug Pricing Investigation: Industry Spending on Buybacks, Dividends, and Executive Compensation', Committee on Oversight and Reform, US House of Representatives, July 2021.

33 David Moore, 'Pharma Companies Spend Billions More on Stock Buybacks than Developing Drugs', *American Prospect*, 15 July 2021.

34 Fernandez, 'Private Gains We Can Ill Afford'.

35 Robert King, 'House Dems' Report Slams Drugmaker Stock Buybacks as Pelosi Presses to Give Medicare Negotiating Powers', *Fierce Pharma*, 9 July 2021, at fiercepharma.com.

36 Committee on Oversight and Reform, 'Drug Pricing Investigation'.

37 Ibid.

38 Ned Pagliarulo, 'How Biotech and Pharma Companies Pay Their CEOs, and Their Workers', *BioPharmaDive*, 8 September 2020, at biopharmadive.com.

39 William Lazonick, Öner Tulum, Matt Hopkins, Mustafa Erdem Sakinç and Ken Jacobson, 'Financialization of the US Pharmaceutical Industry', Academic-Industry Research Network, 2 December 2019.

40 Shayla Love, 'Psychedelic Patents are Broken Because the Patent System Is Broken', *Vice*, 9 May 2022.

41 Luke Hawksbee, Martin McKee and Lawrence King, 'Don't Worry About the Drug Industry's Profits when Considering a Waiver on Covid-19 Intellectual Property Rights', *British Medical Journal*, 31 January 2022.

42 Mariana Mazzucato, 'The People's Prescription: Re-imagining Health Innovation to Deliver Public Value', UCL Institute for Innovation and Public Purpose, October 2018.

43 Billy Kenber, 'From Cancer to Rare Diseases, Big Pharma Puts Profit Before Patients when Deciding on New Drugs', *I News*, 12 October 2021, at inews.co.uk.

44 Mazzucato, 'People's Prescription'.

45 Ibid.

46 William Lazonick, 'Big Pharma Spends on Share Buybacks, but R&D? Not So Much', *New York Times*, 14 July 2017.

47 Lazonick et al., 'Financialization of the US Pharmaceutical Industry'.

48 Emily H. Jung, Alfred Engelberg and Aaron S. Kesselheim, 'Do Large Pharma Companies Provide Drug Development Innovation? Our Analysis Says No', *StatNews*, 10 December 2019, at statnews.com.

49 'Research and Development in the Pharmaceutical Industry', Congressional Budget Office, April 2021, at cbo.gov.

50 AbbVie, '2018 Annual Report on Form 10-K and 2019 Notice of Annual Meeting and Proxy Statement', investors.abbvie.com/static-files/47b78f29-de86-46fd-ae82-83878c1a72f1.

51 Billy Kenber, *Sick Money: The Truth about the Global Pharmaceutical Industry* (Edinburgh: Canongate, 2021), pp. 283–4.

52 Niko Lusiani, 'Hazardous to Your Health: How the Trump Tax Cuts to Big Pharma Widen Inequality and Undermine the Health of Women and Girls', Oxfam America, 9 April 2019, at oxfam.org.

53 Marc Iskowitz, 'Cash-Rich Biopharmas About to Go on a Shopping Spree', Haymarket Marketing Communications, 16 December 2021, at mmm-online.com.

54 Silke Koltrowitz, 'Cash-Flush Novartis Launches New Share Buyback of Up to $15 Bln', Reuters, 16 December 2021; Fraiser Kansteiner, 'Bristol-Myers Squibb, After Massive Celgene Takeover, Plots $15B Buyback Plan', *Fierce Pharma*, 13 December 2021, at fiercepharma.com.

55 Hawksbee et al., 'Don't Worry about the Drug Industry's Profits'.

56 Ibid.

57 Fred D. Ledley, Sarah Shonka McCoy and Gregory Vaughan, 'Profitability of Large Pharmaceutical Companies Compared With Other Large Public Companies', JAMA Network, 3 March 2020, at jamanetwork.com.

58 Robert Frank, 'The Wealthiest 10% of Americans Own a Record 89% of all US stocks', *CNBC*, 18 October 2019; Juliana Kaplan and Andy Kiersz, 'The Wealthiest Americans Now Own Almost All of the Stock Market – 89% to Be Exact', *Business Insider*, 19 October 2021.

59 Julia Horowitz, 'Inequality in America Was Huge Before the Pandemic. The Stock Market Is Making It Worse', *CNN*, 17 June 2020.

60 Kenber, *Sick Money*, p. 180.

61 Ibid., Chapter 6.

62 Ibid., p. 183.

63 James Angel, Nick Dearden and Heidi Chow, 'The Horrible History of Big Pharma: Why We Can't Leave Pharmaceutical Corporations in the Driving Seat of the Covid-19 Response', *Global Justice Now*, 18 December 2020.

64 Press Release, 'CMA Fines Pfizer and Flynn £90 Million for Drug Price Hike to NHS', UK Competition and Markets Authority, 7 December 2016, at gov.uk.

65 Competition and Markets Authority vs Flynn Pharma, Royal Courts of Justice Court of Appeal, Case No. C3/2018/1847 & 1874, 10 March 2020.
66 Press Release, 'CMA Accuses Pharma Firms of Illegal Pricing', *UK Competition and Markets Authority*, 5 August 2021.
67 Jillian Ambrose, 'Pfizer and Flynn Accused of Overcharging NHS for Anti-Epilepsy Drugs, *Guardian*, 5 August 2021.
68 Matthew Herper, 'Pfizer's CEO Faces the Drug Pricing Firestorm', *Forbes*, 13 October 2015.
69 Andrew Ward, 'Ian Read: The Pragmatist Out to Transform the Drugs Industry', *Financial Times*, 2 May 2014.
70 Öner Tulum, 'Innovation and Financialization in the US Biopharmaceutical Industry', University of Ljubljana Faculty of Economics, doctoral dissertation, 2018.
71 Jennifer Rankin, 'Pfizer Ends Attempt to Buy AstraZeneca', *Guardian*, 26 May 2014; Matthew Herper, 'Pfizer's CEO Faces the Drug Pricing Firestorm', *Forbes*, 13 October 2015.
72 William Lazonick, Matt Hopkins, Ken Jacobson, Mustafa Erdem Sakinç and Öner Tulum, 'US Pharma's Financialized Business Model', *Institute for New Economic Thinking*, Working Paper No. 60, 13 July 2017.
73 Ransdell Pierson, Bill Berkrot, 'Pfizer to Buy Allergan in $160 Billion Deal', Reuters, 24 November 2015.
74 Caroline Humer, Ankur Banerjee, 'Pfizer, Allergan Scrap $160 Billion Deal after US Tax Rule Change', Reuters, 6 April 2016.
75 Lazonick et al., 'Financialization of the US Pharmaceutical industry'.
76 William Lazonick and Öner Tulum, 'Global Tax Dodging Just One Part of Pfizer's Corrupt Business Model', *Institute for New Economic Thinking*, 3 December 2015, at ineteconomics.org.
77 My calculations based on Pfizer's annual report data, 2016–20.
78 Jeffrey Sachs, 'The Cure for Gilead', *Huffington Post*, 3 August 2015.
79 Lazonick et al., 'US Pharma's Financialized Business Model'.
80 Sarah Boseley, 'Hepatitis C Drug Delayed by NHS Due to High Cost', *Guardian*, 16 January 2015.
81 *Just Treatment*, 'Solidarity, Progress and System Change', 15 March 2019, at justtreatment.org.
82 *Just Treatment*, 'Michelle's Story', 16 February 2018, at justtreatment.org.
83 'Briefing, Pharma 101: A Primer', *Public Citizen*, 6 August 2019, at citizen.org.
84 Steven Knievel, 'How Much Is Enough for Gilead?', *Public Citizen*, 5 August 2015, at citizen.org.

85 Sachs, 'Cure for Gilead'; Press Release, 'Gilead Loses Monopoly Control of Its Blockbuster Hepatitis C Medicine in China', Médecins Sans Frontières, 16 August 2018, at msfaccess.org.

86 Press Release, 'Wyden Press Conference Remarks on Investigation into Gilead's Pricing of Hepatitis Drug Sovaldi', US Senate Committee on Finance, 1 December 2015.

87 Angel et al., 'Horrible History of Big Pharma'.

88 Ed Silverman, 'Gilead Pricing for Sovaldi Hepatitis C Drug Slammed by Senators', *Stat News*, 1 December 2015, at statnews.com

89 William Rice and Frank Clemente, 'Gilead Sciences: Price Gouger, Tax Dodge', *Americans for Tax Fairness*, July 2017.

90 Sachs, 'Cure for Gilead'.

91 Fact sheet, 'Gilead's Chronic Hepatitis C Treatment Restrictions', *Médecins Sans Frontières*, March 2015, at msfaccess.org.

92 *Just Treatment*, 'Michelle's Story'.

93 My calculations based on Gilead's annual report data, 2016–20.

94 Kyle Blankenship 'The Top 20 Drugs by Global Sales in 2019', *Fierce Pharma*, 27 July 2020, at fiercepharma.com.

95 Dzintars Gotham, Chris Redd, Morten Thaysen, Tabitha Ha, Heidi Chow and Katy Athersuch 'Pills and Profits: How Drug Companies Make a Killing Out of Public Research', Global Justice Now/Stop Aids, October 2017, at stopaids.org.uk.

96 Committee on Oversight and Reform, 'Drug Pricing Investigation Industry Spending on Buybacks, Dividends, and Executive Compensation', Staff Report, US House of Representatives, July 2021, at oversightdemocrats.house.gov.

97 Ibid.

98 Sally Turner, 'Humira: The Highs and Lows of the World's Best-Selling Drug', *Pharmaceutical Technology*, 4 September 2020; Blake Brittain, 'AbbVie Wins Appeal in Antitrust Case over Humira "Patent Thicket" ', Reuters, 2 August 2022.

99 Committee on Oversight and Reform, 'Drug Pricing Investigation'.

100 Gotham, et al., 'Pills and Profits'.

101 Committee on Oversight and Reform, 'Drug Pricing Investigation'.

102 My calculations based on AbbVie's annual report data 2016–20.

103 Dan Mangan, 'Judge Rejects Bid by "Pharma Bro" Martin Shkreli to Delay Paying More than $24.6 Million in FTC Lawsuit Related to Medication', *CNBC*, 17 March 2022; James Langton, 'SEC Hits Martin

Shkreli with Director and Officer Ban', *Investment Executive*, 28 February 2022.

104 Jan Hoffman, 'Sacklers and Purdue Pharma Reach New Deal with States Over Opioids', *New York Times*, 3 March 2022; News Agencies, 'Opioid Crisis Victims Confront Purdue Pharma's Sackler Family', *Al Jazeera*, 10 March 2022.

3. It Was Greed, My Friends

1 Press Association, ' "Greed" and "Capitalism" Helped UK's Vaccines Success, Says PM', BBC News, 24 March 2021.

2 Laura Kuenssberg, 'PM's Vaccines Comments Set Tongues Wagging', BBC News, 24 March 2021.

3 Boris Johnson, 'Boris Johnson's Keynote Speech – We're Getting On with the Job', The Conservative Party, 6 October 2021, at conservatives.com.

4 For example, Mike Davis, *The Monster at Our Door: The Global Threat of Avian Flu* (New York: New Press, 2005), pp 18–24.

5 Karl Polanyi, *The Great Transformation* (New York: Farrar & Rinehart, 1944).

6 Press Release, 'Ten Richest Men Double Their Fortunes in Pandemic While Incomes of 99 Percent of Humanity Fall', *Oxfam International*, 17 January 2022, at oxfam.org.

7 Mike Davis, *Late Victorian Holocausts: El Niño Famines and the Making of the Third World* (London: Verso, 2000).

8 Davis, *Monster at Our Door.*

9 Eric Levitz. 'Why Humanity Will Probably Botch the Next Pandemic, Too', *New York Magazine*, 30 April 2020.

10 Uri Friedman, 'We Were Warned', *Atlantic*, 18 March 2020.

11 Robin Marantz Henig, 'Experts Warned of a Pandemic Decades Ago. Why Weren't We Ready?' *National Geographic*, 8 April 2020.

12 Charlotte Kilpatrick, 'COVID-19 Has Shown How Big Pharma Is Broken', *Salon*, 20 February 2021.

13 Ibid.

14 Author interview with Zain Rizvi of Public Citizen, 11 March 2022.

15 James Hazel, 'R&D for COVID-19 Has Increased, Yet Other Pandemic Risks Go Unaddressed', Access to Medicine Foundation, 2021, at accesstomedicinefoundation.org.

16 Ellen 't Hoen, 'Coronavirus: The Latest Problem Big Pharma Won't Solve', *Barron's*, 7 February 2020, at barrons.com.

17 David Cox, 'A Covid Breakthrough Could Fix the Broken Economics of Vaccines', *Wired*, 27 April 2021.

18 Jessica Davis Pluess, 'With No Prospects for Profits, Big Pharma Neglects New Infectious Diseases', SwissInfo, 6 March 2020, at swissinfo.ch.

19 Helen Branswell, 'Who will answer the call in the next outbreak? Drug makers feel burned by string of vaccine pleas', *StatNews,* 11 January 2018.

20 Mike Ludwig, 'Big Pharma's Blindspot: Before COVID-19, Vaccine and Antiviral Research Went Neglected', *Salon*, 25 April 2020, at salon.com.

21 Tahir Amin, Rohit Malpani, 'Covid-19 Has Exposed the Limits of the Pharmaceutical Market Model', *StatNews*, 19 May 2020, at statnews.com.

22 Clive Cookson and Tim Bradshaw 'Davos Launch for Coalition to Prevent Epidemics of Emerging Viruses', *Financial Times*, 18 January 2017.

23 Francis Collins, 'NIH at 80: Sharing a Timeless Message from President Roosevelt', National Institutes of Health, 29 October 2020, at directors-blog.nig.gov.

24 Ekaterina Galkina Cleary, Jennifer M. Beierlein, Navleen Surjit Khanuja, Laura M. McNamee and Fred D. Ledley 'Contribution of NIH Funding to New Drug Approvals 2010–2016', PNAS, 12 February 2018, at pnas.org.

25 Jim Dryden, 'Cutting NIH Budget Could Cripple Drug Development', Washington University School of Medicine in St Louis, 16 November 2017, at medicine.wustl.edu.

26 Robin Seaton Jefferson, 'How the Largest Public Funder of Biomedical Research in the World Spends Your Money', *Forbes*, 21 December 2018.

27 Dryden, 'Cutting NIH Budget Could Cripple Drug Development'.

28 Ibid.

29 James Angel, Nick Dearden and Heidi Chow, 'The Horrible History of Big Pharma: Why We Can't Leave Pharmaceutical Corporations in the Driving Seat of the Covid-19 Response', *Global Justice Now*, 18 December 2020.

30 Daniel Boffey, 'Exclusive: Big Pharma Rejected EU Plan to Fast-Track Vaccines in 2017', *Guardian*, 25 May 2020; Renewable Carbon News, 'In the Name of Innovation: Industry Controls Billions in EU Research Funding, De-Prioritises the Public Interest', 3 June 2020, at renewable-carbon.eu.

31 Author interview.

32 Stephanie Baker and Cynthia Koons, 'Inside Operation Warp Speed's $18 Billion Sprint for a Vaccine', Bloomberg, 29 October 2020.

33 Ibid.

34 Ibid.

35 Adam Leaver and Richard Murphy, 'Financial Engineering and the Productivity Crisis', *Productivity Insights Network*, 2020, at productivity-insightsnetwork.co.uk.

36 Madeleine Hoecklin, '€93 Billion Spent by Public Sector on COVID Vaccines and Therapeutics in 11 Months, Research Finds', Health Policy Watch, 12 January 2021, at healthpolicy-watch.news.

37 David Wallace-Wells, 'We Had the Vaccine the Whole Time', *New York Magazine*, 7 October 2020.

38 Andrew Stroehlein, 'Interview: The World Desperately Needs More Covid-19 Vaccines', Human Rights Watch, 15 December 2021, at hrw.org.

39 Damian Garde, 'The Story of mRNA: How a Once-Dismissed Idea Became a Leading Technology in the Covid Vaccine Race', *StatNews*, 10 November 2020, at statnews.com.

40 Damian Garde, 'Ego, Ambition, and Turmoil: Inside One of Biotech's Most Secretive Startups', *StatNews*, 13 September 2016, at statnews.com.

41 Ibid.

42 Jonathan Ponciano, 'Moderna Stock Crash Intensifies: Losses Top $130 Billion', *Forbes*, 21 January 2022.

43 Press Release, 'COVID Vaccines Create 9 New Billionaires with Combined Wealth Greater than Cost of Vaccinating World's Poorest Countries', Oxfam International, 20 May 2021, at oxfam.org.

44 Yahoo Finance, 'Moderna Reports Fourth Quarter and Fiscal Year 2021 Financial Results and Provides Business Updates', 24 February 2022, at finance.yahoo.com.

45 Press Release, 'Pandemic of Greed: A Wake-Up Call for Vaccine Equity at a Grim Milestone', Oxfam International, 3 March 2022, at oxfam.org.

46 Anna Marriott and Alex Maitland, 'The Great Vaccine Robbery', People's Vaccine Policy Brief, 29 July 2021, at oxfamamerica.org.

47 Bob Herman, 'Moderna Skirts Disclosures of Coronavirus Vaccine Costs', *Axios*, 5 August 2020, at axios.com.

48 Julie Steenhuysen, 'Moderna COVID-19 Vaccine Patent Dispute Headed to Court, US NIH Head Says', Reuters, 11 November 2021.

49 Sheryl Gay Stolberg and Rebecca Robbins, 'Moderna and US at Odds Over Vaccine Patent Rights', *New York Times*, 11 November 2021.
50 Ibid.
51 Blake Brittain, 'COVID-19 Patent Challenges Mount as Moderna Faces New Vaccine Lawsuit', Reuters, 28 February 2022.
52 Reuters, 'Moderna Sues Pfizer and BioNTech Over Coronavirus Vaccine', *Guardian*, 26 August 2022.
53 Kathryn Ardizzone, 'BARDA Responds to KEI, Public Citizen Letter Asking BARDA to Enforce Moderna Contract', Knowledge Ecology International, 5 August 2020, at keionline.org.
54 Public Citizen, 'Statement: Moderna Vaccine Belongs to the People', 16 November 2020, at citizen.org.
55 Adam Tooze, 'Chartbook #77: More than 7000 Deaths per Day . . . and We Talk as Though It Is Over', *Substack*, 2 February 2022, at adamtooze.substack.com.
56 Elie Dolgin, 'The Tangled History of mRNA Vaccines', *Nature*, 14 September 2021.
57 Riley Griffin and Drew Armstrong, 'Pfizer Vaccine's Funding Came from Berlin, Not Washington', Bloomberg, 9 November 2020.
58 Hannah Kuchler, Donato Paolo Mancini and David Pilling, 'The Inside Story of the Pfizer Vaccine', *Financial Times*, 30 November 2021.
59 BBC News, 'Prof Sarah Gilbert: The Woman Who Designed the Oxford Vaccine', 23 November 2020.
60 Samuel Cross, Yeanuk Rho, Henna Reddy, Toby Pepperrell, Florence Rodgers, Rhiannon Osborne, Ayolola Eni-Olotu, Rishi Banerjee, Sabrina Wimmer and Sarai Keestra, 'Who Funded the Research Behind the Oxford-AstraZeneca COVID-19 Vaccine?', *BMJ Global Health 2021*, 10 April 2021.
61 Public Citizen, 'Letter Urging J&J to Share COVID Vaccine Technology', 2 March 2021, at citizen.org.
62 Press Release, 'Monopolies Causing "Artificial Rationing" in COVID-19 Crisis as 3 Biggest Global Vaccine Giants Sit on Sidelines', Oxfam Inteernational, 5 February 2021, at oxfam.org.
63 Adam Taylor, 'Why Covax, the best hope for vaccinating the world, was doomed to fall short', *Washington Post*, 22 March 2022
64 Sergey Brin, 'Heroes & Icons', *Time*, 30 April 2009.
65 Press Release, 'GAVI Should Stop Awarding Special Funds to Pfizer and GSK for Pneumonia Vaccine', Médecins Sans Frontières, 26 August 2019, at msfaccess.org.

66 GAVI staff, 'The GAVI COVAX AMC Explained', *Gavi*, 15 February 2021, at gavi.org.

67 Unicef, 'COVID-19 Vaccine Market Dashboard', 31 December 2021, at unicef.org.

68 Adam Taylor, 'Why Covax, the Best Hope for Vaccinating the World, Was Doomed to Fall Short', *Washington Post*, 22 March 2022.

69 Médecins Sans Frontières, 'COVAX: A Broken Promise to the World', 21 December 2021, at msfaccess.org.

70 Taylor, 'Why Covax, the Best Hope for Vaccinating the World, Was Doomed to Fall Short'.

71 Rosa Furneaux, Olivia Goldhill and Madlen Davies, 'How Covax Failed on Its Promise to Vaccinate the World', Bureau of Investigative Journalism, 8 October 2021, at thebureauinvestigates.com.

72 Médecins Sans Frontières, 'COVAX: A Broken Promise to the World'.

73 Ann Danaiya Usher, 'A Beautiful Idea: How COVAX Has Fallen Short', *Lancet*, 19 June 2021.

74 Médecins Sans Frontières, 'COVAX: A Broken Promise to the World'.

75 Ibid.

76 Harris Gleckman, 'COVAX: A Global Multistakeholder Group that Poses Political and Health Risks to Developing Countries and Multilateralism', Friends of the Earth International, March 2021, at foei.org.

77 James Love, 'President and Minister of Health of Costa Rica ask WHO to create global pool for rights in COVID-19 related technologies', *Knowledge Ecology Online*, 23 March 2020.

78 WHO briefing, 'Sharing Tools to Fight COVID-19 "the Best Shot the World Has" ', World Economic Forum, 29 May 2020, at weforum.org.

79 Ibid.

80 William Worley, 'WHO and Costa Rica Launch COVID-19 Technology Access Pool', Devex, 29 May 2020, at devex.com.

81 Amnesty International, 'A Double Dose of Inequality: Pharma Companies and the Covid-19 Vaccines Crisis', September 2021, at amnesty.org.

82 Ed Silverman, 'Pharma Leaders Shoot Down WHO Voluntary Pool for Patent Rights on Covid-19 Products', *StatNews*, 28 May 2020, at statnews.com.

83 World Health Orgnization, 'WHO and MPP Announce the First Transparent, Global, Non-Exclusive Licence for a COVID-19 Technology', *ReliefWeb*, 22 November 202, at who.int.

4. The Pandemic Begins

1 Author interview with Nabil Ahmed, 29 April 2022.

2 Andrew Jack, 'Winnie Byanyima: "It's Powerful to Be Different. I Never Hesitate to Be Myself" ', *Financial Times*, 11 July 2021.

3 James Ashton, 'Winnie Byanyima Interview: "We Don't Think Charity Is the Way to Resolve Global Inequality" Says Oxfam International Boss', *Independent*, 25 January 2015.

4 Winnie Byanyima, 'We Must Have a #PeoplesVaccine, Not a Profit Vaccine', UN Aids, 9 December 2020, at unaids.org.

5 Author interview.

6 Sharon Lerner and Lee Fang, 'Factory Owners Around the World Stand Ready to Manufacture Covid-19 Vaccines', *Intercept*, 29 April 2021, at theintercept.com.

7 Press Release, 'Pandemic of Greed: A Wake-Up Call for Vaccine Equity at a Grim Milestone', Oxfam International, 3 March 2022, at oxfam.org.

8 Third World Network Trust (India) et al., 'Indian Civil Society Letter to Johnson & Johnson', 16 September 2021, at accessibsa.org.

9 Editorial, 'Danish Company Offers to Help with Covid-19 Vaccine Production', The Local DK, 2 February 2021, at thelocal.dk.

10 Lerner and Fang, 'Factory Owners Around the World Stand Ready'.

11 Benjamin Blanco, 'With One Simple Decision, the Canadian Government Can Save Lives', Al Jazeera, 28 September 2021, at aljazeera.com.

12 Human Rights Watch, 'Experts Identify 100 Plus Firms to Make Covid-19 mRNA Vaccines', 15 December 2021, at hrw.org.

13 Achal Prabhala and Alain Alsalhani, 'Pharmaceutical Manufacturers Across Asia, Africa and Latin America with the Technical Requirements and Quality Standards to Manufacture mRNA Vaccines', 10 December 2021, at accessibsa.org.

14 Press Release (Oxfam), 'Pandemic of Greed'.

15 Press Release, 'An Average of 7 in 10 Across G7 Countries Think Their Governments Should Force Big Pharma to Share Vaccine Know-How', Amnesty International, 5 May 2021.

16 Bird & Bird, 'COVID-19: New German Legislation to Fight Pandemic May Affect Granted German Patents', 10 May 2020, at twobirds.com; Laura Eggertson, 'Canada Can Override Patents to Combat Drug, Equipment Shortages during the Pandemic', CMAJ News, 2 April 2020, at cmaj.ca.

17 Jamie Dettmer, 'EU Threatens Vaccine Export Ban, Prompting UK, Australian Backlash', VOA News, 17 March 2021, at voanews.com.

18 Press Release, 'Most of Pfizer's Vaccine Already Promised to Richest, Campaigners Warn', Global Justice Now, 11 November 2020, at globaljustice.org.uk.

19 Press Release, '78% of Moderna Vaccine Doses Already Sold to Rich Countries', Global Justice Now, 16 November 2020, at globaljustice.org.uk.

20 Oxfam America, 'A Shot at Recovery: Measuring Corporate Commitments Towards a Free, Fair, and Accessible COVID-19 Vaccine', 23 October 2020, at oxfam.org.

21 Bill and Melinda Gates, 'Vaccine Fairness Will Make Us All Safer', *Financial Times*, 15 September 2020.

22 Press Release, 'Pharmaceutical Giants Shell Out Billions to Shareholders as World Confronts Vaccine Apartheid', Oxfam International, 22 April 2021, at oxfam.org.

23 US Embassy and Consulates in the United Kingdom, 'Statement from Ambassador Katherine Tai on the Covid-19 Trips Waiver', United States Trade Representative, 5 May 2021, at uk.usembassy.gov.

24 Pharmaceutical Research and Manufacturers of America, 'PhRMA Special 301 Submission 2022', PhRMA Policy Paper, 13 October 2022, at phrma.org.

25 Ibid.

26 Ann Danaiya Usher, 'A Beautiful Idea: How COVAX Has Fallen Short', *Lancet*, 19 June 2021, at thelancet.com.

27 Press Release, 'UK Secures Extra 60 Million Pfizer/BioNTech COVID-19 Vaccines', Department of Health and Social Care, 28 April 2021, at gov.uk.

28 Guy Faulconbridge, Alistair Smout and Kate Holton, 'Britain to Slow Vaccine Rollout Due to Supply Crunch in India, Testing of Big Batch', Reuters, 18 March 2021.

29 Samuel Lovett, 'An Absolute Scandal': UK Threw Away 600,000 Vaccine Doses After They Passed Expiry Date', *Independent*, 15 November 2021.

30 Press Release, 'G7 Vaccine Donations Will Cover Just 11% of World's Unvaccinated Population', Global Justice Now, 11 June 2021, at globaljustic.org.uk.

31 David Bol, 'Gordon Brown: G7 Has Committed "Unforgivable Moral Failure" over Vaccines', *Herald*, 13 June 2021, at heraldscotland.com.

32 Sabah Meddings, 'Interview: I Was Right to Fight Off Pfizer, Says Astra Zeneca Boss Pascal Soriot', *The Times*, 23 September 2018.

33 Angus Liu, 'AstraZeneca Investors Hit Back at CEO Soriot's 2021 Pay Plan After COVID Vaccine Stumbles', *Fierce Pharma*, 5 May 2021, at fiercepharma.com.

34 Press Release, 'Antitrust: Commission Welcomes Court of Justice Judgment in the AstraZeneca Case', European Commission, 6 December 2012, at ec.europa.eu.

35 Press Release, 'Pharmaceutical Giant AstraZeneca to Pay $520 Million for Off-Label Drug Marketing', United States Department of Justice, 27 April 2010, at justice.gov.

36 Janice Hopkins Tanne, 'AstraZeneca Pays $520m Fine for Off Label Marketing', *British Medical Journal*, 29 April 2010, at bmj.com.

37 Richard Wachman, 'AstraZeneca Agrees to Pay £505m to Settle UK Tax Dispute', *Guardian*, 23 February 2010.

38 Ed Silverman, 'AstraZeneca Loses Court Battle to Prevent Generic Versions of Crestor', *StatNews*, 20 July 2016, at statnews.com; Emma Court, 'Big Pharma Games the System to Make Generic Drugs More Expensive', *Market Watch*, 3 August 2018, at marketwatch.com.

39 Nathan Vardi, 'AstraZeneca's Pascal Soriot Was the Hottest CEO in Pharma. Now He's in the Hot Seat', *Forbes*, 19 March 2021.

40 Andrew Ward, 'Big Pharma Balks at Investment in TB', *Financial Times*, 23 March 2014.

41 Press Release, 'MSF Responds to News of Pull Out of Neglected Disease R&D by AstraZeneca', Médecins Sans Frontières, 31 January 2014, at msfaccess.org.

42 Press Release, 'Funding and Manufacturing Boost for UK Vaccine Programme', Department for Business, Energy and Industrial Strategy, 17 May 2020, at gov.uk.

43 Eric Sagonowsky, 'AstraZeneca Scores $1.2B from US, Signs Up to Deliver Hundreds of Millions of COVID-19 Vaccines', *Fierce Pharma*, 21 May 2020, at fiercepharma.com.

44 David D. Kirkpatrick, 'In Race for a Coronavirus Vaccine, an Oxford Group Leaps Ahead', *New York Times*, 2 May 2020.

45 Svět Lustig Vijay and Elaine Ruth Fletcher, 'Gates Foundation: Technology Transfer, Not Patents Is Main Roadblock To Expanding Vaccine Production', Health Policy Watch, 14 April 2021, at healthpolicy-watch.news.

46 Reuters, 'S. Africa to Pay Big Premium for AstraZeneca COVID-19 Vaccine from India's SII', 21 January 2021; Esther Nakkazi, 'Uganda Defends Price Paid for AstraZeneca COVID19 Vaccine', Health Policy Watch, 3 February 2021, at healthpolicy-watch.news; Prabha Raghavan and Anil Sasi, 'Serum Institute's Rs 600/Dose for Covishield in Private Hospitals Is Its Highest Rate the World Over', *Indian Express*, 25 April 2021.

47 Tom Espiner, 'AstraZeneca to Take Profits from Covid Vaccine', BBC News, 12 November 2021.

48 Simon Jack, 'AstraZeneca Vaccine – Was It Really Worth It?', BBC News, 30 March 2021; Vardi, 'AstraZeneca's Pascal Soriot Was the Hottest CEO in Pharma'.

49 Thiru, '23 February 2021: South Africa's Interventions at the WTO TRIPS Council', *Knowledge Ecology International*, 1 March 2021.

50 Sara Jerving, 'Over 70% of African Nations Didn't Reach Global COVID-19 Vaccine Goal', Devex, 30 September 2021, at devex.com.

51 World Health Organisation, 'WHO Director-General's Opening Remarks at 148th Session of the Executive Board', 18 January 2021, at who.int.

52 António Guterres, 'Secretary-General's Address to the 76th Session of the UN General Assembly', United Nations, 21 September 2021, at un.org.

53 UN Web TV, 'Peru – President Addresses General Debate, 76th Session', 21 September 2021, at media.un.org.

54 'Statement of President Rodrigo Duterte at the High-Level General Debate, 76th Session of United Nations General Assembly', United Nations, 21 September 2021, available at rappler.com,

55 'Address by HE Yoweri Kaguta Museveni, President of the Republic of Uganda at the General Debate of the 76th session of the United Nations General Assembly', United Nations, 23 September 2021, at youtube.com.

56 Kerry Cullinan, 'Massive Increase in COVID-19 Vaccine Production May Mean Dose Surplus by Mid-2022, Says IFPMA', Health Policy Watch, 08 September 2021, at healthpolicy-watch.news.

57 Hannah Kuchler, Donato Paolo Mancini and David Pilling, 'The Inside Story of the Pfizer Vaccine', *Financial Times*, 30 November 2021.

58 Annalisa Merelli, 'Europe Sent Nigeria Up to 1 Million Near-Expired Doses of Covid-19 Vaccine', *Quartz*, 10 December 2021, at qz.com.

59 Azfar Hossain, Stephen Asiimwe and Louise Ivers, 'Claims of Vaccine Hesitancy in African Countries Are at Odds with the Reality on the Ground', *StatNews*, 21 December 2021, at statnews.com.

60 Yannick Markhof, Shelton Kanyanda, Philip Randolph Wollburg and Alberto Zezza, 'Sustainedly High Levels of COVID-19 Vaccine Acceptance in Five Sub-Saharan African Countries', *World Bank Blogs*, 6 December 2021, at blogs.worldbank.org.

61 Max Kozlov, 'COVID Vaccines Have Higher Approval in Less-Affluent Countries', *Nature*, 22 July 2021.

62 Manas Mishra and Michael Erman, 'Pfizer's COVID Product Sales to Top $50 Bln This Year, Investors Want More', Reuters, 8 February 2022.

63 Ceri Thomas, 'Pfizer's War', *Tortoise Media*, 27 September 2021, at tortoisemedia.com.

64 Ed Silverman, 'After a Long Battle, Pfizer Drops the Price of Its Prevnar Vaccine to Humanitarian Groups', *StatNews*, 11 November 2016, statnews.com.

65 Press Release, 'First Alternative Pneumonia Vaccine Breaks Pfizer and GSK's Decades-Long Stranglehold, Promising More Children Protected Against Biggest Childhood Killer', Médecins Sans Frontières, 20 December 2019, at msfaccess.org.

66 Charlotte Hu, 'These Are the Most – and Least – Reputable Drug Companies in the US', *Business Insider*, 19 June 2018.

67 David Crow, 'Pfizer Chief Albert Bourla: "We Are the Most Efficient Vaccine Machine" ', *Financial Times*, 13 August 2021.

68 Amnesty International, 'A Double Dose of Inequality: Pharma Companies and the Covid-19 Vaccines Crisis', September 2021, at amnesty.org.

69 Riley Griffin and Drew Armstrong, 'Pfizer Vaccine's Funding Came from Berlin, Not Washington', *Bloomberg*, 9 November 2020.

70 Nathan Vardi, 'The Race Is On: Why Pfizer Might Be the Best Bet to Deliver a Vaccine by the Fall', *Forbes*, 20 March 2020.

71 Kuchler et al., 'Inside Story of the Pfizer Vaccine'.

72 *Dispatches*, 'Vaccine Wars: Truth About Pfizer', Channel 4, 10 December 2021.

73 Press Release, 'Pfizer's £2 billion NHS Rip-Off Could Pay for Nurses' Pay Rise SIX TIMES Over', Global Justice Now, 23 November 2021, at globaljustice.org.uk.

74 John Siddle, 'Pfizer Made Nearly £2bn in Profit from Cash-Strapped NHS for Its Covid Vaccine', *Daily Mirror*, 25 November 2021.

75 Kuchler et al., 'Inside Story of the Pfizer Vaccine'.

76 Eric Sagonowsky, 'Pfizer Eyes Higher Prices for COVID-19 Vaccine after the Pandemic Wanes: Exec, Analyst', *Fierce Pharma*, 23 February 2021, at fiercepharma.com.

77 Kuchler et al., 'Inside Story of the Pfizer Vaccine'.

78 Jon Ungoed-Thomas, ' "Wall of Secrecy" in Pfizer Contracts as Company Accused of Profiteering', *Guardian*, 5 December 2021.

79 Michael Erman, 'Pfizer Expects to Hike US COVID Vaccine Price to $110–$130 Per Dose', Reuters, 21 October 2022.

80 Jake Johnson, ' "Daylight Robbery": Pfizer Condemned for Hiking US Covid Vaccine Price by 10,000% Above Cost', *Common Dreams*, 21 October 2022, at commondreams.org, 21 October 2022.

81 *Dispatches*, 'Vaccine Wars: Truth About Pfizer'.

82 Amnesty International, 'Double Dose of Inequality'

83 Press Release, 'A Dose of Reality: How Rich Countries and Pharmaceutical Corporations Are Breaking Their Vaccine Promises', UN Aids, 21 October 2021, at unaids.org.

84 Thomas, 'Pfizer's War'.

85 *Dispatches*, 'Vaccine Wars: Truth About Pfizer'.

86 Thomas, 'Pfizer's War'.

87 Ibid.

88 Kuchler et al., 'Inside Story of the Pfizer Vaccine'.

89 Thomas, 'Pfizer's War'.

90 Reuters, 'Lebanese Parliament Passes Law to Pave Way for Coronavirus Vaccine Deals', Reuters, 15 January 2021; Kuchler et al., 'Inside Story of the Pfizer Vaccine'.

91 Madlen Davies, Rosa Furneaux, Iván Ruiz, Jill Langlois, ' "Held to Ransom": Pfizer Demands Governments Gamble with State Assets to Secure Vaccine Deal', *Bureau of Investigative Journalism*, 23 February 2021, at thebureauinvestigates.com.

92 *Dispatches*, 'Vaccine Wars: Truth About Pfizer'.

93 Corporate Europe Observatory, 'Still Not Loving ISDS: 10 Reasons to Oppose Investors' Super-Rights in EU Trade Deals', 16 April 2014, at corporateeurope.org.

94 Kuchler et al., 'Inside Story of the Pfizer Vaccine'.

95 Amnesty International, 'Double Dose of Inequality'.

96 Rohit Malpani and Alex Maitland, 'Dose of Reality: How Rich Countries and Pharmaceutical Corporations Are Breaking Their Vaccine Promises', *People's Vaccine*, 21 October 2021, at peoplesvaccine.org.

97 Anna Marriott and Alex Maitland, 'The Great Vaccine Robbery', People's Vaccine Policy Brief, 29 July 2021, at oxfamamerica.org.

98 Damian Garde, 'Ego, Ambition, and Turmoil: Inside One of Biotech's Most Secretive Startups', *StatNews*, 13 September 2016, at statnews.com.

99 Matt Egan and Robert Kuznia, 'Moderna's Coronavirus Vaccine Announcement Set Off a Frenzy on Wall Street. Now Some Are Calling for an Investigation', CNN, 1 June 2020.

100 Ibid.

101 Ibid.

102 David Meyer, 'Moderna Wouldn't Share Its Vaccine Technology, So South Africa and the WHO Made a COVID Jab Based on It Anyway', *Fortune*, 4 February 2022.

103 Wendell Roelf and Julie Steenhuysen, 'Moderna Patent Application Raises Fears for Africa COVID Vaccine Hub', Reuters, 17 February 2022.

104 Jamie Smyth, Hannah Kuchler and Andres Schipani, 'Moderna Vows Never to Enforce Covid Jab Patents in Policy U-Turn', *Financial Times*, 8 March 2022.

105 Ashleigh Furlong of *Politico Europe* on *Twitter*, as @ashleighfurlong, 8 March 2022.

106 Bryce Baschuk, 'WTO's Future Grows Cloudier in a World Shattered by Covid', *Bloomberg*, 29 November 2021.

107 Alexandra Topping, 'UK, EU and US "Get More Covid Vaccines in Six Weeks than Africa Has All Year" ', *Guardian*, 23 December 2021.

108 Press Release, 'Covid-19: Big Pharma Fuelling Unprecedented Human Rights Crisis – New Report', Amnesty International UK, 21 September 2021, at amnesty.org.uk.

109 Unicef, 'COVID-19 Vaccine Market Dashboard', 31 December 2021, at unicef.org.

110 Press Release, 'Omicron Variant Made $10 Billion in a Week for Top Moderna and Pfizer Shareholders', Global Justice Now, 7 December 2021, at globaljustice.org.uk.

111 Ibid.

112 See Chapter 7, below.

113 Max Kozlov, 'Why Scientists Are Racing to Develop More COVID Antivirals', *Nature*, 21 January 2022.

114 Ann Danaiya Usher, 'The Global COVID-19 Treatment Divide', *Lancet*, 26 February 2022, at thelancet.com.

115 Public Citizen, 'The Real Story of Remdesivir', 7 May 2020, at citizen.org.

116 Yaniv Heled, Ana Santos Rutschman and Liza Vertinsky, 'The Problem with Relying on Profit-Driven Models to Produce Pandemic Drugs', *Journal of Law and the Biosciences*, January–June 2020.

117 Kyle Blankenship, 'Gilead Asks FDA to Rescind Remdesivir Orphan Drug Tag After Public Backlash', *Fierce Pharma*, 25 March 2020, at fiercepharma.com.

118 Gilead Annual Report, 4 May 2022, at wwwam10.gilead.com; Angus Liu, 'Gilead's Long-Awaited Remdesivir Price Is $3,120, in Line with Watchdog Estimates', *Fierce Pharma*, 29 June 2020, at fiercepharma.com; Junzheng Wang, Jacob Levi, Katie Heath and Joseph Fortunak, 'Minimum Costs to Manufacture New Treatments for COVID-19', *Journal of Virus Eradication*, April 2020.

119 Drugs for Neglected Diseases Initiative, 'Pfizer Blocking Research to Generate Evidence on Optimal Use of Novel Antiviral for COVID-19 Patients in Low- and Middle-Income Countries', 15 March 2022, at dndi.org.

120 Public Citizen, 'Letter Urging Pfizer to Address Paxlovid Inequality', 24 January 2022, at citizen.org.

121 Médecins Sans Frontières, 'Removing Intellectual-Property Barriers from COVID-19 Vaccines and Treatments for People in South Africa', 8 March 2022, at msfaccess.org.

122 Public Citizen, 'Letter Urging Pfizer to Address Paxlovid Inequality'.

123 Press Release, 'Reaction to Pfizer's Announcement of Voluntary Licenses of Its COVID-19 Oral Antiviral Treatment Paxlovid to the Medicines Patent Pool', Oxfam International, 16 November 2021, at oxfam.org; Press Release, 'MSF Response to License Between Pfizer and Medicines Patent Pool for New COVID-19 Treatment Paxlovid', Médecins Sans Frontières, 16 November 2021, msfaccess.org.

124 Médecins Sans Frontières, 'Latin America: How Patents and Licensing Hinder Access to COVID-19 Treatments', 8 March 2022, at msfaccess.org.

125 Press Release, 'Pfizer Is Building a "Paxlovid Patent Wall", New Research Reveals', *Public Citizen*, 18 February 2022, at citizen.org.

126 Drugs for Neglected Diseases Initiative, 'Pfizer Blocking Research to Generate Evidence on Optimal Use of Novel Antiviral'.

127 Ibid.

128 Médecins Sans Frontières, 'Removing Intellectual-Property Barriers from COVID-19 Vaccines'; Press Release, 'MSF Responds to Latest WHO Recommendation for a COVID-19 Therapeutic, Baricitinib', 13 January 2022, msfaccess.org.

129 Médecins Sans Frontières, 'Latin America: How Patents and Licensing Hinder Access to COVID-19 Treatments'.

130 Médecins Sans Frontières, 'MSF Response to License Between Pfizer and Medicines Patent Pool'.

131 Press Release (Oxfam), 'Pandemic of Greed'.

132 Freda Kreier, 'Morgue Data Hint at COVID's True Toll in Africa', *Nature*, 23 March 2022.

133 See Chapter 7, below.

5. Recolonising the Global Economy

1 Author interview with Tahir Amin, 6 February 2022.

2 Naomi Klein, *No Logo: 10th Anniversary Edition* (London: Picador, 1999).

3 Graham Dutfield, *That High Design of Purest Gold: A Critical History of the Pharmaceutical Industry, 1880–2020* (Singapore: World Scientific, 2020), p. 170.

4 Ibid., p. 205.

5 Billy Kenber, *Sick Money: The Truth About the Global Pharmaceutical Industry* (Edinburgh: Canongate, 2021), p. 36.

6 Ibid., p. 35.

7 Alexander Zaitchik, *Owning the Sun: A People's History of Monopoly Medicine from Aspirin to COVID-19 Vaccine* (Berkeley: Counterpoint, 2023), p. 47.

8 Christopher Klein, '8 Things You May Not Know about Jonas Salk and the Polio Vaccine', *History*, 28 October 2014, at history.com.

9 Dutfield, *That High Design of Purest Gold*, p. 166.

10 Maki Sagami, 'China Goes on an Intellectual Property Offensive, *Financial Times*, 26 September 2021.

11 Ellen 't Hoen, 'Private Patents and Public Health: Changing Intellectual Property Rules for Access to Medicines', Health Action International, 2016, p. 20, at haiweb.org.

12 Alexander Zaitchik, 'Long, Strange TRIPS: The Grubby History of How Vaccines Became Intellectual Property', *New Republic*, 1 June 2021.

13 Susan K. Sell, 'Trips and the Access to Medicines Campaign', *Wisconsin International Law Journal*, Summer 2002.

14 't Hoen, 'Private Patents and Public Health', p. 24.

15 Zaitchik, 'Long, Strange TRIPS'.

16 Author interview with Walden Bello, 11 February 2022.

17 Médecins Sans Frontières, 'The Doha Declaration @ 20: The Quest for Solutions to Overcome Access Barriers Created by the TRIPS Agreement', 15 December 2021, at msf-access.medium.com.

18 Analysis taken from 't Hoen, 'Private Patents and Public Health'.

19 Ibid., p. 45.

20 Médecins Sans Frontières, 'Doha Declaration @ 20'.

21 't Hoen, 'Private Patents and Public Health', p. 54.

22 Public Citizen, 'Leaked Cables Show US Tried, Failed to Organize Against Ecuador Compulsory Licensing', 10 May 2011, at citizen.org.

23 't Hoen, 'Private Patents and Public Health', pp. 61, 67; *i-Base*, 'Glaxo Blocks Importation of Generic Combivir into Ghana', 17 January 2001, at i-base.info; Press Release, 'Novartis Must End "Bullying Tactics" over Life-Saving Medicines', Global Justice Now, 1 March 2018, at globaljustice.org.uk.

24 Médecins Sans Frontières, 'Spotlight On: TRIPS, TRIPS Plus, and Doha', n.d., at msfaccess.org.

25 Oxfam International, 'US Bullying on Drug Patents: One Year after Doha', 1 November 2002, at policy-practice.oxfam.org.

26 Rohit Malpani, 'All Costs, No Benefits: How TRIPS-Plus Intellectual Property Rules in the US–Jordan FTA Affect Access to Medicines', Oxfam International, 21 March 2007, at oxfamilibrary.openrepository.com.

27 Rachel Tansey, Heidi Chow and Radhika Patel, 'Pharma Trade Secrets: The Truth about a Trade Deal with Trump', Global Justice Now, 26 November 2019, at globaljustice.org.uk.

28 Zaitchik, 'Long, Strange TRIPS'.

29 Nasir Tyabji, 'Gaining Technical Know-How in an Unequal World: Penicillin Manufacture in Nehru's India', *Technology and Culture* 45: 2, April 2004.

30 Vandana Shiva, 'Living on the Frontline', *Guardian*, 8 September 2003.

31 Achal Prabhala and Alain Alsalhani, 'Pharmaceutical Manufacturers Across Asia, Africa and Latin America with the Technical Requirements and Quality Standards to Manufacture mRNA Vaccines', 10 December 2021, at accessibsa.org.

32 Author interview with Prabhala.

6. The Hospital That Became a Trading Floor

1 Owaahh, 'Customers, Not Patients: The Nairobi Women's Hospital Saga', *Elephant*, 6 February 2020.

2 *Business Daily* (Kenya), 'Hospital CEO Talks Money, Zeal, Silence', 10 November 2016.

3 Anna Marriott and Jessica Hamer, 'Investing for the Few: The IFC's Health in Africa Initiative', Oxfam International, 9 September 2014, at oxfam.org.

4 *Nairobi News*, 'Day Uhuru Called Hospital Boss to Release Body of Dead Patient', 11 November 2016.

5 Dasha Afanasieva, 'Review: The Dark Side of Stakeholder Capitalism', Reuters, 9 July 2021.

6 Global Justice Now, 'Doing More Harm than Good: Why CDC Must Reform for People and Planet', 15 February 2020, at globaljustice.org.uk.

7 Landon Thomas, Jr, 'Leading Private Equity Firm Accused of Misusing Funds', *New York Times*, 2 February 2018.

8 Simeon Kerr, 'US Prosecutors Widen Probe into Collapse of Abraaj', *Financial Times*, 14 June 2019.

9 Arif Sharif, 'What's Been Learned and Who's Charged in Abraaj Collapse', *Bloomberg*, 7 September 2019.

10 *Economist*, 'The Biggest Collapse in Private-Equity History Will Have a Lasting Impact', 18 May 2019.

11 Saeed Azhar, 'TPG-Backed Evercare Eyes Expansion of Ex-Abraaj Healthcare Business', Reuters, 13 December 2021.

12 Owaahh, 'Customers, Not Patients'.

13 Ben Zimmer, 'The Rise and Fall of the Term "Third World" ', *Wall Street Journal*, 1 May 2015.

14 World Health Organization, 'Dr Halfdan Mahler's Address to the 61st World Health Assembly', 20 May 2008, at who.int.

15 Nitsan Chorev, *The World Health Organization between North and South* (Ithaca, NY: Cornell University Press, 2012), p. 110.

16 Ibid., p. 67.

17 Ibid., p. 125.

18 United Nations Development Programme, 'Human Development Report 2003', 1 January 2003, at hdr.undp.org.

19 World Health Organization data, Medical doctors (per 10,000 population), accessed 02/03/23 at who.int.

20 Kamran Abbasi, 'Changing Sides', *British Medical Journal* 318 (27 March 1999).

21 See for example Gavin E. R. Wilson, 'Billions to Trillions: Financing the Global Goals', 24 September 2015 accessed on blogs.worldbank.org or the World Bank's new 'Business Enabling Environment (BEE)' project at worldbank.org.

22 Sarah Boseley, 'Half of Lesotho Health Budget Goes to Private Consortium for One Hospital', *Guardian*, 7 April 2014.

23 Chorev, *World Health Organization between North and South*, p.136.

24 World Health Organisation, 'Programme Budget 2022–2023', 31 May 2021, at apps.who.int; Editorial, 'The WHO Deserves More Money for Its Core Mission – and More Respect', *Nature*, 1 February 2022.

25 Author interview with David Legge, 3 May 2022.

26 Tim Lewis, 'Bill Gates: "Vaccines Are a Miracle. It's Mind-Blowing Somebody Could Say the Opposite" ', *Guardian*, 15 May 2022.

27 Mark Curtis, 'Gated Development: Is the Gates Foundation Always a Force for Good?', Global Justice Now, June 2016, at globaljustice.org.uk.

28 University of Manchester Global Development Institute, 'What Covid-19 Reveals about 21st Century Capitalism with Susan Sell', youtube.com, 4 February 2021.

29 Jens Martens and Karolin Seitz, *Philanthropic Power and Development: Who Shapes the Agenda?* (Aachen: Bischöfliches Hilfswerk Misereor, 2015).

30 Benjamin Mayo, 'Apple, Microsoft and Others Group to Lobby Against Upcoming Patent Troll Legislation', *9to5Mac*, 3 April 2014, at 9to5mac.com; Sara Morrison, 'Microsoft Avoided the Latest Round of Big Tech Antitrust Scrutiny. Then It Bought a Company for $69 billion', *Vox*, 27 January 2022.

31 John Vidal, 'Are Gates and Rockefeller Using Their Influence to Set Agenda in Poor States?', *Guardian*, 15 January 2016.

32 Max Lawson, 'Vaccines Save Lives but Is S Getting Value for Money?', From Poverty to Power blog, 13 June 2011, at frompoverty.oxfam.org.uk.

33 Bill Gates, *How to Prevent the Next Pandemic* (London: Allen Lane, 2022).

34 Oxfam International, 'Public Good or Private Wealth?', January 2019, at oxfam.org.

35 Kelsey Piper, 'Bill Gates Is Committed to Giving Away His Fortune – But He Keeps Getting Richer', *Vox*, 23 April 2019.

36 Nitasha Tiku and Jay Greene, 'The Billionaire Boom', *Washington Post*, 12 March 2021.

37 Martens and Seitz, *Philanthropic Power and Development*.

38 Daniel Willis, 'Healthcare for All? How UK Aid Undermines Universal Public Healthcare', Global Justice Now, 27 January 2021, at globaljustice.org.uk.

39 Willis, 'Healthcare for All?'

40 Oxfam International, 'Blind Optimism: Challenging the Myths About Private Health Care in Poor Countries', 1 February 2009, at policy-practice.oxfam.org.

41 Marriott and Hamer, 'Investing for the Few'.

42 Author interview with Dr T. Sundararaman, 19 May 2022.

43 Willis, 'Healthcare for All?'

44 Ibid.

45 Shweta Marathe, Shakuntala Bhalerao, Kanchan Pawar, Dhananjay Kakade and Abhay Shukla, 'Patients' Voices During the Pandemic: Stories and Analysis of Rights Violations and Overcharging by Private Hospitals', Support for Advocacy and Training to Health Initiatives, March 2022, at sathicehat.org.

46 Ashlin Mathew, 'Profit in Times of COVID-19: Is It Time to Take Over Private Hospitals?', *National Herald India*, 20 June 2020.

47 Owain David Williams, 'COVID-19 and Private Health: Market and Governance Failure', *Development* (Rome) 63: 2–4 (17 November 2020).

48 *Daily News Egypt*, 'Some Private Hospitals Sell COVID-19 Plasma at Inflated Prices: MP', 13 June 2020.

49 *SABC News*, 'Eastern Cape Health Condemns Refusal to Treat COVID-19 patients', 9 May 2020; Joseph Muraya, 'Private Hospitals Warned Against Overcharging Patients on COVID-19', *Capital News* (Kenya), 6 April 2020.

50 Williams, 'COVID-19 and Private Health'.

51 Ibid.

52 Gabrielle Appleford, Isaac Theuri and Edward Owino, 'Brokering Accreditation in Kenya's National Hospital Insurance Fund: Lessons Learned from Marie Stopes Kenya's AMUA Social Franchise Network', Marie Stopes International, n.d., at msichoices.org; Rebecca Riddell, 'Why Is the US Trying to Export Its Flawed Health-Care Policies Around the World?', *Washington Post*, 10 January 2022.

53 Oxfam International, 'Blind Optimism'.

54 Owen Smith, 'Sri Lanka: Achieving Pro-Poor Universal Health Coverage Without Health Financing Reforms', World Bank, 1 January 2018, at documents.worldbank.org.

55 Anne-Emanuelle Birn, 'Universal Health Coverage Can Best Be Achieved by Public Systems', *British Medical Journal* (blog), 24 August 2018, at blogs.bmj.com.

56 Oxfam International, 'Blind Optimism'.

57 Ban Ki-moon, 'Secretary-General Hails Cuba for Training Medical "Miracle Workers", Being on Frontlines of Global Health', United Nations, 28 January 2014, at press.un.org.

58 Oxfam International, 'Public Good or Private Wealth?'

59 Phillip Inman, 'Should Africa Let Silicon Valley In?', *Guardian*, 19 May 2018.

60 John Greenwood, 'Amazon Launches into Employee Benefits as a Healthcare Provider', *Corporate Advisor*, 22 March 2021.

61 Author's interview with Dr. T. Sundararaman, 19 May 2022.

7. A New Hope

1 Author interview with Fatima Hassan, 17 January 2022. All subsequent quotes are from this interview.

2 Author interview with Gregg Gonsalves, 18 February 2022.

3 Ruth Mayne, 'South Africa vs. the Drug Giants: A Challenge to Affordable Medicines', Oxfam, 1 February 2001, at policy-practice.oxfam.org.

4 Stephanie Nolan, 'Yes, a Raging Pandemic Can Be Quelled. Recent History Shows How', *New York Times*, 12 January 2022.

5 Mayne, 'South Africa vs. the Drug Giants'.

6 Ibid.

7 Ibid.

8 See Chapter 5, above.

9 Mark Heywood, 'The Unravelling of the Human Rights Response to HIV and AIDS and Why It Happened: An Activists' Perspective', from 'AIDS Today: Tell no lies, claim no easy victories', International HIV/Aids Alliance, October 2014, at globalfundadvocatesnetwork.org.

10 Author interview with Diarmaid McDonald, 27 January 2022.

11 Author interview with Els Torreele, 25 February 2022. All subsequent quotes are from this interview.

12 Author interview with Catherine Kyobutungi, 23 February 2022.

13 Author interview with Tian Johnson, 18 February 2022.

14 Jessica Bassett, 'Long-Acting PreP Is a Necessity, Not a Luxury: ViiV's Greed Is Still Blocking Global Access to Injection that Could Transform HIV Prevention and Help End the Pandemic', Health GAP, 4 April 2022, at healthgap.org.

15 Ibid.

16 Matthew Kavanagh and Eamonn Murphy, 'New Medicines May Help End AIDS – But High Prices and Monopolies Could Keep the Poor Locked Out', Inter Press Service, 18 May 2022, at ipsnews.net.

17 Ibid.

18 Alex Boyd, 'Why South Africa's Plans to Make Continent's First COVID-19 Vaccine May Upend a Broken Global System', *Toronto Star*, 17 February 2022.

19 Author interview with Fabrizio Chiodo, 22 April 2022.

20 Sam Meredith, 'Why Cuba's Extraordinary Covid Vaccine Success Could Provide the Best Hope for Low-Income Countries', CNBC, 13 January 2022.

21 Author interview with Achal Prabhala, 19 January 2022. All subsequent quotes are from this interview.

22 Unicef, 'COVID-19 Vaccine Market Dashboard', 31 December 2021, at unicef.org.

23 Thanks to Ho-Chih Lin for this analysis.

24 Jon Cohen, 'China's Vaccine Gambit', *Science* 370: 6522, 11 December 2020.

25 Henry Tillman, Yu Ye and Yang Jian, 'Health Silk Road 2020: A Bridge to the Future of Health for All', Shanghai Institutes for International Studies, 31 March 2021, at papers.ssrn.com.

26 Zoe Leung, 'Fill, Finish and Beyond: The Chinese Vaccine Developers Exporting Their Ambitions Overseas', Pharma Boardroom, 29 March 2022, at pharmaboardroom.com.

27 Ahmed Morsy, 'Manufacturing Vaccines Locally', *Ahram Online*, 25 February 2022, at english.ahram.org.eg.

28 Leung, 'Fill, Finish and Beyond'.

29 Interview with Amy Goodman, ' "A Vaccine for the World": US Scientists Develop Low-Cost Shot to Inoculate Global South', *Democracy Now*, 3 January 2022, at democracynow.org.

30 Goodman, 'A Vaccine for the World.'

31 Joe Palca, 'A Texas Team Comes Up with a COVID Vaccine That Could Be a Global Game Changer', NPR, 5 January 2022.

32 Goodman, 'A Vaccine for the World.'

33 Goodman, 'A Vaccine for the World'.

34 Neil Savage, 'An mRNA Vaccine Industry in the Making', *Nature*, 27 October 2020.

35 Amy Maxmen, 'The Fight to Manufacture COVID Vaccines in Lower-Income Countries', *Nature*, 15 September 2021.

36 Amy Maxmen, 'South African Scientists Copy Moderna's COVID Vaccine', *Nature*, 3 February 2022.

37 World Health Organization, 'Recipients of mRNA Technology from the WHO mRNA Technology Transfer Hub', at who.int.

38 Alex Boyd, 'Why South Africa's Plans to Make Continent's First COVID-19 Vaccine May Upend a Broken Global System', *Toronto Star*, 17 February 2022.

39 Amy Maxmen, 'South African Scientists Copy Moderna's COVID Vaccine', *Nature*, 3 February 2022.

40 Reuters, 'Moderna to Build mRNA Vaccine Manufacturing Facility in Kenya', 8 March 2022.

41 Press Release, 'BioNTech Introduces First Modular mRNA Manufacturing Facility to Promote Scalable Vaccine Production in Africa', BioNTech, 16 February 2022, at investors.biontech.de.

42 Priti Patnaik, 'The EU's Vaccine Production Race in Africa; Delaying Tactics Risk Irrelevance of The TRIPS Waiver Newsletter Edition #125', *Geneva Health Files*, 18 March 2022, at genevahealthfiles.substack.com.

43 Madlen Davies, 'Covid-19: WHO Efforts to Bring Vaccine Manufacturing to Africa Are Undermined by the Drug Industry, Documents Show', *British Medical Journal* 376: 304, 9 February 2022.

44 Ibid.

8. Reach for the Moon

1 Mariana Mazzucato, *The Entrepreneurial State: Debunking Public vs Private Sector Myths* (London: Anthem, 2013).

2 Tim Harford, 'The iPhone at 10: How the Smartphone Became So Smart', BBC News, 26 December 2016.

3 Mariana Mazzucato, 'The People's Prescription: Re-imagining Health Innovation to Deliver Public Value', UCL Institute for Innovation and Public Purpose, October 2018.

4 Jeremy Corbyn, ' "Together, We Can Take on the Privileged, and Put the People in Power" – Corbyn's conference speech', reproduced on *LabourList*, 24 September 2019, at labourlist.org.

5 Author interview with Diarmaid McDonald, 27 January 2022. All subsequent quotes are from this interview.

6 Press Release, 'NHS England Concludes Wide-Ranging Deal for Cystic Fibrosis Drugs', NHS England, 24 October 2019, at england.nhs.uk.

7 Mike Marqusee, *The Price of Experience: Writings on Living with Cancer* (New York: OR Books, 2014).

8 Alison Kodjak, 'How a Drugmaker Gamed the System to Keep Generic Competition Away', NPR, 17 May 2018; Shayla Love, 'Psychedelic Patents are Broken Because the Patent System Is Broken', *Vice*, 9 May 2022.

9 Author interview with John McDonnell MP, 6 May 2022.

10 Press Association, 'Nationalised Drug Companies May Be Needed to "Fix Antibiotics Market"', *Guardian*, 27 March 2019.

11 Ibid.; Clive Cookson, 'Industry Must Turn Words into Action on Superbugs, Says Jim O'Neill', *Financial Times*, 27 March 2019.

12 Madeline Drexler, 'Seeking the Path of Least Resistance', *Harvard Public Health*, Spring 2019, at hsph.harvard.edu.

13 BBC News, 'Global Antibiotics "Revolution" Needed', 19 May 2016.

14 Benjamin Plackett, 'Why Big Pharma Has Abandoned Antibiotics', *Nature*, 21 October 2020.

15 World Health Organization, '2019 Antibacterial Agents in Clinical Development: An Analysis of the Antibacterial Clinical Development Pipeline', 15 January 2020, at who.int.

16 Chris Dall, 'WHO Report Highlights Shortage of New Antibiotics', Center for Infectious Disease Research and Policy, University of Minnesota, 15 April 2021, at cidrap.umn.edu.

17 Hannah Devlin, 'Antibiotic Resistant Superbugs "Will Kill 90,000 Britons by 2050" ', *Guardian*, 7 November 2018.

18 James Gallagher, 'Take Over Pharma to Create New Medicines, Says Top Adviser', BBC News, 27 March 2019.

19 Jonathan Gardner, 'UK Bid to Battle Antibiotic Resistance Yields First Subscription-Style Plan', Bio Pharma Dive, 12 April 2022, at biopharmadive.com.

20 Megan Ford, 'NHS Poised to Roll Out Two New Antibiotics for Drug-Resistant Infections', *Nursing Times*, 13 April 2022.

21 Tae Kim, 'Goldman Sachs Asks in Biotech Research Report: "Is Curing Patients a Sustainable Business Model?" ', CNBC, 11 April 2018.

22 Billy Kenber, *Sick Money: The Truth about the Global Pharmaceutical Industry* (Edinburgh: Canongate, 2021), Chapter 10.

23 Charlotte Kilpatrick, 'COVID-19 Has Shown How Big Pharma Is Broken', *Salon*, 20 February 2021, at salon.com.

24 Examples taken from Labour Party, 'Medicines for the Many: Public Health before Private Profit', 1 September 2019, at labour.org.uk.

25 Thomas Hanna, Miriam Brett and Dana Brown, 'Democratising Knowledge: Transforming Intellectual Property and R&D', *Common Wealth*, 19 September 2020, at common-wealth.co.uk.

26 NL News, 'Amsterdam Hospital to Make Its Own Generic Versions of Rare, Expensive Medicines', 11 February 2019.

27 White House, 'Remarks of President Joe Biden – State of the Union Address as Prepared for Delivery', 1 March 2022, at whitehouse.gov.

28 Author interview with Peter Maybarduk, 22 April 2022. All subsequent quotes are from this interview.

29 Andrew Perez and David Sirota, 'Big Pharma Has a Powerful New Shill, Kyrsten Sinema, Fighting Drug Price Reform', *Guardian*, 11 October 2021.

30 Reuters, 'US Congressional Democrats, Biden Reach Deal on Drug Prices', 3 November 2019.

31 Ahmed Aboulenein, 'Analysis: US Move to Negotiate Drug Prices a Rare Defeat for Big Pharma', Reuters, 13 August 2022.

32 Leigh Phillips, 'Are We at the Dawn of "Insulin Socialism"?', *Jacobin*, 8 March 2022, at jacobin.com.

33 Ibid.

34 Jamie Smyth, 'Eli Lilly to Cut Price of Insulin Drugs by 70%', *Financial Times*, 1 March 2023.

35 Raisa Santos, 'WHO Welcomes US Move to Share COVID-19 Technologies with C-TAP Patent Pool Medicines & Vaccines', Health Policy Watch, 4 March 2022, at healthpolicy-watch.news.

36 Zephyr Teachout, speech to 'Rebalancing Power' conference, Berlin, 12–13 May 2022.

37 Michelle Meagher and Nicholas Shaxson, 'The US Is Taking On Its Corporate Monopolists – Now the Rest of the World Must Follow', Open Democracy, 17 September 2021, at opendemocracy.net.

38 White House, 'Remarks by President Biden at Signing of an Executive Order Promoting Competition in the American Economy', 9 July 2021, at whitehouse.gov.

39 Barry C. Lynn, 'Antimonopoly Power: The Global Fight Against Corporate Concentration', *Foreign Affairs* 100: 4, July–August 2021.

40 Duncan McCann, 'Commoning Intellectual Property: Public Funding and the Creation of a Knowledge Commons', *Common Wealth*, 29 July 2020, at common-wealth.co.uk.

41 Dean Baker, Arjun Jayadev and Joseph Stiglitz, 'Innovation, Intellectual Property, and Development: A Better Set of Approaches for the 21st Century', Center for Economic and Policy Research, July 2017, at cepr.net.

42 Annalisa Merelli, 'How Much Blame for Global Vaccine Inequity Should the WTO Bear?', *Quartz*, 19 April 2022, at qz.com.

43 Author interview with Tahir Amin, 6 February 2022.

Index